CARDINAL

CARDINAL

*A Contemporary Anthology
of Fiction and Poetry
by North Carolina Writers*

Edited by
RICHARD KRAWIEC

Poetry Editor
PAUL JONES

Associate Editor
CAROL COLLIER

JACAR PRESS
Wendell, North Carolina   1986

Library of Congress Catalogue Card Number
85-081407

ISBN 0-936481-00-5

Manufactured in the United States of America
by MacNaughton and Gunn, Inc.
Ann Arbor, Michigan

Cover Photo by Cathy Crowell

Typesetting and Book Design by
Bull City Studios, Durham, North Carolina

Acknowledgments

Reynolds Price, "Waiting at Dachau," from *Permanent Errors*, Copyright 1970. Reprinted with the permission of Atheneum Publishers, Inc.

Elizabeth Cox, "Snail Darter," from *Familiar Ground*, Copyright 1984. Reprinted with the permission of Atheneum Publishers, Inc.

Some of these stories and poems have appeared, or are forthcoming, in the following publications:

Antaeus, Atlantic Monthly, Bloomsbury Review, Callaloo, Carolina Quarterly, Crescent Review, Hambone, Georgia Review, Iowa Review, Ironwood, Kayak, Kenyon Review, The Literary Review, Negative Capability, The New Yorker, Ohio Review, Poetry Northwest, Prairie Schooner, Pulpsmith, St. Andrews Review, Southern Humanities Review, Yellow Silk, and others.

The following works have been reprinted with the permission of their authors, and appear in the books listed.

Adcock, Betty, "The Swan Story," from *Nettles*, LSU Press.

Barrax, Gerald, "Another Fellow," from *A Different Rain*, University of Georgia Press. "Death of Another Fellow," from *The Deaths of Animals and Lesser Gods*, Callaloo Poetry Series, University of Kentucky.

Deagon, Ann, "Basic Rescue," from *There is No Balm in Birmingham*, Godine, Inc. "Women and Children First," from *Women and Children First*, Iron Mountain Press.

Eaton, Charles Edward, "Slip of the Tongue," from *The Work of the Wrench*, Cornwall Books. "Sentimental Education," from *The Thing King*, Cornwall Books. "The Parrot," from *On the Edge of the Knife*, Abelard Schulman.

Guy, David, "Chapters From . . ." *The Man Who Loved Dirty Books*, NAL Books.

Hedin, Robert, "Waiting for Trains at Col D'Aubisque," "On Tuesdays They Open the Local Pools to the Stroke-Victims," and "Tornado," from *County O*, Copper Canyon Press.

Kenney, Richard, "Speed of Light," "Fourth," "In June," from *Orrery*, Atheneum.

McFee, Michael, "Possumma," from *Light Year '86*, Bits Press, Cleveland.

Smith, Lee, "Selections From . . ." *Oral History*, Putnam.

Personal mail orders should be addressed to
Jacar Press P O Box 4, Wendell, North Carolina 27591

CARDINAL

CARDINAL

SPEED OF LIGHT
Richard Kenney

The radium in luminescent numbers
painted on my watchface fades: no time,
and no things in the closed-in cosmos now,
but these: the massive plow looming ahead,
the soft churn of chains in snow, eccentric
scythings of his hazard lights like amber
helicopter blades above, the close
cones of headlamps pressed against the blizzard's
high wall. I've followed him for miles now,
watched the spume combing off his cutwater,
the great V-plow, speeding, sparks spurting
underneath its tempered edge and drifting
up the windscreen now in strange and unfamiliar
constellations, changing—
                                        A universe
in one dimension only, love, this road:
the black trace reeling off his rear wheels here
like new creation dragging off its spool—
This is the limiting velocity:
I thread this white cloud-chamber as I can,
I etch this line across what curvature
of space and time still separates us, now,
and night dilates, all night, all night the plow
grinds the stone road bed like my heart
grinding through this last bad month alone
without you, in the dark or in the light—

FOURTH
Richard Kenney

Time out of mind— false
dawn it might be, breaking— embers,
stars, salutes;
a cloud of burning metal salts . . .
My son follows
long stems up until they burst
and star and fall,
a fall of fire— He'll be embarrassed
later on
an ash lights on his cheek, his arm;
it's nothing, skin
a paper lantern-cloth, and earth
is unfamiliar
to him still, and so he cries.
Just now I think
we've seen a million million years
break by, seen novas,
all the heavy atoms thickened
deep inside
the ancient stars— seen all the stuff
of man and earth
come sifting down the sky to stove-
black here, and hearth-
stone here— The urn of light. An iron
sun's repose.
So vapor trails collapse to roses,
rise, and burn,
and set again. Who counts the blank
spots in the sky?—
but these are who we are, who lie

across coarse blankets
here— as I did by my father
on the Fourth
another life of warm Julys . . .
The stars blink out.
Show's over; time to go. The sleight
of fire that jewels
the dark in memory is done,
and here my son
is fast asleep, tears dry. I lift
him, yawning, yearning
too for life, for the high falsework
of the light
that arches under heaven's fall—
and feel the drift
of ash, the sieve, that limes the sleeper's
upturned eye,
that sleeves us all, in time, in time.

IN JUNE
Richard Kenney

Now the earth is warmer than the air.
The eyes adjust, but slowly; for a while, still,
dark is all but absolute. Remember—
somewhere to our left, and close, a deer
woke up— he came out of his dream disturbed
and curious; we heard him stand, stamp,
snorting, close, hooves jarring through our backs
and ribcages like heartbeat in the ground—
and let our breath out long and slowly as we
could, and held—
                          I felt your throat catch air—
as though the heart could hold its teacups-full
quite motionless above this pearly planet
here, oh, how we rattle, and I nearly
laughed out into that queer dark that leaves
the unconcerning household of the flesh
so clamorous—
                          We lay a long while yet.
The night was sweet with timothy we'd crushed,
and uncut all around us so, it seemed
to rise like grey earth-light— in time, it might
have cast our single shadow out among
the summer stars. This was in June. The stars
adjust. The moon had not then risen, but
its turbid light welled up and billowed like
a cool current furled in warmer water,
which appeared to stir some clouds a little,
water lilies on the near horizon—
Then, the dream: that you had moved away,
had balanced there and let your legs into

that light, cool scarves of it across your open
lap and belly and throat and thrown-back cheek—
and the planet strung, then, crescent in the curve
between your spine's arch and the straight line, nightfall,
black hair back to earth.
                          The deer has gone
up in some new and unlit constellation
by this time, and all his timothy
turned milk, or corn, or antler-silk torn loose
in the high Coal-Sack; and we have changed, as well,
and yet— the memory is so strong now
it startles me a moment, lying here,
my arms around you, not to feel the slight
wax-quilled insignature, the water-mark,
the grass impression on your shoulder blades
and strangely perfect back.

selections from
ORAL HISTORY
Lee Smith

GRANNY YOUNGER

From his cabin door, Almarine Cantrell owns all the land
he sees. He's not but twenty-two years old now. Young, then—
you could call him young for owning this much land and
that's a fact, but they's other ways Almarine is not young
now and never was young atall. He growed up right here,
right on this place. Nobody ever knowed what he was up to.
Where's Almarine? they allus said, and who told the an-
swer to that? Not his mama, nor his daddy, nor yet those sorry
brothers of hisn, nor even me over here where I live on the
south side of Hurricane Mountain where I have been aliving
praise God for more years than I could tell you if I was to sit
down and try to count them which I won't. I been here a
long time. Years. I know what I know. I know moren most
folks and that's a fact, you can ask anybody. I know moren I
want to tell you, and moren you want to know. And if I never
knowed exactly where Almarine was when he was little, I
could of give you a good idea.
He'd be down on Grassy Creek all by hisself most likely,
seeing how the water ran over the rocks and how cold it kept
even in summer, or he'd be up in the crook of the biggest
sycamore there at the bend afore the trace starts down
through the spruce-pines, a-setting up there still as a little old

owl for hours and hours just waiting to see if anybody ever
come up the trace, which nobody ever did, or he was out
back in the dugout where they kept the meat all winter on
the cold dirt floor, and potatoes and onions down in the straw
in the grabbling holes, but him not a-grabbling neither, just
sitting there still as you please and breathing that musky salty
smell in there, a dark smell like something too old to figure
whatever it mought have been.

Well, that was Almarine. Almarine fell down between the
cracks in the family like some children will.

In spite of him being so pretty, with all that pale-gold hair,
in spite of him being no trouble to a living soul. Almarine was
said to spend nights in the laurel slick over by Frenchman's
Cave, nights by hisself out there when he was not but nine or
ten. Now that's the wild side of Black Rock Mountain. And
Almarine knowed where Grassy Creek starts, away up high
on Hurricane behind this land of mine, away up there where
it comes a-bubbling and a-snorting like a regular fountain right
out of the ferny ground. Almarine went beyond that spring,
too, straight up the rocky clift where the trees won't grow
and this little fine green grass grows all around in a perfect
circle. A lot of folks won't go up there. But Almarine went
and lived to tell it and went again, and nobody marked his
comings or goings in particular, or cared how he could scream
in the night like a painter until the painters all around were
screaming back. Almarine trained a crow one time, till it
could talk. It could say about fifteen words when his brother
Riley kilt it with a rifle, out of spite. That's how Riley was.
But Almarine! Almarine had the lightest, biggest eyes when
he was a child. It seemed like he never blinked. He liked to
look out on some distance.

Almarine didn't need nobody, is what it was, and there's
folks won't take to a child like that. Still and all, he was sweet
when nobody else in that family was, so this was a part of it
too. People don't like somebody to be so sweet it makes
them look bad, that's a fact. Which he was. I mean he was
that sweet. In fact Almarine was that kind of sweet moony
child who'll likely end up without a thing in this or any other
world, without a pot to piss in.

How Almarine ended up with all this land is a curious
thing.

His daddy, Charles Vance Cantrell, was a big old man as mean as a snake and hard on women and children. He had him one gold tooth in the front. Charles Vance Cantrell was Irish or so he said at one time. He had him a long gold chain with a big watch on it that had some dates and "Dublin" carved into the back, but don't you know he lost it in a poker game at old man Joe Johnson's store like he lost those mules and everything else he owned sooner or later except his land, and Lord knows it's surprising how he never lost that too. He never put up his land. Anyway, Charles Vance Cantrell—they called him Van—was a fat old man who gambled a lot and would just as soon strike you as speak. He come by ship, he said, and then by wagon, and they was religion mixed up in it someway, but of course you couldn't never prove it by Van Cantrell. He brung that wife of hisn, that Nell, from Ireland with him, or so we thought, although wasn't nobody sure since she was so ashy-pale and she never said a word until Van went off to fight in the war after which she perked up considerable. It would of been all right with me if she had not, now that's the truth. I never give a fig for that Nell.

Anyway, Van went off through Indian Grave Gap, over Snowman Mountain and down into West Virginia, where he joined up with the Union. Nobody knowed if he joined with the Union out of principle or because, what I thought, it was the quickest army to get to, and Van Cantrell ever loved a fight. Now some men hereabouts took up on one side, and some the other. They was nary a slave in the county. So they done what they felt to do. It split some families down the middle, I'll tell you that. Churches too. They is a church in Abingdon that to this day has got one door for those who stood with the Union in the war and one door for Johnny Reb, and this is true, and I'll swear it. To this day.

Van Cantrell stayed with the army as long as he could, and lost one leg above the knee afore he come home. Things was different when he got back, he found out right away. Old Nell Cantrell, who had not done a thing but lay in the bed having a sick headache since the day he carried her in that wagon up the trace, Old Nell was up and farming! She had planted her some cabbage and some corn; she had three hogs on the side of Hurricane Mountain. She never got back in the bed neither. She didn't have to, since Van was laid up hisself and couldn't get around like he used to do. Thank God! is what she thought. But she needed some help of course, and so she had them three boys right in a row—stairstep boys, with Almarine in the middle. The other two, Riley and Shelby Dick, took after their daddy, and they growed up a-fighting and a-fussing just like him. They would throw your wash off the line, I've seed it, they tromped on their mama's beans. It was clear from the beginning that they would kill each other or get kilt theirselves before they was through, which is near-about what they did.

But this happened first. Van Cantrell's leg started up ooz-ing a clear liquid where it had been cut off and healed over. It was a clear smelly liquid, not like pus, which seemed to ooze right out of the very skin without no break that you could find atall. You never saw the beat of it. They called me, of course, and I done what I knowed, but nothing I knowed done any good. The first thing I done was lay me a spider web acrost it, hold it on with soot and lard. Now this had no effect. The next thing I done was what my mama showed me and which I am knowed for everywhere in these parts, what I do to stop bleeding. They will call me anytime, day or night, and when I hear who it is I start saying the words even afore I get my bonnet on, I start saying the words which I know by heart from my mama, and when I get there, most times, the bleeding's already stopped. It is Ezekiel 16, sixth verse, what I say. I done this for Van Cantrell too, done it two days run-ning with nary result. But it is for bleeding, like I said, and not for no smelly old ooze.

"Hit ain't going to work," I told Nell when the sun come up. Then she sent Riley off for old Doc Story, but by the time he got acrost Black Rock Mountain, Van was dead. We had to burn sulfur in there for two weeks to get the smell outen the cabin.

Anyway, without no old man to keep him in line, Riley got hisself in trouble over a girl and had to leave this county fastern squat. This left Shelby Dick, who was the youngest, and Almarine, but him and Almarine fell out someway over a knife and whose it was, or who knows what it was they fell out about, but pretty soon Almarine was gone too, leaving Shelby Dick to farm with his mama. Now this was fine with Shelby Dick and with old Nell Cantrell too. Nobody took much to Almarine as I have said, and even when he was there it was like he wasn't really there so twerent much difference atall with him gone. Almarine allus wanted something—who knows what?—and that's why he kept staring out beyond them hills.

He was gone almost five years. And whatever happened to him in between, that's his story. He never did tell a word. Almarine went off sweet and shy and distant, like I said. He come back all of them things—not changed in any way you could put your finger on—but with another set to his jaw and a hard look sometimes around his eyes. He appeared tired. He appeared oldern he should have been, for his age. Old man Joe Johnson said he heard that Almarine had been in prison someplace, and the way Almarine looked, you could feature it. Of course folks'll say anything but it's true, a man is his father's son. Anyway it was clear that they had been some hard times, even if we never knowed what they was, just like when Almarine was a little boy and you couldn't guess what he was up to.

So I am telling how Almarine come back one day in August 1902, a-walking up the trace in mincy shoes and a snow-white shirt without one thin dime to his name. He just missed burying his mama, who had died about five days prior. His face never changed a bit when he found this out, but I for one couldn't fault him on it since the sweetness and goodness you find in most women were not present, it has to be said, in old Nell Cantrell. Not at the first when she was young and laying in the bed so sickly and down in the mouth, nor yet later when she took to farming herself and smoked that pipe. I smoke a pipe too and you know it. The pipe's not the point. It was the way she gone about everything, like she was too smart for this world, like she couldn't be bothered to smile. She sulled around all the time. A decent woman, folks said. Hard-working, could hoe her corn like a man. But any sweetness in the family, it went straight to Almarine. I see I have forgot to mention Shelby Dick. He died in a whorehouse fire in Roseann, West Virginia, two years before Almarine come a-walking up the trace in that soft white shirt.

Shelby Dick broke his mama's heart.

So Almarine got it all.

And Almarine sits now in the cabin door in his daddy's

chair, and he owns all the land he sees. Truly this holler is so much a part of Almarine that he doesn't even think of owning it, not any moren a man would thnk of owning his arm nor yet one of his legs. The whole time Almarine was gone, most of him stayed right here. He wasn't nothing but a half-boy, a half-man I guess you'd say, but now he's come back here with all of them dead as stumps and he won't have to leave again, he won't have to go noplace, ever again. Almarine's soul swells out over this whole holler. He rolls a cigarette outen rabbit tobaccy and gets up and goes in to the fire and lights it and comes back out. Dragging the smoke in deep, he tilts hisself back in the chair and runs his hand through his long light hair. Then he blows smoke out the cabin door, smoke so blue it gets lost in that blue haze that comes creeping up the holler of an evening, like right now.

Leave him be.

Let Almarine set awhile. He's not but twenty-two years old, and look at what-all he owns. Hoot Owl Holler is the prettiest holler on God's green earth, the way this creek runs through. Most hollers don't have no creek. And Almarine's cabin sets high, high up in the head of the holler, it gives him a view. Most hollers don't have no view. Almarine's daddy mought of been a son of a bitch, but he was a strong man and he knowed how to build a cabin. This cabin is here to stay. It's got a puncheon floor instead of pure dirt, which most don't. A front room, a back room, a lean-to and a big high loft where old Nell's beans have been strung into leather-britches since July, a-drying against the winter, alongside her strings of apples and peppers, pears and tobaccy twists. She's saved the seed in gourds, there at the back. She's got them lined up on the farthest wall. A fireplace in the front room, little old jumping fire. Beds with corn-husk ticks on them, quilts. Jacob's Ladder, Poplar Leaf, Bear Paw, Star. The quilts is real pretty and bright in the lights and shadows throwed up by that little fire. One of the beds has got a down tick on it, and that one will be Almarine's. Many's the time he held the goose while Old Nell plucked the down—and got bit, too, over and over, for all his trouble—but never has he slept on down his whole life long.

So let him. It's his house.

Let him look out the door past the ash-hopper nailed on

the tree, where they ran their lye, out past the big black kettle on the tripod, where Old Nell boiled her clothes. It's all hisn, now. It's all hisn including Hoot Owl Mountain behind the cabin, them apple trees and pear trees at the foot of it, the burying ground up on top. Old Nell's up there already, along with the other two. He owns that mountain now. He owns a strip on the side of Hurricane Mountain too, that strip running next to me where the dogwood's so thick in the spring. He owns the garden on the other side, and starting up Snowman Mountain, he owns them blackberry bushes all in a tangle there where the garden stops and the mountain starts. Now these three mountains is all different, let me say, Hoot Owl and Hurricane and Snowman, with Hoot Owl Holler smack in the middle of them three like a play-pretty cotched in the hand of God.

Hoot Owl Mountain looks like how it sounds, laurel so thick you can't hardly climb it atall, in fact you plumb can't do it iffen you don't know the way. They's not but one trail up Hoot Owl Mountain and it goes on to the burying ground. So you start up that trail through the laurel and it's so dark in there you can't hardly see your way. You get through that laurel and then you're climbing, see, but climbing slow—it's a big mountain, and the trail goes round and round. They's trees up Hoot Owl biggern you ever saw in your life, they's ferns nigh as tall as a man. On up, they's caves in the rocky clift and one cave a man got lost in, so they say. They say you can hear him holler. Now the burying ground on the top of the mountain is a flat grassy bald, and it's real pretty. They's a wind that blows all the time. I like that burying ground. But I mislike Hoot Owl Mountain myself and don't go up it lessen I have to, but you can find yellowroot there, and ginger, heartleaf and pennyrile, red coon for poison ivy. What I need. Hoot Owl Mountain is a dark mountain though, maybe it's all them pines, and it don't get hardly no sun. Fog will hang on the north side all day long, with that blue mist spread over the top. Moss grows everywhere under them pines, moss thick enough to sleep on if you cared to. Not me, mind you. They is something about Hoot Owl Mountain makes a body lose heart. If you laid down to sleep on that pretty moss, you mought never wake up again in this world. It's no telling where you'd wake up. They was never anybody knowed to court on Hoot Owl neither, you see for why. I keep a buckeye in my pocket, traveling Hoot Owl. I get right along.

But up on Hurricane, where I live, now that's as pretty a place as you please. Grassy Creek running down it, all them little falls, why it is music to your ears just a-walking up Grassy Creek. It is pussywillow and Indian paint, Queen Anne's lace and black-eyed Susan. It is swimming holes with water so clear you can see straight down to the bottom. They never was any water bettern Grassy Creek. Then you get on up, you've got your oak, your chestnut, your tulip tree. Big old trees all spreaded out which lets the sun shine through. The mast under these trees is so good it's what they call hog heaven up here on Hurricane Mountain, everybody lets their hogs run here. Hurricane Mountain is a fine mountain and they's other folks lives here too, you can see for why. Now I've got my own holler, mind. Nobody ever lived in it but me and mama, and mama's dead. But I've got my neighbors up here on Hurricane, not like Almarine. They's a bunch of Horns, been here forever, and some Justices, some Rameys, Davenports. They is one-eyed Jesse Waldron lives all by hisself in the Paw Paw Gap. Rhoda Hibbitts not far from me with them two ugly mealy-mouth daughters of hern, and no man in sight. That wouldn't bother me none if I was Rhoda. I'd not put up with a regular man if you paid me. But it grieves Rhoda considerable. Take 'em to town, I says. Well, that's another story.

And Snowman, over on the other side of Hoot Owl Holler, why Snowman's the biggest of all. They's a rocky clift the other side of Snowman, looking down into West Virginia, that's the spitting image of a man, and that rocky clift is so high that snow will stay on it nigh into April sometimes, why they call it Snowman. If you want to go to West Virginia, you follow the trace over Indian Grave Gap and down Coon Branch and into Roseann where the lumber company's at. It'll take you a day and a half to get over Snowman from here if you walk it steady. Mought be it'll take you two days. And they's folks all over Snowman—Ratliffs and Presleys, Ashes, Stacys, and Skeens. There's moren I know including lately them foreigners come in with the lumber trade.

This is not to mention old Isom Charles nor yet Old Isom's red-headed Emmy up there on Snowman Mountain, that same red-headed Emmy who's to be the ruination and the end of Almarine. I'll get to them. Nobody knows them anyway, half-crazy a-living way off up there under the Raven Clifts. I'll get to them in my own sweet time.

Anyway here's Almarine, not knowing any of that. Almarine a-looking out the door of his cabin where the creek goes down the holler, and down, and down again in front of the cabin until it turkey-tails out in the bottom and runs along flat down there so far you can't hardly see it, beyond that stand of sycamores where it flows on through the spruce-pines and from there down the Meeting House branch and into the Dismal River at Tug, where the store is.

Almarine looks past the creek and the dropping-off holler, Almarine looks out on space. Away acrost his valley he sees Black Mountain rising jagged to the sky—county seat beyond it, Black Rock where the courthouse is—and if he looks to the left on past it, he sees all the furtherest ranges, line on line. Purple and blue and blue again and smoky until you can't tell the mountains apart from the sky. Lord, it'll make a man think something, seeing that. It'll make a man think deep.

And Almarine is thinking, I seed him from the trace. Tilted back and thinking, a-smoking that cigarette, with night coming on like it does.

"Well Almarine," I says.

And Almarine says, "Granny."

Then he says, "Come and set with me, Granny," and I was proud to do it. I set in the chair and Almarine hunkered down in the doorway smoking, he hunkered down there just like he used to do as a little set-along child. It seemed like no time since he was borned. But he had growed up into the finest-looking man you ever laid your eyes on, that's a fact. All that pale gold hair and them light blue eyes, and so tall and so straight. Everbody else around here is mostly dark complected and mostly slighter than Almarine.

"Air ye going to stay now?" I asked him, and Almarine said he was.

He said he was home for good.

That did not surprise me none, as Almarine was made for this holler and it for him, iffen he left it or no. I could see how he knowed it for home.

We set out there while the fog rolled up in the bottom and

the lightning bugs commenced to rise all along the banks of the creek. "Ever thick fog in August means a heavy snow come winter," I says, and Almarine grins. It was getting so dark I couldn't hardly see him, white tooth-shine in the dark. "Old Granny," he said. "I misremember all of that." "Don't make no differ," I said. "Old woman like me." I stands up to go. "What you need is a girl," I says to Almarine. "What you need around here is some children on this land, and a woman's touch in the house. You better find you a girl," I says.

Then I left, off up Hurricane, how I go.

Later, I wished I'd of bit off my tongue.

Sometimes I know the future in my breast. Sometimes I see the future coming out like a picture show, acrost the trail ahead. But that night I never seed nothing atall. If I had, it would of been graves and dying, it would of been blood on the moon. And I never saw a blessed thing in the night but them lightning bugs a-rising from the sally grass along by Grassy Creek.

Because of course Almarine went right out and done it, what I said. Everbody does what I say. Almarine went a-courting. He courted on Hurricane, he courted over in Black Rock. He courted until he run acrost Isom's red-headed Emmy, and that was the end of him. I'll tell it all directly.

I'll tell it all, but don't you forget it is Almarine's story. Almarine's, and Pricey Jane's, and Lord yes, it's that red-headed Emmy's. Mought be it's her story moren the rest. Iffen twas my story, I never would tell it at all. There's tales I'll tell, and tales I won't. And iffen twas my story, why I'd be all hemmed in by the facts of it like Hoot Owl Holler is hemmed in by them three mountains. I couldn't move no way but forward. And often in my traveling over these hills I have seed that what you want the most, you find offen the beaten path. I never find ary a thing. But I am an old, old woman, and I have traveled a lot in these parts. I have seed folks come and I have seed them go. I have cotched more babies than I can name you; I have put the burying quilts around many a soul. I said I know moren you know and mought be I'll tell you moren you want to hear. I'll tell you a story that's truer than true, and nothing so true is so pretty. It's blood on the moon, as I said. The way I tell a story is the way I want to, and iffen you mislike it, you don't have to hear.

LITTLE LUTHER WADE

I was out in the yard working on that old truck we got off of Giles Hogg when Daddy come back from town and come over there and told me what old man Rife had told him that morning. I'd been out there working on that truck since dinner nearabouts, and my hands had like to froze off. I had some gloves up at the house, but I didn't give a damn. That whole winter I was a fool for work, it seemed like I couldn't get enough, and I couldn't do nothing else. I couldn't sit in a chair. And I never played no music all that time. So I was under there working when Daddy come.

"Son!" Daddy hollered. "Get out from under that truck and mind what I'm telling you," Daddy hollered out in the yard.

"I done heard you the first time," I said.

"Then get out from under there," Daddy said, "and get on up to the house."

"I'll be there in a minute," I told him. "You go on."

"What?" Daddy hollered. His hearing is going bad.

"You go on," I hollered back. "I said I'll be up there directly."

I watched from under the truck where I could see his boots, which stayed right where they was for a while and then I could see he had done give up on me when he turned and left. I stayed under there for a while longer though, thinking things over, afore I come out myself. Thing was, I never knowed that Daddy knowed what I'd been projecting, until he said. So I was kindly surprised-like, that he knowed what I'd had in my mind, what I was fixing to do. Thing about Daddy is, he's so old and all, and he acts like he can't hear much, but I guess he hears what he wants to, like the rest of us. I guess he hears enough. Anyway I laid under there in the cold and I was sorry I wasn't going to do it, at first, and then

I was glad, I guess, even though I was sorry too. If ever a man needed killing, that was the feller, and now he had done got away. I stayed under there and thought about it, I stayed till my face worked right.

Then I got out and got my tools and went up to the house and they was all in there, Mama and Daddy and Earl was, anyway, and Earl's little girl Blanche, and they was all acting like they was so goddamn busy, like they wasn't nothing atall going on.

I put the tools in the box and got the keys to the other truck and told them I'd see them after while.

"Hit's coming on for dark," Mama said. "I saved you some supper," she said next. "Why don't you just stay home?" Mama's the kind can drive you crazy without even trying.

"Let him be, Mary," Daddy said, and then he tells me there's a icy patch on the road at the Paw Paw Gap and to watch out for it.

"I ain't goin that way," I said. But seeing as how they already knew so goddamn much anyway, it looked like, I'd be damned if I'd give them any more satisfaction and say where I *was* going. I don't reckon I knew myself, until I got ahold of those keys, and then it come to me. All I wanted to do was drive over to where I could see the spur line, coming from Claypool Hill, and see that train pass by. Iffen he was on it, and Aldous said he was going to put him on it, why then I wanted to see it pass. It was a long way and a crazy idea and I knew I had better get going.

"Mama says Dory is ruint," Blanche said.

Blanche was holding the yarn up and Mama was winding a ball. I looked at Mama and she wouldn't look back, and then Blanche said, "What's *ruint?*"

"You shut your mouth," I said. Daddy was acting like he couldn't hear none of this. Then I got my rifle and my guitar and then I left. I know they was wondering what I wanted with all of that, and I was wondering too. It was like my head was a-spinning around. I throwed everthing in the truck and then I clumb in too, and pulled that thing what throws the seat forward—I have to sit way up, on account of my leg—and it come up so fast I knocked my gun in the floor, give me a big scare. It could of gone off and kilt *me*, and then wouldn't that be a sight? I got to grinning, thinking about it, cranking the truck. I hadn't grinned in such a while, it was like it was hurting my face. So I don't have to shoot nobody after all, I thought, not even myself. But still I wanted to see him pass.

I went by Wall Johnson's store and him and Merle and some other fellers was coming out the door and they tried to wave me down but I drove on, I wasn't stopping for nothing, and I drove on past Tug and through the Paw Paw Gap where they wasn't no ice atall, Daddy just made that up, and then I drove over the mountain to Claypool Hill and pulled off at that bend of the Levisa River where you can see the stretch where the railroad track comes when it goes out of town. It took me a hour or so to get there, and I still didn't have no gloves, I just wanted to see him pass.

By then it was dark for sure. I got my gun and got out of the truck and walked over there by the river so I could see better. It was cold, Lord! I blowed on my hands and stomped my feet, but didn't nothing help. I wondered if Dory knew he was leaving, too, if she was thinking about him. I wondered how she felt and what she thought. It was cold as a bitch that night and I got to wishing I'd of shot him anyway, then I wouldn't have to stand out here and wait no more. Then I got to whistling till my lips got too cold to whistle. First I'd feel alright, and then I'd feel awful. Things was confused in my mind. I thought how Mama had said Dory was ruint, which was just about what you could figure Mama'd say, but I knowed she weren't never ruint. I thought on Wall Johnson saying he wouldn't take no man's leftovers. Well by God I'll take what I can get, I thought all of a sudden. I'll take it and be damned, I thought, and then I heard it coming far away around Black Rock Mountain, and then I heard it coming closer. By and by I seen the light, coming around the bend, and then before I knowed it, here it was going by me kicking up the awfulest ruckus you ever heard way out here in the night. Steam pouring outen the engine, and you could see the men in there, stoking the fire, one of them looked like Bill Horn's boy. They was not but five cars and a caboose, and two of the cars looked to be empty, from what I could tell in the dark. But I knowed in my bones he was on it someplace, up there in the engine with them or else in one of them other cars. I knowed he was on that train. It went on with a great big roaring racket and leaving smoke in the air. I pulled my

gun up to my shoulder then and sighted down it, just for the
hell of it, at the swinging light on the back of the caboose. It
swang back and forth, back and forth, in and out of the sight,
and then the train was gone and him with it. I went back and
got in the truck and got my guitar and made up this song, my
fingers was too cold to pick, but anyway I made up this song.

> Darlin' Dory stands by the cabin door
> Standing with her Bible in her hands
> Darlin' Dory stands by the cabin door
> A-pinin' for her city man.
>
> You can throw that Bible down on the floor
> You can throw it out in the rain
> Prayin' for him all night long won't do no good
> For he ain't a-comin' back again.
>
> Well he ain't a-comin' back to the meetin'-house
> and he ain't a-comin' back to the school
> City feller gone with a head full of dreams
> Oh, why can't you see him for a fool?
>
> Dory let me dry those tears away
> Dory come back in and shut the door
> A month or two don't add up to a life
> A slip or two don't make you a whore.
>
> Dory come back to your own true love
> A month or two don't add up to life
> Dory let me dry them tears away
> Dory let me make you my wife.

It took me nearabout a hour to make it up. I knowed I
wouldn't never sing it to nobody, least of all to her, but any-
way I made it up and then I knowed what I was going to do
and I felt good, I tell you, I got to feeling like myself again
for the first time all winter. I laughed out loud in the dark
and cranked up that old truck. She was my girl afore she was
hisn, whether she knowed it or not. I allowed as how she was
my girl now, whether she knowed it yet or not, either. I
knowed then that she might not love me as much as I loved

her, but that was all right with me too. She'd love me more than she thought. A girl needs a man she can depend on, and by God there's worse things than that. By God there is, I says to myself, gunning that truck back home, and she'll come to know it afore she's through. In a way I still wish he hadn't of left, though, I was going to shoot him dead as soon as he walked out of Justine Poole's no doubt about it. I had been laying for him. I wondered how Daddy knew. You have to get up mighty damn early to get ahead of Daddy. I rode along grinning, and it was cold as a witch's tit. But I tell you, it wouldn't have turned a hair on my head to shoot him, that's a fact.

SALLY

There's two things I like to do better than anything else in this world, even at my age—and one of them is talk. You all can guess what the other one is.

A while back, Roy and me were in the bed—that's my husband, Roy—and I said this out loud to him it is something I have thought to myself for a while.

"Roy," I said, "when you get right down to it, honey, there's not a lot worth doing, is there, outside of this and talking?" and Roy wrinkled up his eyes in that way he has, and thought for the longest time, and then he said, "Well, Sally, I guess there's sports." Sports! I laughed so loud.

But that's Roy for you. He'd roll over and die if he missed a bowl game on TV. One time he didn't get up from that recliner for seven hours solid and his knees went right out from under him when he stood up when the news come on.

Roy has a good time, that's the thing I like about Roy. He's a lineman for the Appalachian Power and he likes that job fine, no complaints, turned down a promotion because it meant he'd have to wear a tie and spend half time at the office.

"Count me out," was what Roy said.

Roy likes his sports and he likes my kids and he likes pepperoni pizza and he likes to have some beer of an evening—I do too—and he'll grow him some tomatoes every year out there by the garage, he likes tomatoes, and he likes engines better than any man you ever saw. Any kind of engine. He made Davy the cutest little dune buggie, and got him a helmet to go with it. Roy likes cars and boats. And Roy can fuck your eyes out, Roy can, and talking all the time. "Talk to me," he says. Well I like that.

My first husband came from a family up in Ohio that didn't believe in talking to women and he never said one word, just roll over and go to sleep.

I didn't run into Roy until I was over the hill—I had this other husband first, as I said—but by God I know a good thing when I see it.

I jumped right on it.

Because him and me we are two of a kind and sometimes when we're there in the bed it's like it all gets mixed up some way, like you kind of forget where your body stops and his starts or who did what to who and who came when and all that. I said we are two of a kind.

Another way we are, Roy and me, is *down to earth*. I've always been like that basically and so has Roy, even before we took up with each other. Sometimes we play a little poker with Lois and Ozell Banks and sometimes we go to Myrtle Beach. We don't want the moon.

Not like Almarine, who is all the time trying to get us to go into the AmWay business with him and Debra. The more people they get, see, the closer him and Debra get to being a diamond distributor, or a ruby or a emerald distributor, or whatever the hell it is he wants so bad.

"I'll buy your soap," I said, "and I'll buy your oven cleaner," I said, "but by God that's it and you might as well take all those cosmetics right out of this house."

I am not about to go fooling around with any soap cosmetics.

I told Almarine that, too, right to his face.

"I don't buy a thing but Mary Kay," I said. "Now get that straight." Roy was laughing and laughing. Lord, I love the way that man can laugh. And Almarine leaning forward, just so serious, he was sitting right there on that couch.

"Tell me your dreams," he said. Almarine learned that at the AmWay convention, they tell you to say that and write them down.

"I dreamed I went to a demolition derby in my Maidenform bra." Roger said that—that's my grandson, Roger, with the smart mouth. We were all in here in the family room looking at Almarine sitting on the couch with all that soap and air fresheners and nail polish and God knows what-all spread out around him like he was a regular store. And putting on weight, too, I noticed—Almarine used to be a tackle in high school and now he's got this real big neck.

"No, I'm serious." He held his pencil up in his hand like he was back in tenth grade, taking a spelling test. "Tell me your dreams," he said.

"Shit, Almarine," Roy said. "Come on."

So finally Almarine got up and went home. If he had any sense he would of known he'd never get anyplace with me and Roy who are the only people on our street who haven't ever planted any grass in our yard so we won't have to mow it. That's how we are.

But Almarine is always telling people that if they go in the AmWay business their life and their marriage will improve.

"It's a couples business," Almarine says.

Shows you how much he knows.

But my whole family is like that. People say they're haunted and they are—every one of them all eat up with wanting something they haven't got. If it's not being a double ruby it's something else. Roy says that watching my family carry on is better than TV. They've *always* been like that—not Ora Mae, of course, but she's another case altogether, and not Pappy, that's Luther—any more since he's gotten so old and crazy he's forgotten what it was that he wanted so bad although all the rest of us remembers it real well as you might imagine. But the rest of them, Lord!

When Roy fell off of the truck about a month ago and got his knee smashed up so bad, I told him the whole story, I never had told it before, Roy sitting home in a leg cast so he couldn't do anything else *but* talk.

"Listen," I said, and I got him a beer, "I'll start at the beginning," I said, which I did, and although I told it the best I could, I'm still not sure I got it straight. It took me a day to tell the whole thing. ■

ANOTHER FELLOW
Gerald Barrax

The almost whole skin
Lay right outside the window of my basement
Where I'd been entombed for more than a year.
Whenever it happened, if I had raised myself
And looked out of the groundlevel window
I'd have seen it crawling out of its year-old skin;
It would've seen a face marveling and envious
Up from a book behind the screen,
But it would've been too busy
Doing what it was supposed to do
To stop for me;
My ancestors, considering its immortality,
Would've welcomed it with food and drink
When it came as spirit of the living-dead from the forest
To visit their huts;
And I would've sacrificed a book to its wisdom
In return for a poem.
     Dear Emily,
That was in September, months ago.
The grass after days of rain was high, wet, still growing
And had to be cut once more for the year. I cut it
In anticipation, wondering if I would drive it
Into the square of the yard, or out,
Half dreading both but needing
One or the other. This year I will be 43.
I found neither the spotted shaft in the high grass
Nor in my room your worm transformed
And ringed with power. I found an empty skin
That I threw over the fence.

THE DEATH OF ANOTHER FELLOW
Gerald Barrax

1. It's April, the month I can't escape,
Thick with paradoxes, when
So many things have ended or begun.
I am pulling the lawn mower through the back door
When the sun blinks and freezes the space
Where my unwitting sinister eye sees the black shape
Vanishing between the two concrete blocks laid end to end
On the sloping earth beneath my window.

Now I unwillingly know the secret
Of his hiding place: he hadn't been far from home
When he'd left those shed skins
Along the rear wall of the house
Those years before. Not far at all.
And the warm driveway was his porch,
Where he'd surprised Helen
Once too often. It must be killed
Because of the girls, she told me.
How can she let them go out into the yard?

But until he became so careless
He never revealed where he lived.
And I swear: I thought I didn't know.

2. It's a simple, mindless chore, cutting grass.
You can easily lose yourself in meditation
Going back and forth across a yard
As I do this Sunday morning.
It's less easy if you're being constantly
Watched, back and forth,

As I am.
> *I know who you are, African forebear*
> *coming to give me corn and fertility;*
> *incarnation of our dead, unborn children;*
> *Indian ancestor, great grandsire, spear*
> *of the war gods, rain-bearer;*
> *and you, the more "civilized" of my burdens,*
> *tempting me with wisdom and guilt.*

I have little enough of one, none of the other.
Because I wasn't meant to be alone
I married twice, but continued to burn.
Now there are old lost loves to remember,
To wonder what became of,
For whom I might have been cutting this grass.
And sons, who might have been doing it for me.

The farther away from him I get
The further he comes up, black and straight,
From between the stones, outlined
Against the house, watching me
In a curious, friendly way.
In spite of the enmity
It's hard to resist that functional beauty,
The symmetry of its purpose in living.
> *I see you, old buddy. At this distance*
> *are you following only the sound of the mower*
> *back and forth, or is it me?*

You play with fire. And your children burn.
For the love I found wholly incarnated in Cathy's arms,
Eve's breasts, Kay's hair, Suzy's lips,
Annie's thighs my sons burned without their father.
Alas, alas that ever love was sin!
But that *was* love, the better part of wisdom;
Nevertheless, why keep the grass cut
And the yard fenced in

And free of snakes if there are no children?
> *But you are inside the fence*
> *and that's as far as I can go*
> *before I must come back to you.*
> *And still you rise from your hole*
> *the farther away I go,*
> *my fixed foot leaning after me*
> *but vanishing if I approach you.*
> *I need the distance more than you;*
> *but there's this goddamned fence.*

And here in the corner of the yard, the mowing
Is difficult where Helen had the garden plot
The year before the first baby was born.
The grass has overgrown it now, and surrounded
By the drainage ditch, and raised higher
Than the level of the yard, it resembles an island
Or burial mound.
But she made things grow there in profusion.
Lettuce, beans, tomatoes, squash, eggplant, corn.
And the fruit in the woods beyond the fence:
She never went over there, afraid of the snakes.
And she wants the yard free, her home safe.
I tell her
> *he is harmless, and replaces*
> *small, lesser, more numerous, flabby evils*

(and maintains a balance in my nature)
She says: it is better to marry than to burn,
But I was not meant to burn with you.
Nor will I let my children.

3. I leave the mower running out of his
sight, behind the redwood fence that extends
twelve feet from the wall of the
house into the yard.
I go into the basement for the

B.B. gun, a rake and spade, out the
front door around the side of the
house, behind him. At the corner of the
house I peer around, brace myself against the
house, and sight the gun on the opening
between the two blocks. His head emerges, waving
toward the sound of the still running
mower. I aim at the back of the
small head and try to stop wavering. I
miss the first shot and he
vanishes. I cock the gun, feeling cowardly, and
foolish, hoping no neighbors see me.
He emerges again and I steady
myself. Another
miss? So, I've got to face him.
I go through the gate, carrying my
rake and long-handled spade. I pull over one of the
concrete slabs with the rake, and then the
other, and in the hollow space underneath
> *from the mass of black coils*
> *the head comes up and the spade goes*
> chuk chuk chuk (*Stop!*) chuk chuk *through*
> *the body*
> *into the cool clayey earth.*
> *The sun is blinking, freezing the images*
> *of his movements; his lidless, unblinking eyes*
> *mock and accuse me in cold intelligence,*
> *its sacrifice transforming it into Serpent.*
> *The head falls back among the coils and guts,*
> *the mouth opening and closing in gasps,*
> *as if to localize the pains.*
> A small movement. A nest? Young ones? A
> family?
> No. Serpents are solitary, live alone.
> That is its tail.

I cover him with dirt,
Bury it there under my window and replace the stones.
It was so helpless after all,
So easy to kill.
And my own fears.

4. Now it's June. Walking up the front steps
With my oldest daughter, I hear rustling
In the dry leaves at the side of the porch.
I look over the wrought iron rail
And see a black snake, smaller than the one
I killed, moving along the front wall. Above it,
On a bush, a mockingbird is chirping at it
In agitation, feathers ruffled, wings outspread.
I take my child into the
House, tell her to stay there while I
Kill a snake. I get the spade from the basement
And go back out to the front yard.
It has gone. And so has the bird.
I go around the house and find nothing.
Back inside, my daughter asks if I killed it.
No. It was gone.
But Daddy, it was harmless anyway and wasn't
Going to hurt anybody.
I look at her, unbelieving. No, I said,
It wasn't going to hurt anybody.

> *Then what was it I killed, what is buried*
> *in the backyard under my window?*

YAKOV
Larry Rudner

How I loved Yakov Szmul Milutsky!

Milutsky the painter of oversized watercolors, the sketch artist who would drag me out in the middle of the night to make a quick drawing of something he'd seen on one of his long walks away from the shop—an iron railing by a church, a broken wooden table leaning against a shed in the Market Square, the spot where yeshiva boys would gather for a few moments of air after so much time studying Torah. Or Milutsky the collector of Russian and Yiddish poetry, recalling from memory a fragment from Blok or Moishe Leib Halpern ("he left us, Mendel," Yakov told me, never forgiving Halpern for leaving, "and now we have to look for his words across the ocean!"), booming verses out across the crowded coffee house for all to hear, his voice raw from too much brandy and acrid-smelling cigarettes. And Milutsky: engraver, printer of posters, handbills and broadsheets for any number of Zionist groups, the man who took me into his shop as an apprentice, demanding of me only that I spend my time reading and drawing while I listened to his long tales about the Palestine he had only imagined in his sketches and dreams.

"You can stay with me for life, if you want to," Yakov would tell me nearly every morning when we opened the shop for business. "After all, Mendel, I know God commanded us to make good art, and since I'm as good a Jew as anyone here (Yakov always found a new commandment for us), we two will follow this law for life. Now, my young artist friend —to work!"

Yakov's shop was situated on a narrow street not too far from the Market Square. Although he inherited the shop and what remained of a poor business from his father, Yakov improved the trade while he expanded his own interests from the occasional commercial posters his father printed on an ancient press at the rear of the shop, to a now-flourishing business in poster design and production that served Poles as well as Jews. Everyone knew him, used the shop as a meeting place, tolerated his politics (he kept his own large charcoal sketch of Rosa Luxemburg directly over the counter, arranging a fresh bouquet of poppies beneath for all to see!), and even bought his watercolors of Jerusalem and the Dead Sea.

There was a time when Yakov tried to put the shop in order. When he first took me in after my father's moods and anger became intolerable, Yakov had me cleaning, arranging, and cataloging the charcoals, inks, reams of various-sized paper, and the half-completed posters he stacked everywhere or just dropped where he had been working at the time. I would go to the back of the shop to the large storeroom that served as studio and printing room and settle myself around the glass containers filled with inks so exotic in name and color ("Bombay Blue" or "Flower of the Gold Coast"), that I would, much to the joy of my employer, spend my time opening the containers and sampling the colors as I spread them on the always available blank paper. "That's it," Yakov shouted when he caught me. "Mix them together and see what you come up with . . . like so." Pushing me aside, he put his finger in one pool of ink while a second finger swam in another color; and when he pressed his dripping fingers together he created strange tints he quickly smeared on a sheet of paper, so pleased at the result he urged me to do the same as he hunted along the dusty shelves for brightest colors he could find after years of neglect. We often sat together for hours playing with the inks like children, sometimes unaware of the wildly-ringing set of bells signaling the appearance of one of Yakov's customers in the front of the shop. "A moment," Yakov always yelled from where we sat hunched over scattered sheets of paper on the floor, "the young genius and his teacher are working hard. Be patient. Take a roll from the basket or come back here with us!''

Yakov's frequent absences from the shop to search for new customers kept him away for hours at a time, leaving the management of the business to Meyer Hershkovitz, a master printer and the only one of us brave enough to operate the groaning, thumping press, or to Jerzy Fiatkowska, a Pole Yakov employed for his special genius as a photographer and darkroom technician. It was uncommon for a Jewish artisan like Yakov to work so closely with a Pole, especially during the awful years of the economic boycott against Jewish businesses, but Yakov valued his assistant, paid him well and was careful to allow Jerzy time off even for the most minor of Catholic holidays and celebrations (''He always brings me a piece of cake,'' Yakov told me, ''so why shouldn't he go whenever he wants?''). When Jerzy returned from taking photographs of some Zionist athletic team whose faces would soon appear on a large poster, Yakov insisted Jerzy print the film straight away and display them for everyone to see on the black felt board by the front door. Calling us from the back room, Yakov would pour cheap vodka into the tiny crystal glasses he saved for our frequent celebrations of ''art.'' He made a toast to his ''right arm,'' congratulated the Pole on another ''victory'' for the good eye and steady hand of Jerzy Fiatkowska. Jerzy's eyes would tear over and he followed with a pledge of loyalty to the business and, above all, to Yakov Szmul Milutsky.

My employer insisted I divide my working time into periods in which I was taught all phases of the business. I arrived at the shop before anyone else and immediately began to arrange the various orders Yakov solicited all over Lodz, making sure I noted the time allowed for any particular job and sketching preliminary designs for posters Yakov inevitably changed, always for the better. When Hershkovitz forced open the front door carrying a steaming pot of dark tea and balancing a sack of freshly-baked rolls, I was through with the morning orders. I then joined Hershkovitz for the refreshments before we put on our aprons to prepare the press for the day's run of material. Since I was nervous about working the press, Hershkovitz put me in charge of inking the printing plates and the rubber rollers, stacking the cheap paper that would soon be covered by announcements of concerts, political rallies, poetry readings at the university, or Left Zionist meetings. "Ready, Mendel," Hershkovitz said, positioning himself in front of the machine as his hands held tightly to the iron levers—and before I could answer, the master printer kicked the three meter long handle that sent the press into its rumbling operation while the wooden floor seemed to sway under the weight of the shaking machine. The noise was so overpowering at times, Hershkovitz had to yell at me to stay in my place until each poster was finished. When I removed the wet posters from the rack at the base of the press I had to run to the drying stand and carefully hang the posters to avoid any smudges.

Printing was over by late morning, the time when Yakov would burst into the shop to inspect our work. Though he frequently called for a new run of posters at the last moment, he never let anything leave the shop until it was perfect. He insisted we all sit together for another tea break—I on the low stool facing Yakov, while Hershkovitz balanced his cup and rolls on top of the press, eating with one hand and using the other to clean and oil some unknown gear only our printer could locate. Yakov spent the next three hours at the shop with us and left only after he was certain I was concentrating on what he called, "your jewel time of the day." You see, Yakov insisted I spend a part of my time studying with him. For two years, the same subjects: Polish grammar and literature; basic lessons in drawing and anatomy; hours spent listening to Yakov talk about the history of art (we never got past Goya!) with examples taken from his expensive collection of painting texts he wrapped in leather and tied with a heavy cord; rudimentary mathematics Yakov allowed Hershkovitz to explain; and finally, my "writing lessons" drawn from the work of Yakov himself, from the poetry and short plays he wrote based on Biblical stories, "the only themes worth considering," he told me, "and written for the only audiences worth having—children!"

Along with his painting, Yakov wanted to be known as a writer in the Yiddish circles he associated with. He saw his writing—the poetry and plays he wrote at home in the darkroom when Jerzy was out—as something that gave him life. "What are you working on now, Yakov?" I would always ask, knowing the answer would take at least thirty minutes, including a recital of some of the work-in-progress. But he used his work, and especially the plays for children, as examples of well-written Yiddish (though he occasionally translated his work into Polish) that, as he told his fellow Yiddishist Hershkovitz, "are as clear as a bell on a winter night."

Whenever he was at work on a new play, Yakov paid us countless early morning visits, shouting over the noise of the press. "Hershkovitz, listen to this. Tell me what you think or I will stay here all day." Hershkovitz dutifully shut down the press and we all stood and became Yakov's first, and sometimes best, audience.

"I have in mind . . . now listen carefully . . . doing something with Genesis, with the creation."

"Genesis," Hershkovitz broke in. "How can you possibly make a story like that clear in a play, Yakov? First of all you won't be able to use many characters, unless you have the fish talking. Or maybe the rocks and sky can add a bit of dialog, eh?" Hershkovitz looked over at me and forced a wink. But when he saw how serious Yakov was, he settled into a chair and listened. Yakov never took criticism very well.

"No, no, you don't understand. I can have characters by putting character into everything that appears in Chapter 1, with my children playing the roles of that which has been created. Do you understand now?"

"Yes, Yakov, who wouldn't understand that. Please, go on," Hershkovitz answered, as anxious as I to see how our friend would accomplish this miracle.

Yakov walked to the center of the room and began to kick aside wooden boxes, piles of old papers, even a neatly-stacked order of posters. He brought a ladder from the closet and set it in the middle of the floor. "Do we have any bolts of cloth here?" he asked me, "anything we can use as a cloud?"

"This is a printing shop, Yakov, not the heavenly throne," Hershkovitz said, smiling at me. Our printer knew our work break would take longer than usual while Yakov prepared his "stage!" While Yakov ran around the shop finding the materials he needed for his first presentation, Jerzy walked in and stumbled across the crates next to the ladder. "Careful, my friend," said Hershkovitz, "You've just pushed aside the firmament . . . kindly have some respect for the divine creation." Gathering his camera case and lens boxes from the floor, Jerzy—as used to these dress rehearsals as the rest of us —sat on a high stool overlooking our new stage, rubbing his hurt knee and hissing some Polish curse (he would have spit on the floor to ward off the evil eye, but Yakov forbade such peasant superstition in the shop).

"Now, quiet, all of you. I want you to close your eyes for a moment," Yakov called out from behind the closet door where he had hidden away. "You have to imagine the stage set with brown and green cloth covering the floor; smoke will drift in from the wings of the stage and a small backlight will reflect through this haze . . . you must see this as haze."

Yakov waited until we were quiet. From inside the closet I heard a swishing sound and the scrape of another ladder being moved across the floor. When the second ladder was in place Yakov told us to open our eyes. Except for a small candle burning to my left, the room was dark, and I noticed a long, black cord that wound across the floor and up the ladder where Yakov, beneath a canvas dropcloth, was hunched over, balancing precariously over the top rungs of the two ladders. Once my eyes were used to the semi-darkness I watched my friends staring at the ladder—Hershkovitz trying to restrain his laughter while Jerzy, who always looked at Yakov's plays with great seriousness, made the sign of the cross as Yakov (now God) spoke in perfectly-accented Yiddish with the aid of a megaphone.

"Let there be . . . be . . . (I could see the cord being pulled closer to the ladder)."

"Light, Yakov," Hershkovitz cried. "It's light!"

"Shush, Meyer," said Jerzy. "He knows what it is."

"Light! Yes. Light!" Yakov raised his voice and the megaphone threw the sound around the walls of the backroom. With one quick jerk Yakov pulled the switch he'd installed at the end of the cord and the swaying overhead electric fixture above us was turned on, a white glare showing everything with the help of a powerful new bulb.

Rising to his full height over the laddertop, God's amorphous shape began to move and groan. Yakov was punching the sides of the canvas covering, looking as if he wanted to escape from his heavenly prison. The moving stopped after a few moments. "This I will call the day that I have made," the hollow voice said. "And this (God's left arm rose within the cloth until it pointed out at us) I shall divide into the darkness."

Climbing down from the ladder so quickly I was sure he would trip over the cord and the boxes strewn everywhere, Yakov ran over to the wooden boxes at the far end of the room. "A moment, please . . . you have to imagine that someone on the stage will now shut off several of the big lights I will set up over half the area here. When God says he wishes to make the darkness, the lights over this half of the stage will go out. Poof!"

Hershkovitz turned to me and whispered: "He's got it wrong, Mendel, since our Lord apparently created stagehands before the appearance of Adam in this play."

"Then, God's voice will come from over here," Yakov continued. "I will have his voice drift around the room when he says, 'Let there be a firmament in the midst of the waters, and let it divide the waters from the waters.'" Yakov was now inside one of the large packing crates and was closing the lid. "His voice will be everywhere, you see. Now, listen to these lines:

"Oooh, oooh, what a place I have made. What more can I make for this place I am creating?" the boxed God said. "For I am surely excited by all of this business."

"Yakov, you'll have to excuse me," Hershkovitz broke in. "But where in Genesis did you ever see our God say that? Did he groan? Was he ever excited?"

"This is for children, Meyer, can't you see that? This is the problem with all of you former yeshiva boys—too literal! Art, after all, goes for the splendor and, dear friend, the excitement—if I might use the word again—of creation. Think for a second: Can you imagine a God who *wouldn't* be overwhelmed by what he was accomplishing here. *A world . . . he is creating a whole world*, Hershkovitz! Try to be less than petty and lose yourself in the idea and the dream of this splendid affair." Yakov still spoke from within the box.

"That's right," Jerzy agreed, "everything about God is rapture and emotion. How could it be anything but this?"

Ignoring Hershkovitz, Yakov continued. He opened the lid and called out the remaining directions of Creation. "Now

I will have my children who will be hiding beneath either blue or brown cloth—large, flowing pieces all around them—take on the central roles of land and water. Watch how this will happen: first, God's lines."

Yakov closed the lid. The Lord was back in the box. "Oooh but it is time to bring all of this together . . . to make this world I have thought about for so long. And *this* is what I shall do: Let these new waters under heaven, my home, be gathered in one place and . . ." Bursting out of the box, Yakov asked me to get the blankets from the closet. "Bring them quickly, Mendel—you are to be the water." I ran and got the motheaten woolen blankets so beloved by Jerzy during his frequent rest periods in the darkroom. "Here, over here," Yakov said, pulling me toward one side of our stage. "Drape this one over yourself and, when I speak my lines, you answer with this." He handed me a sheet of paper with the scene clearly marked and circled. "Remember, not until I finish speaking."

I heard Yakov ask Jerzy to play the part of the land, his place beneath the other blanket several meters away from me. "You two," Yakov warned, "shuffle along the floor until you touch one another."

I felt Jerzy bump into me and could hear him practicing his one line. Safe within his box, Yakov began to speak.

"I have made the land and the water appear. With the power I have in my person as God, these two creations will break apart making the fundments of this world of mine." God stopped, and I heard Hershkovitz laughing in the background. I was scratching my face so much I forgot to listen for my cue. "Now, Mendel, it's time," my director reminded me. "Stand up and speak, water, given of life from now on. *Speak!*"

I rose to my full blanketed height. "So shall I be, Lord, and forever more give life to your creatures."

"That's good, my water. To the land. Rise up, my land!"

"I am the place of dryness," Jerzy said, his voice lowered solemnly to suit this grave moment. "My creation, too, is part of the process of life" (Jerzy forgot to speak in Yiddish).

I sat still under my water-blanket until I heard what had to be the final line in the beginning stages of my friend's creation. "I pronounce what I have done as good . . . oooh, so good."

"Let them breathe, Yakov," Hershkovitz said. "We have to get back to work—or do you plan a seven day festival of Genesis?"

"Yes, fine," Yakov, the Lord director, answered. "You both did well. How do you like it so far?"

"It takes chutzpah to revise Genesis," Hershkovitz called out, "and I'm worried about what you've added."

"You still don't see through those horse-blinders you wear!" Yakov was becoming angry, his voice rising to a high-pitched squeal, always a certain sign of his emotional state as well as the opening of any defense. Yakov never let the slightest criticism of his work pass even if these critics were the young sons and daughters of his Zionist friends; he had to be prepared for anything.

"Think for a moment about this. First, picture this stage I have suggested to you: the floor covered with cloth bunched together to simulate formlessness; low lighting from the sides and rear of the stage, a mysterious atmosphere children can appreciate because *only they* can see the value of what is to come. *A mystery*, Meyer Hershkovitz—can't you see a mystery here?

"Then this God: he broods from the moment he appears beneath his own formlessness, certain of only one thing to be done, the creation he has been dreaming of since he invented his own time. He asks at one point, 'What shall I do with all of this? What form shall it take? Who is to be here and what will they be like?' And so what do I as writer, director, place here? For everything to be created, a child has a role—he sits beneath a blanket and is made. Rises up. Thanks God and receives instructions for his future. Fruit, Hershkovitz. And seeds, fish, fowl, beasts, many creeping things!"

"Man, too, Yakov," Jerzy noted, caught up in the passion of Yakov's appeal. "Man comes along!"

"Yes, of course—we didn't even get to that today. I have carefully worked out the players I will need, thirty-six in all. I can help them with their costumes, their lines. Think of your son, Leybel, Hershkovitz—you who tell him about Zion every night before he goes to bed—think of Leybel as a bird adorned with feathers under his own blanket. By the fifth day your Leybel will be thanking his God and flying about the stage, his wings moving back and forth as he joins with the other creatures I have made for this world. Won't he be excited? Won't he move with joy? Won't the audience join with him?"

"Yes, but . . ."

"Nothing more to say. You just think about Leybel and you'll understand. A play is not truth revealed, my old friend," Yakov said as he began to gather his props from around our stage. "On the contrary, it is only a kind of truth hinted at, something for the imagination to remake in its own way in the mind of those *who can imagine*. See if you can grasp this subtle point, and you tell me: Have I revised Genesis beyond repair?"

Without waiting for an answer, Yakov walked over each part of the stage we used and pointed. "Here I will have little Sora Gittleman as a rock along with Rive-Mindl, her sister and companion rock; they will touch one another. While here, not too far from the place where I want the waters to separate, Dovid Sosnovsky will become a seed and I will cover his body with thick butcher paper painted brown. Dovid will join several other seeds . . . children, that is, like Yosel Sukenick and his cousin, Oyzer, and Rivke-Gitl, Moyshe Strayber."

Yakov ran from place to place and marked each spot where his children would stand with a cross in the dust of our uncleaned floor. "And here, Hershkovitz, right over here so the audience can follow their every movement, I will put Leon Ablezer and his twin sister, Tsalke, my first creeping things pushing themselves out of the ooze. Everyone and everything with a few lines to say to God and his audience. And maybe if I talk sweetly to her, I can convince Nokmen Aizer's tiny daughter to be one of the stars. Can't you see it now?—Close your eyes and envision that little Sarah perched atop a ladder with a light shining in front of her costume made of silver. Amazing!"

When he finished his tour of the workshop area, Yakov gathered his handwritten script pages together and folded them into the leather binder he used for his plays. Hershkovitz had started the press and avoided any eye contact with us, content to busy himself with his own work. The press seemed louder than ever before as the printer pushed the machine to a higher speed, causing posters to fall into the metal tray. I saw Jerzy go into his darkroom carrying a load of chemicals and mumbling his one line from the play over and over, at one point yelling out his line with arms raised in a new interpretation in Polish and Yiddish of Yakov's birth of the world. Since the day's "study time" had been taken up by the play reading, I joined Meyer at the Press and began to stack the posters he let fly on the floor.

"Mendel, come with me," Yakov said from the center of the room where he remained. "I want you to copy over part of this script from Yiddish into Polish before I have the whole business typed out; don't worry about Hershkovitz, he can brood and simmer for a time by himself. Please, come."

Yakov's office was nothing more than a hastily walled-off section his father built to store food during the World War. Retreating to this shelter when he wanted to write, sketch or paint, Yakov often worked there all night. He refused to use electricity in the office, preferring the light given off by three kerosene lanterns he insisted "illuminate like the sun." On the large oak desk inherited from his father, Yakov gave me a place to do my work with him, and he even built a small cubicle at the side of the desk to hold the gift he presented me with on my nineteenth birthday last year: a folding easel that held a beautiful set of Austrian paintbrushes, charcoals and three finely-made Swiss pens. We called our place here, "the studio."

"The play, my young artist, did you like it?"

"Yes, of course, but I do wonder how people will react to it," I answered, aware of how Yakov was pacing back and forth behind me.

"People? By 'people' you mean the adults or the children? Who is most importnat? It doesn't matter at all. You should only pay attention to what I tell you, to my instructions. So this is what you do for the rest of the morning." Yakov opened his leather play folder and handed me five or six sheets of heavy writing paper. "As you begin your exercise with my play, whenever you come across a descriptive passage, find two, maybe three other phrases to use in its place. This will be good practice for an aspiring writer, and your work may even help me to come up with a satisfactory conclusion to this little play of mine."

"Yakov, you haven't finished? There's no ending yet? But I thought you always wrote everything before you read to us.

What is . . ."

Yakov walked behind me and quickly turned to the last page of his unfinished script. "Look at this," he said as he jabbed and poked at the paper. "It's so puzzling, you see. Notice how I have copied the exact text from the Genesis chapter out in my script so I could understand that last verse. Such a problem. Listen: 'And God saw everything he had made, and, behold, *it was* very good.' What do you make of that, Mendel—tell me."

It seemed obvious to me what the intent of the passage was. I couldn't understand Yakov's confusion with the words. "God has finished his work after six days," I said. "Now after so much work, he prepares for a rest. His world is finished, and the seventh day is upon him. Just a rest, nothing more."

"But the italicized words, *it was* lead me to believe the creator considered his work to be past tense, yes? Perhaps . . . perhaps he was beginning to worry about the results of what he had made, thinking it might go wrong somewhere. I have thought about this again and again: I write an ending—and keep in mind the children on the stage—with a satisfied God overflowing with accomplishment. He makes the children laugh, makes a rainbow or two for their pleasure, blows the little birds around with his winds. All his work was good."

Yakov resumed his pacing. He began to read from his several versions of the play's ending scene, always pausing over the final line. With each succeeding reading Yakov's God became more and more sullen, almost angry, until he openly brooded about the future: he shook his ladder, refused to listen to the pleas of his creatures—even the rocks spoke in Yakov's play—for another rainbow, and once he even shouted, frightening all of his many creations! Just as I asked Yakov to read that last version one more time, Hershkovitz bolted into the room and grabbed the script from Yakov's hands.

"So! This is what you have written . . . I have heard every word. I ask you, Yakov Milutsky, entertainer of our children, whether those are the words you want our children to hear, you who wishes to give the little ones a sense of wonder? Yakov backed away from the angry printer and sat in a low chair next to me. "I'm listening, Meyer, see what you can make out of it."

"First, let's have our Polish compatriot join us. Maybe,

Pan Fiatkowska will be able to see some hope in the midst of this angry God's mumblings to our children."

Hershkovitz called Jerzy from the darkroom. The photographer stopped at the doorway of the office, fell to his knees, and shouted out his one line from the play. "I am the place of dryness. And my creation, too, is part of the process of life!" This time, Jerzy's Yiddish was perfect.

"No, Jerzy, sit for a moment as Meyer reads. We want to hear what you think about this passage." Yakov pointed to a stool beside him and patted the seat. Jerzy looked confused and hurt. "Should I have said it in Polish?" he whispered to me.

I had never seen Meyer Hershkovitz so angry before. He waited until all of us were silent, though Jerzy kept whispering his line, convinced he had left out a crucial verb somewhere. Meyer climbed onto the bench facing the window. "Now, I want you to picture this: Yakov's God has just made the world; children playing all of the living things have been dancing around the stage, excited by their prospects. Rocks, land, water are in place, and even a little child-butterfly graces this youthful world. Our God smiles on all of this from his heavenly mist, he 'oohs' because it has all gone so very well and passes this sound down to an audience we assume must share in the Lord's tremendous creation. What, I ask you, could be better?

"Hard work? Of course! Does God have to rest after six days? Any child from his first day of cheder knows this day will be blessed for the generations, not troubled over. A Loving God, my colleagues; the God who somehow called upon Yakov Milutsky to make water and rocks and lizards out of children in a play. And what do we have here from the pen of our mentor? This:

'I have given all that I can to this place. Look, there are seeds, water, green herbs for meat, and creatures that grace my air with their presence and abundance, their sleekness. Time, too, has come with day made from the night and many lights to shine upon all that I have made.
(*God pauses; climbs down from ladder to see a world in motion in front of him; children are*

> *moving everywhere on stage and, thinking*
> *God has come to celebrate with them, they*
> *gather around Him.*)
> 'I must rest from my work. What I have made was good.
> (*God lifts a child to His shoulders.*)
> 'What will happen to you who are so new and good?
> (*God's question causes children to become*
> *quiet. He walks from center stage to wing; re-*
> *peats question.*)
> 'What will happen to you who are so new and good in
> the time I will make to follow?'
> (*Lights Dim and Out; Children Bow, some cry*)"

We were as silent as the stage directions required. Hersh-
kovitz looked at Yakov. "This you cannot tell children! It's
enough that you invent your own Genesis, Yakov, but even
allowing for 'art' as you see it, there is no room for this. If
you want my Leybel in your play, you choose the ending in-
tended by the book itself to be glorious. Your secularist non-
sense will frighten those too young to understand."

Hershkovitz folded the script into his apron pocket. "Now
there can be no more, do you see," he shouted. "no more.
Ever!"

The printer and the photographer left the office together.
The noise of the press was soon echoing throughout the room
as Hershkovitz kicked and swore at its gears. Yakov waved me
back to my work while he gathered what remained of his
script into a pile. From the side of the press where I stood
watching Yakov straighten the office furniture, Hershkovitz
was already yelling out his own interpretation of Genesis to a
bewildered Jerzy. Yakov moved his own large painter's easel
into the storeroom and covered the wooden slats with a large
sheet of drawing paper. Sketching quickly and shifting from
one pastel chalk to another, he called Hershkovitz over and
showed him what Leybel would look like in his costume. "He
will be a plant, my friend, such has never been seen before on
the stage!" Hershkovitz nodded approval when Yakov cupped
his hand over the printer's ear and spoke for a few minutes.

When Hershkovitz slowed the press enough so we could
hear him, he told us about Leybel's costume. "Yakov says it
will all work out. God will see that everything is good, and

then my Leybel will walk to God and give him a leaf, maybe a branch. Next, they embrace as all the children on stage clap and cheer. He says it will be beautiful to watch."

With all his doubts about Yakov's play removed, Hershkovitz was a contented man. He even worked up the original idea for a poster advertising the play, paying special attention to the ornate lettering he printed by hand with precision along the top of the paper. The blue lettering was bordered by white trim, with the initials of the Young Zionist Organization boldly leading into the play's title. Hershkovitz read the title to us, one he especially liked: "The Wonder of Creation Revealed," to be presented, Jerzy was quick to point out as he penciled in the date, "On August 3, 1934."

"The date is very important," he reminded us, "because everyone who comes to see his child perform in this play will want to have a souvenir poster to take home."

Yakov smiled. He approved Hershkovitz' idea and ordered a run of five hundred play posters as soon as we could set type. "Show my sketch of the bird costume to Leybel," he shouted to Hershkovitz. "After all, the boy will want to know what he will look like at the beginning of time." ■

THE FUNNIES
Edison Dupree

It's the old story: Nancy has
floored Sluggo with her baseball bat,
and he lies snoring. The lump pops out
on his brow and gleams, a tumorous
small moon: whatever was jarred loose
from the thick pudding between his ears
is trying to punch through to the stars
that hover in front of Sluggo's eyes
like incandescent bugs. But Sluggo's
luggage, and Nancy's leaving. The lump
is down, or waning. And now the damp
is taking its countless places. The sky's
ink wash descends, and Nancy is lonely,
as Sluggo, beginning to move, will be.

BREAKFAST WITH NEWS OF A SHIPPING ACCIDENT
Edison Dupree

The spoon holding the clod of sugar,
the brown sugar I like, just under
the brown tea surface, teaches
something about those wretches
on the downed tanker. Checking their watches
like mad, they just can't wait any longer.
Look, their breath to its vast brother
the sky begins to climb, through water
darker and colder than any tea
I've ever drunk. Don't ask me
the color of last thought,
or how the lungs explode with salt.
I'm drinking my own tea. Pearls
of sweetened air rush up to the world.

A RAPID TRANSIT
Edison Dupree

Before I go,
I'd like to know why everything
keeps speeding up. Who's causing these winds,
who's driving Nebraska's tall windmills
crazy? And what's the government doing
about the Vacuum Zones?

My new apartment has air and all
electric kitchen, why am I driving
away on the Interstate so fast
the speedometer pops open? Oh springs
and gears fly out the window *zip*!
—then fall like Gretel's breadcrumbs
to the squabbling roadside crows.
Hours later the dominant beak
still dangles the steel bauble.

◇

Forget It and Keep Moving,
that's the motto I swear I read
as a kid in the flame-orange
tiny right angles of Grandma's sampler,
—or else I'm embroidering things.
Anyhow, what I'm sure of
is the silver jet that unaccountably
streaked in over our bush-league park
that day as we roared the double play.
Now *that's* what I call sudden: our flushed
faces drained, a deafening black

shadow swept over the stands and snatched
our hearts all upward to where the jet

had been. It was an F-4
Phantom, I think, from the nearby base;
escort there for heavily-laden
B-52's. We used to salute them
late at night, as the signoff anthem
ended the Mystery Theater.

AUSTIN
Catherine Petroski

Last night after the show closed up at twelve on the dot
Binny give me something special in his trailer. I could tell he
was holding something behind his back so as I couldn't see it
so I guessed he was hiding a surprise for me. He teased me
like he always does, making fun of me because he says I'm just
a kid that doesn't know anything but I know he's only play-
ing that way. What he give me was a pretty sea-shell necklace
only Binny told me right away that it wasn't exactly a sea
shell like most. It's pink, nice shiny plastic, and it hangs on a
silverish chain round my neck and I don't think I'll never
take it off cause it's from Binny and it was a real surprise.

Anyway Binny must have read up on that little sea shell
that isn't a sea shell cause he told me all about what kind it
was. Called a sand dollar, Binny said. That the real ones are
little animals that live in the sea. How they're supposed to
break, the real ones, and out flies supposed to be five doves
for peace. How they're really sea urchins, them little animals,
just like you, he said. And that made me feel kind of bad for
a minute. So I said to Binny, this one's better than a real one
cause it won't break like that. Binny laughed and said maybe
we could try finding a real one and break it open and see what
happens when we get to Corpus. Last year when the show
was in Corpus I was where I used to call home. I never been
there, Corpus. I didn't even know the show or Martha or
Binny was alive last year.

Binny said, it is right pretty. It'll go with all the pink clothes you got, he said, and that pearly pink nail polish I got the Saturday before I left what used to be home. Binny laughed when I said that I didn't never want to take off the sand dollar, and said, don't never say never. But Binny will see I'm wearing it and maybe he will know I'm wearing it to say thank you for being so nice.

This Austin here is a pretty town and where we're at on the lake front is a real pretty spot. Not like Dallas where we was all hemmed in by old buildings that must have looked real modern once upon a time. That fairground has some nice things, like its aquarium. It's real dark there and you can watch the fish glowy in their tanks. And the splotchy harbor seals, but they have cataracts on their eyes like grandma and that ruined the aquarium for me. But I like this much better. Out in the open like, with the lake and the sky and lots of clean air and friendlier people. A lot of people just aren't nice to folks with the traveling shows. Call us carneys and treat us like we aren't human beings. Like my folks never let me go when we was at the State Fair once. I was little then and I can only remember so many people I never saw before. It wasn't a good time but it seems like we never had a good time together cause we was always worrying about what's next. Which is why I left after we had a bad fight and why I joined the show. The people here don't seem to worry much about the next thing—the next day, the next town, the next anything. They just take it like it comes.

Sometimes I guess I get to missing them because I guess I should miss home like in all the songs and I get to feeling lonesome. Even though there's Martha, who I work for and who's been real good to me. And Binny. But if you got to be lonesome Austin is a nice place to be it cause this here lake is real pretty. They call it Town Lake I guess because the town is around it but it ain't really a lake. It's really some river, and last week when we was setting up they found a man floating in it. I seen them drag him out. They put him on a stretcher all blue and grey and took him away one afternoon about three o'clock. And nobody knew who he was cause there wasn't nobody missing in particular. When it happened with the ambulances and police and all, Binny just about had his spin-art stand ready to go and Martha had me blowing up balloons until I was blue in the face. Just like any other time we set up for a stand, all day metal hitting metal over at the rides. But finding the man did make it a little different. I was glad for the break, but it was sad about the guy they found in the river. Even the guys on the rides got to stop work for that.

Spring is funny, I told Martha, but she acted like she didn't hear and maybe she didn't. She's getting older and sometimes people that old can't hear. Sometimes they can, too, and pretend when it's convenient not to hear. But I guess Martha didn't want to talk about spring. You look across the lake and see the fruit trees blooming out like that and redbuds and grass all bright and green and even though it's pretty, somehow it can make you sad. Maybe that's why Martha didn't answer. And things go on and on, always balloons to blow up, darts to keep putting feathers on. Martha's been doing it a long time. You got to wash your hair, go to the laundromat, do your bunk, then you get to thinking, What if I didn't.

But now it's getting on to evening and the night is when we make most of our money. The lights attract the people like moths, Martha says. It's you that gets people to play Martha's game, Binny says. I don't know if I'll last as long as Martha. She's been in this business for forty-three years this coming June. But Martha says it's just like anything else. You do your job, you make your money, she says. Sometimes you're happy, sometimes you're sad. Sometimes you win, sometimes you lose, she says. Being a carney doesn't make you different from other people, Martha says. She says regular people think we're all cheats and sharps, but Martha says carneys aren't any more that way than anybody else. Everybody cheats somewhere along the line, and most more than me, Martha says. Martha reads the papers and always listens to the news. Binny told me Martha's fixed real good, that she knows about the stock market, the one in New York. That old gal could buy and sell us all, Binny told me. What I really would like is to stick with Binny, but he says, You stick with her and you'll do all right. After all, Binny says, all he has is a spin-art trailer, fifty cents a shot, and a 1957 Harley that don't start, but Martha's got a balloon game and knows a lot about people. Binny is a funny guy. He laughs and says the spin-art stand will come and go, but the balloon game will last forever. I hope it don't rain tonight.

There is this guy with a camera and I can't figure him. At first I thought he was taking pictures of his little girl on the pony ride. Then a lady asked him, why are you taking a picture of my little girl? and then her husband asked him, how'd you like somebody to bust that Nikon, boy?, so then he moved on away from the pony ride, around the back of the merry-go-round and down one side of the midway, the other side. He was a funny-looking guy, almost looked like an Indian. Not a redman, but an Indian Indian. He had long hair in a ponytail but it was thin like him and clean so as you'd hardly notice it was long. I could keep an eye on him all the way down the midway he was so tall and he was looking for somebody else to take pictures of I guess and he must of found some because he really took a long time to work his way around to the balloon stand. He stopped for a while at Binny's spin-art, I could see that. He looked at the samples Binny had tacked around the top and looked into the painting holes that Binny lines with fresh foil every morning of the world and I guess he looked at Binny. He might of taken a picture of Binny cause he really seemed interested in Binny's stand. But probably what really held him up was old Okie. Maybe not Okie himself, cause I couldn't see if he went in to see him, but how everybody stood around listening to the swampman pitch. Like to be hypnotized. I don't know if the camera man would even be allowed in, with that camera slung on his neck. Anyway when he come around by here, I felt like asking him if he wanted to take my picture but I didn't because I had already figured out that that was the odd thing about his pictures. You weren't supposed to know he was taking them.

As he come by the balloons he stopped for a minute to listen to Martha, far away in the middle of the alley. She called out to him, but he acted like he don't hear. Like most.

You know Binny has red hair and he says that's why he has such a short temper. But this afternoon the fellow come around again with the camera with the ponytail. And instead of taking Binny's picture again, he took mine while I wasn't looking and Binny saw it and got mad. Called the camera man a hippy and said I was being used. About fifty times. And asked me if I enjoyed being used.

Binny's been saying that a lot lately. He says how everybody uses me. That Martha uses me. He says if Martha stood in the balloon booth maybe people would look after they heard her spiel but once they took a look at her, they wouldn't pay no attention. Never play. Maybe Binny's right. I tell Binny what my grandma said, the one with the cataracts. One hand washes the other, she always said. I use Martha, she uses me, only I never said that right out, just the thing about the hands. That's how the world goes around, I told Binny. Binny didn't laugh and said I was too young to be a cynic, but I don't get his meaning. It probably wasn't good. Binny has his moods.

So when Binny gets like that, I get mad and tell him off, like I don't know how he can sit around with all them catsup squirters of paint, trying to get people to do that silly spin painting. Course I just say that when I'm mad at him. Really I think the spin paintings is pretty, some of them after you practice. Binny can make beautiful ones, but when he's in one of them moods I won't tell him that.

What made the fight worse was I brought up going to look at the azaleas. Thought it would help. We would get over our fight. Binny told me we should stay with our own kind, but I kept going on how one of the girls told me the azaleas was blooming in the rich part of town. How she told me all about how to get there and I asked Binny would he take me there some morning when we was all ready. So Binny blew up and said, don't you even know enough to stay out of where you're not wanted, and don't you even know enough not to want things you can't have, and don't you even know enough to keep with your own. Don't go getting any ideas, Binny told me. Which confused me cause I always thought Binny had lots of ideas that didn't necessarily work out. And which got me real mad cause it's a free country and the roads is public, after all, which is just what I said to Binny. But there ain't any arguing with Binny. If he guesses you might win the argument he stomps away. Says you're a kid, and what do you know.

It didn't come to that this time, but no, Binny said, no. I ain't taking you to any rich part of town to look at azaleas.

Just a bunch of ugly pink flowers in ugly green tubs, he said. Said he wouldn't have such an ugly color as them in his catsup squirters. Said the reason he really hates them is they don't grow natural, that them plastic tubs is the only reason they grow, that the ground here ain't right, that it's all artificial. Just look across the lake, Binny told me, at them fruit trees growing natural in the ground. That ought to be good enough, Binny said, cause that's the best you can get.

So I did. I didn't say no more about driving out to see no flowers, and all them trees budding out across the lake was pretty and I remembered what I heard about what was over there and asked Binny if it was true there was an animal shelter over there. Just to make conversation. It was the Humane Society, he told me, over by some baseball fields. I told him the baseball fields didn't hold any fascination to me but maybe could we go on a walk to the Humane Society some morning.

Well, that was how it all started, with Binny saying people used me. I don't get the connection. So after the fight with Binny I went in Martha's trailer where I live and put on my pink silky top that looked nice with the sand dollar and combed my hair nice and brushed my teeth and put on some nice perfume somebody I don't want to remember give me once, and that almost spoiled everything for me, and then without thinking too much or looking back to see if anybody was watching me go, I started walking by myself across the bridge and then turned left down to where the Humane Society ought to be if I figured right.

I got about half way there and here comes Binny. What you think you're doing girl, Binny asks me. Taking a walk, I say. He knows perfectly well what I'm doing, where I'm going.

You going to the Humane Society, he says. Could be, I say. Martha sent me looking for you, Binny says. She says she needs you to go get change. Binny looks at me funny, then he says, you coming with me, half asking, half telling.

Well, I say, if Martha needs me, guess I better. And when we got back, Martha told me to stick around when there was work to be done.

If you say everybody uses me, I asked Binny this afternoon, what about you, Binny? He looked at me for a long time, funny. Didn't answer. So I asked him again, and finally he said, if I was using you, would I tell you about it?

Then he got up and left.

Shut down the sides of the spin-art and just took off, like that. He was gone about forty minutes. I didn't see where he went, what he took with him. But when he come back, he had something stuck into the front of his jacket. Pretty soon I could see it was something alive, moving in there. Made me think of a mare about to foal. Then I knew where he had been. I knew he was over to the Humane Society.

Here, Binny says, here. This is how I use you. Go on, he says, it's for you. He opened up his jacket and pulled out a puppy all fluffy and white.

It's yours, he said. From Binny. I gotta get the spin-art open now. And just like that Binny left. I can't figure him out, he's such a funny guy, but he sure give me a nice puppy. Just a mutt, I guess, but going to be a pretty dog. So now I know for sure Binny went to the Humane Society for me, got me this dog, and give him to me, like the sand dollar. Except I can't wear the dog.

Well, he ain't going to live in no trailer with me, Martha said. You might just as well take him right back to that Humane Society or whatever it was where that crazy Binny got him. Martha was hopping mad. She was all red in the face. Her voice got hoarse. I never seen her in such a fit.

Why, Martha, I asked her. I don't see no reason for her to take on so about a little dog. Somehow it don't seem right. But asking her why only made her all the madder. Just let me tell you why, Martha says. I never lived with no animal yet and I ain't about to start now. And, she says, that's final.

He's already broke, Martha, I tell her, and look how scared he's got. But it didn't do no good talking to Martha about the dog. She wouldn't have none of him, and told me if I was to keep on in the balloon game and being her helper and all the dog would have to go. She said I'd either have to take him back to the Humane Society or give him to Binny to take care of. And, Martha said, let off with that Binny while you're at it.

Which surprised me kind of. So I don't know what I'm going to tell Binny. Can't tell him about how nasty she got,

especially about him, how she called him a redhead hippy
and a misfit and the things she said about his spin-art, how it
was ugly and silly and he was nuts with his foil linings and
catsup bottles and how it wasn't even really any fun for the
people.

And I couldn't get a word in edgewise. While she was at it
she said some awful things, things about me, not that I never
heard them things before just not from her and where I heard
them before I left, and the worst part is she said them just to
hurt because she knows for a fact they aren't true. About
Binny and me. Binny says some things, kidding like, but they
don't really hurt, and when he says I don't know nothing,
that's different than what Martha said. And I got to thinking,
Binny's said some not nice things about Martha, but my
grandma always told me, the one with the cataracts like the
seals, have a good word for people and they'll have a good
word for you. It didn't turn out that way with Martha. I al-
ways thought grandma was the smartest best person in the
world. And then Martha too. Sometimes people no matter
how smart you think they are make some bad mistakes.
Sometimes they say such bad things there's no going back,
and things are never the same after. After something like that
happens, there's no trusting anybody. You never know when
they're going to hit you with something else. It's not worth
it. There's no erasing it, like somebody spit on the chalk and
wrote up a blackboard. And now I feel sad, like the same
thing's happened with Martha happened with my family, and
though I'm still sitting here in my bunk in her trailer it's like
I'm not here at all.

There's nothing else for me, and I can't leave Martha.
Binny said it. Nobody'd come if it wasn't for me. I'm the
draw and it's Martha's booth.

It's cold today and looks like all the blossoms on the trees
is going to blow away, clean off the trees. It rained last night,
the way it does around here: one minute it's hotter than
hades, the next comes up a big blue-grey cloud down the
plains and you can see the cold in it coming. The wind starts
in blowing, slow at first, then faster and faster. And you can
see the leaves turn themselves over in the wind. The sky gets
maybe half dark and then it comes, big drops. Not anything

easy or half-noticeable, but big loud drops of rain. Sometimes it stops just as fast as it starts, but last night it kept up for a time. And then this morning it was cold and grey, but it doesn't really bother me that much. I'm going some place in a little while.

When the rain started in last night, Binny come over by the balloon booth and I was gathering up darts. Looks like there won't be much doing now, he said, and I looked and the spin-art was locked up tighter than a drum.

Guess not, I say. So I have to tell him about the dog, but before I get even a chance, Binny looks at me funny and says, What you name that little dog? almost like he could read my mind.

That scared me some, and instead of telling him that I had to give it back or that we had to take it back, that Martha wouldn't let me keep him, I say instead to Binny and I don't know why, I ain't given it much thought.

Then Binny says to me, I was thinking we ought to name him something so we could put something on this. Binny reached in his pocket and pulled out a tag and handed it to me. MY NAME IS and there was a blank and I BELONG TO and another blank. To fill in the names. I couldn't look at Binny just then. The little dog was chewing the leg of Binny's pants, but Binny didn't pay any mind to what he was doing. I guess then Binny could see I was trying not to cry.

Now what you crying for, Binny said, you never pulled that before. That I seen, he said. The trouble was you never know how much to tell a person. So I didn't know what to say, whether he ought to know about Martha and the bad things or just about the dog or about how nothing was coming true for me in my life about good words and such, all the things that weren't ever supposed to be changed. Or even did the dog have to go at all, since Martha and all weren't what I thought. It would be the end of Martha, sort of. It might be the end of Binny. It might be the end of both. Maybe the Humane Society would take me too. I seen things end before.

Things already ended around here. Cause things won't ever be the same with Martha and me, even if I live in her trailer for the next forty-three years, not after everything that happened. Austin, I tell Binny. We can call the little dog Austin, where we are, I said. I don't know why I done that, it made my head feel light.

That's a real good idea, Binny says. We can have the tag filled in, Binny says, maybe tomorrow morning cause there's not going to be much doing around here with this cold front coming through. And I got a little collar for Austin, Binny says, fishing in his jacket pocket. And a leash too, he says.

Binny looks at me funny, trying to figure out what I'm thinking, I guess. I mean, he says, it's your dog and it's o.k. to put the collar on him, ain't it? So I tell him sure it's o.k.

Binny keeps talking, talking. Talking more than I ever heard him. Binny's talking through my thoughts. I hear him but I don't understand him. I'm thinking and what I'm thinking is there's never nothing. One thing ends, another starts up, like them trees across the lake. Some things is nicer than others, that's for sure. But there's always something.

You know you had a right good idea there, naming the little dog Austin, Binny says. That way we can remember when we was in Austin. You still wearing that sand dollar, he says.

And Binny holds out his hand with the MY NAME IS tag and looks at me different like. Binny's face looks glad. And Binny says, you keep this for now, o.k., cause I might lose it or get paint on it, o.k., and when he give me the tag to take care of it was different than with the sand dollar, which wasn't real, and his hand touched mine kind of long. ∎

BASIC RESCUE
Ann Deagon

1. OPEN THE AIRWAY

Green cement has flooded the firehall.
We unfold chairs. The instructor
lays flat a white sheet.
He inflates Resusci-Anne,
pumps till her bent legs kick straight.
LOOK LISTEN AND FEEL FOR BREATHING.
She does not breathe. GIVE FOUR
QUICK BREATHS. We kneel and breathe
turn by turn in a discreet pavane
each of us with her own death in tow.

2. FEEL FOR A PULSE

Each of us with her own death in tow:
the baby turned blue in the highchair
the boy at the bottom of the pool
like a mosaic, the daughter OD'd
the man in the bed not waking up.

We crouch, fingertips to carotid
feeling for pulse we know's not there.
All the world has a single throat.

3. BEGIN COMPRESSION

All the world has a single throat.
See how she lolls, lips parted, knowing
she is born to this, hers to invite
the mouths of strangers. She inhales us
not tasting our garlic or our mouthwash
tasting only our pale clear lives.

The heel of our hand is between her breasts.
We are pumping up the world, see how
its vasty chambers fill. We will breathe
life into the mouths of corpses:
their lungs redden like a forge.

WOMEN AND CHILDREN FIRST
Ann Deagon

While they estimate the damage,
while their great arms pump back the sea,
we have slipped overboard. Girls thin
as oarblades cleave green surface,
fleshed women spiral down
into the salt mother. She bears us up.
We wear our babes like barnacles.
Children skip wave crests, old
women quaff foam like ale.
We have found our element.

Connie, in this sea of women
who sink and swim, yours is the only
form I know. Once when
you did the butterfly across a pool
your lunge out of the breaking water
stopped my breath. The pool has found
its way to sea. You have become
the primal, the Earth-Diver:
yours the bursting journey to pry
out of her deep crevice that stone,
its strata rounded to an eye—
to bear up in your lean hands
that navelstone on which we build
new earth.
        Islanded like Sappho,
an ocean and two continents between us,
I turn this stone, this mandala,
this patterned thumbprint of a god.
Making of worlds is endless. Each word,

each gesture that you make unmakes my world
and makes it new. We are stones
knocking together at the tide's will
in some cleft of an aging sea.
Together we grow round.

SEVERAL WARNINGS IN SEARCH OF A
CONSCIOUSNESS-RAISING GROUP FOR MEN
Lou Lipsitz

"Beware of the man who praises liberated women;
he is planning to quit his job."   —Erica Jong

Beware of the woman poet;
she's waiting to be surprised by a swan

Beware of the woman who keeps coming toward you;
she thinks she's the light at the end of the tunnel

Beware of the woman who won't cook
she'll eat you raw

Beware of the woman who accepts you as you are;
she's weary

Beware of the woman who loves to cook;
she'll make you delve into the leftovers

Beware of the woman with sharp pencils;
she thinks you're a marginal note

Beware of the woman who won't be touched;
she keeps a list of small injuries

Beware of the woman who lifts weights;
she'll let you down

Beware of the unliberated woman;
she knows when to call her lawyer

Beware of the liberated woman;
she's her own lawyer

LEAVING THE PSYCHIATRIST'S OFFICE
Lou Lipsitz

I sit in the car
       and cry
for ten minutes

feeling
    it will never stop
there
    is no bottom

    finally
grabbing hold
of myself, like
           some new
recruit
    in the marines—

the part of me that
            judges
the sincerity
    of weeping
says: this
    is the genuine
thing
    grieving over what
is gone forever:

        twenty years wasted!

    the way lost,
        wandering

through the city like a
homeless one carrying
rags and stones
in an old orange sack

the energy of a boy
purchased finally
by a chicken dealer
who had him sit
by the hour
counting.the feathers
on a stuffed bird

and the thing that
was supposed to be
easiest:
       sexual love —
that would come
so slowly, with
certainty, like a
sunrise
       —became so
complicated
— a prism that seared
the eyes, a shadow
thrown this way and that
on the pavement
by a windblown tree

and something else:
let's call it "knowing"
—as the early fog
burned off
and you could see the ocean
       there!

enormous and majestic
—the easy waves
of what you wanted to do!

but now, I am like two wrestlers
who fall to the canvas together
locked somehow, their arms
and legs twisted beyond releasing;
their fierce energy focused
like a knot pulled tighter
by trying to undo it;
their crushed dance doomed
to last forever.

—"your mother," the doctor
says, "talk about
your mother." and I am here,
turning gray,
              —years old, 44.

THE GIRL WHO GOES TO MUSEUMS
David Michael Kaplan

I.

When I first saw her, the girl who goes to museums was standing by Puvis de Chavannes. *Jeunnes filles au bord de la mer*. In the painting three young women are standing or sitting by the edge of an ocean. One, with her back to us, is holding her hair, pulling it like a shock of spring wheat. Another lies at her feet, hands behind her in an attitude of captivity or surrender. A third, the only one whose face we see, leans on what appears to be a rock and stares into the space beyond the painting. The effect is quite languorous, the kind of seraglio effect Ingres often achieves, except here in open air. I have seen the girl before, in other museums in Paris, and elsewhere. She dresses rather old-fashionedly. Today she was wearing a black dress and a green rainhat, and she carried an umbrella. It had been raining in the morning, and would thunderstorm before one. The girl would walk through the Tuileries before then, stopping to watch the children sail boats in the fountain, while their parents glanced at the sky and spoke of going home before the rain.

The girl who goes to museums does not know that I watch her. At least she has never given me any sign to think so. Often we pass in the corridors without recognition. And it is not her that I watch really—it would be a mistake to give that impression. Rather, I watch what she watches. I see through her eyes. Today she paused a long time before the de Chavannes, then went immediately to the Manets. There was a crowd in the museum—two busloads of Spanish tourists pushing and shoving—so often I lost sight of her. But I know she completely ignored the Degas which used to be her favorite. This puzzled me. I ask myself: does she not like Degas any longer? Or has he taken on the qualities of an old friend that one no longer needs to see? One thinks they will always be there, and that is comfort enough.

II.

In November of that year I attended a *bal masqué* at Comtesse de Severign's estate, and the girl who went to museums was there. She was escorted by two young men wearing crows' heads as masks, with capes of black feathers. One walked on either side of her. Often they would whisper in her ear. She wore a black evening dress and held her mask before her eyes like a lorgnette. She looked most like the night. She nodded to me as she passed, her two attendants also nodding courteously. I am polite in turn.

Later in the evening the Comtesse wishes to show me her *orangerie*, and we descend the stairs into the gardens below. The gardeners had hurried to bring in the trees the past week because of the danger of frost, the Comtesse explains, so they are all inside. She opens the door to the *orangerie* with a large key carried around her neck. She turns on the electric light and we walk among the trees. The smell of oranges makes me giddy. The Comtesse holds my hand and confides to me that she is sad. I say her *bal* is a great success. She shrugs. They are hateful to her, she says. But she is obliged to have them. I could never understand.

"But here," she says, plucking an orange from a tree, "this is from the Philippines. They said it could grow in hardier climates. It is not quite ripe yet, but take it. I fear for the cold weather."

Still later there are fireworks. The girl who goes to museums leans on the balustrade by the south court. I am below her. Suddenly a spotlight is thrown on the pathway between the stone lions. Servants in powdered wigs are pulling a circus cart through the garden. Inside the cart is a rhinoceros. Everyone is delighted, and they applaud. They descend to look at the rhinoceros more closely. He is very quiet in his small cage. He cannot turn, and is probably heavily sedated. Someone reaches in and touches his horn. He does not move. Everyone is greatly amused. One of the ladies asks her masked gentleman to carve a piece of the horn for her. He would, but the Comtesse intervenes. The rhinoceros has been rented from the Circus Haissier for the evening: he must not be damaged. The girl who goes to museums watches through a small pair of opera glasses the color of her mask. She smiles to me from the balustrade. Someone whispers to me that it is rumoured she was once the mistress of a famous painter. I doff my hat to her, much like I imagine a courtier did of old.

III.

My life is much like a triptych, a painting on three folding panels of memory. On one panel, I am a small child in a summer afternoon, standing in the foyer of a great house. I am watching the rain drift through the leaves. A dog is running through the gardens, chasing something I cannot see. People have come in from playing tennis and are laughing in the other room, drinking lemonade and shaking rain from their hats. Beyond the lawn is the garden and beyond the garden is the lake and beyond the lake are the woods. Even now an older man whom I do not know is rowing slowly to the other shore. He is wearing a yellow straw hat and pulls the oars with slow strokes.

In the third panel, I am that old man on the lake, and face across to the young boy standing in the foyer of the great house. I cannot really see him, for he is inside the house, yet I know he is there. I find it strange that I am rowing in the rain—not a very sensible thing to do, but then I have never been a very sensible person. Age has not brought me wisdom. Instead, it's given me a fondness for small foolish things, such as this straw hat. There is a summer pavilion on the other side of the lake. The young boy does not yet know that it is there, so he is puzzled at my destination. On the pavilion a small orchestra is playing gay music. Two or three people are sitting and nodding in time. They do not notice me as I pull the boat in. They also are drinking lemonade, and are talking about Venice. There is a museum there, whose name I forget, that I went to once.

But it is the middle panel that is most wondrous. In it, I am not there at all. The view is of a cavernous museum with a gallery longer than the Grande Gallerie of the Louvre. Paintings are hanging everywhere, from all sides and even from the ceiling. The perspective is quite distorted, so that even these paintings on the ceiling can be seen clearly from below. A man who prefers to be anonymous, since he is shading his head with his hand, strolls along the gallery. Poor man! He looks at the paintings like a thief on a plain. The girl who goes to museums has not yet arrived, but she is coming, she is expected. The dust settles slowly in the museum awaiting her arrival. Someimes, however, she has just left: details change, the paintings change. This is after all only a panel of imagination, and is never truly finished.

IV.

I found a note today from the girl who goes to museums. It bears an address in the Septiéme Quartier. I do not know whether it was meant for me. She left it on a table in a drawing room in the Musée des Beaux Arts. It is there I find it. It is late afternoon in winter. On afternoons like this children skate on ponds, and start fires to keep warm, and drink tea made with melted snow. A party of hunters passes the children. They are carrying a wild deer they have killed. Occasionally blood spurts from the mouth of the deer, who lies on the pole, its tongue lolling out. Its eyes stare at the children. In the Musée there is a tapestry much like this, but more refined.

Now it is late; the museum is closing. The sun appears briefly, illuminating the room and the vases. As I said, I do not know whether the message was meant for me. But I will assume so. I will go to the address indicated, at the hour indicated.

When I arrive, I find a tiny apartment, empty except for a bed, a table, a wardrobe, and some cheap plaster statues of nymphs in the corner. The girl who goes to museums offers me a drink, and we sit on the edge of the bed because there is little where else to sit in the room. She asks me about my love of painting, and I say it is rivalled only by hers. We are great connoisseurs, she and I.

"You are too polite," she says sadly. "I really know nothing about painting. I have never known painters." Her voice is like small shards of glass falling on the evening lawn.

I protest. "You are being modest," I say.

"My dream," she says while pouring me another glass, "is to go to the country and live by a lake. Nature will be my art, my only observed art."

"You will be a shepherdess," I laugh.

This delights her. "Yes, of course, a shepherdess," she says. "I shall live in a cottage and grow old."

She turns out the light and goes now to the high wardrobe. On the inside door is a mirror. In the mirror I see her watching me. It is a game we play. We are old friends, she and I.

Now she takes a printed silk kimono from the wardrobe and puts it on. I have seen this scene before in a painting, in a museum. She will turn now and come to stand beside me. While I watch, she will take off the kimono and stand naked before me. Then she will take off her wig of black hair and place it on the night-table. Her head is smooth as an egg underneath the wig. Then she will take out her eyes, first one, then the other, and carefully place them like jewels next to the wig. Then her nose, and ears, and finally her mouth, until her face is naked and shining in the darkness.

"You are the only one I will ever show this to," she has told me. ∎

WAITING FOR TRAINS AT COL D'AUBISQUE
Robert Hedin

4 a.m. and rain since dark, rain dropping
From the slate roofs onto the stone walkway,
And all of us here—
The middle-aged mother and the child,
The three privates smoking
As only those going off
For good can smoke—
All of us standing at these windows,
Except the young boy out under the archway
Who has brought his father's coffin
Down out of these bare hills,
A small sheepherder's boy
Who doesn't care how old the night gets
Or how long this rain takes hold,
Only that his wool coat
Is folded neatly, and that his head rests
Over his father's shoulder,
For if this boy, this young dark-eyed Basque
From Col d'Aubisque
Whose skin will never again feel as wet
Or as wanted as it is
By all this rain,
If this small boy would talk
He would say we've stood all night
At these windows for nothing,
And that even if the morning comes
And we step out into the cold light,
Finding the world no better or worse
And ourselves still wanting
To be filled with its presence,

The words we've waited all night to say
We will have to turn into breath
And use to warm our hands.

ON TUESDAYS THEY OPEN THE LOCAL POOL
TO THE STROKE-VICTIMS
Robert Hedin

—for my sons

Thank God my own father didn't have to go through this.
Or I'd be driving him here every Tuesday
So he could swim his laps
Or splash around with the others
In the shallow end. Something terrible
Has been bled out of these lives. Why else
Would they be here pulling themselves along on their sides,
Scissoring, having to prove to their middle-aged sons
They can still dance.
                    The last three days I heard water
In the cellar, the rooms below me bumping together
Like dinghies. Somewhere back in my sleep
My father splashes in the shallow end.
All these men, even
The balding ones waiting behind the chain-link fence
Watching their fathers, are down there
At the bottom of the stairs.
They are all gliding like sunlight,
Like trout across the cold floors of their breeding ponds.

TORNADO
Robert Hedin

Four farms over it looked like a braid of black hemp
I could pull and make the whole sky ring.
And I remember there falling to earth that night
The broken slats of a barn, baling wire, straw and hay,
And one black leather Bible with a broken spine.

I think of the bulls my father slaughtered every August,
How he would pull out of that rank sea
A pair of collapsed lungs, stomach,
Eight bushels of gleaming rope he called intestines,
And one bucket of parts he could never name.

In the dream that keeps circling back in the shape
Of a barn, my father has just drained
His last bull. Outside it is raining harder
Than I've ever seen, and the sky is about to step down
On one leg. And all through the barn,
As high as the loft, the smell of blood and hay.
All night, as long as the dream holds,
He keeps turning the thick slab of soap over and over,
Building the lather up like clouds in his hands.

THE PURE IN HEART
Peggy Payne

He would not have said that he was ever 'called' to the ministry. It wasn't like that. Instead, he grew up knowing that it would be so. The church was Swain Hammond's future—unofficially. He got his doctorate at Yale. Then, after one brief stint as an associate minister, he became the pastor at Westside, a good choice for—as he had become—a man of a rational, ethical orientation.

The church, in Chapel Hill, North Carolina, is Presbyterian. It is fairly conventional, though influenced, certainly, by the university community. Swain is happy here. Westside suits him. But it is clearly not the best place to hold the pastorate if you're the sort who's inclined to hear the actual voice of God. Up until recently, this would not have been a problem for Swain. But about eight weeks ago, the situation changed. At that time, Swain did indeed hear God.

He and his wife Julie were grilling skewers of pork and green peppers on the back patio of the stone house they chose themselves as the parsonage. They have no children. Julie works. She is a medical librarian at the hospital, though if you met her you would never think of libraries. You might think of Hayley Mills in some of those movies from her teenage years. She has the same full features and thick red hair. On this particular night, Julie is turning a shish-kabob, which seems to be falling apart. Swain, bare-footed—it is June—is

77

drinking a beer and squinting up the slight hill of their back yard, which they have kept wooded.

"Isn't that a ladyslipper?" he says. "Was that out yesterday?" But Julie is busy; she doesn't look. Swain, his long white feet still bare, carefully picks his way up the hill to examine the flower. It is then, as he stops yards away from the plant—clearly not a ladyslipper—that he hears God for the first time.

The sound comes up and over the hill. One quick cut. Like a hugely amplified PA system, blocks away, switched on for a moment by mistake. "Know that there is truth. Know this." The last vowel, the 'i' of this, lies quivering on the air like a note struck on a wineglass.

The voice is unmistakable. At the first intonation, the first rolling syllable, Swain wakes, feeling the murmuring life of each of a million cells. Each of them all at once. He feels the line where his two lips touch, the fingers of his left hand pressed against his leg, the spears of wet grass against the flat soles of his feet, the gleaming half-circles of tears that stand in his eyes. His own bone marrow hums inside him like colonies of bees. He feels the breath pouring in and out of him, through the damp red passages of his skull. Then in the slow way that fireworks die, the knowledge fades. He is left again with his surfaces and the usual vague darkness within. He turns back around to see if Julie has heard.

She has not. Her back turned to him, she is serving the two plates that he has set on the patio table. A breeze is moving the edge of the outdoor tablecloth. She turns back around toward him, looking up the hill. "Soup's on," she says, smiling. "Come eat." She stands and waits for him, as he walks, careful still of his feet and the nettles, back down to her. Straight to her. He takes her in his arms, ignoring her surprise, the half-second of her resistance. He pulls her close, tight against him, one hand laced now in her hair, one arm around her hips. He is as close as he can get. He has gathered all of her to him that he can hold.

He puts the side of his face against her cheek, so he will not have to see her eyes when he says: "Julie, over there on the grass, I heard something. A voice."

She pulls back from him, forcing him to see her. She raises her eyebrows, half-smiling, searching his face for the signs of a joke. "A voice?" she says. There is laughter ready in her tone. "God," he says. His mouth is dry. "God's voice."

She watches him carefully now, her eyes scanning his eyes, ever-so-slightly moving. The trace of a smile is gone. "What do you mean?"

"Standing up there on the hill," he says, almost irritably. "I heard God. That's what I mean." He watches her, his own face blank. Hers is struggling. Let her question it if she wants to. He doesn't know how to explain.

"So what happened?" she says. "Tell me some more." She pauses. "What did it—what did the voice sound like?"

Swain repeats the words he heard. He does not say then what happened to him: that hearing the voice, he has felt the mortality of his every cell.

They stand apart from each other now. She reaches over and touches his hair, strokes it. If one of us was to hear God, it should have been Julie, he thinks. But a different God—the one he has believed in until today.

She is looking at him steadily. "I don't think you're crazy, if that's what you're worried about." Her uncertainty has left her. "It's all right," she says. "It is."

"For you it would be," he says. He means it as a compliment. He has envied her her imaginings, felt left behind sometimes by the unfocused look of her eyes. Though she will tell him where she is: that she goes back, years back, to particular days with particular weathers. That she plays in the back yard of her grandparents' house, shirtless, in seersucker shorts, breathing the heavy summer air, near the blue hydrangeas. Swain wants to be with her then. He wants to go: "Except ye become as little children, ye shall not enter. . . ." He wants, and yet he doesn't want.

She glances at the food on the plates. They move toward the table. The sweat that soaked his shirt has started to chill him.

"I'm going to get a sweater," he says. "Do you want anything?" She shakes her head 'no.' She sits, begins to eat her cooling dinner.

There are no lights on inside the house, only the yellowish glow of the patio light through the window, shining on one patch of floor in the hall. He goes to the hall closet, looking for something to put on. He finds a light windbreaker. He has his hand in the closet, reaching for the jacket,when he hears the voice again. One syllable. "Son." The sound unfurls down the long hall toward him. He feels the sound and its thousand echoes hit him all at once. He holds onto the wooden bar where the coat hangs, while the shock washes over his back.

He stays where he is, his back and neck bent, his hand bracing him, waiting. Nothing else happens. Again, it is over. Again he is wet with sweat. He straightens, painfully, as if he had held the position for hours. He walks again out onto the patio. Julie, at the table, squints to see his face against the light beside the door.

"Are you all right?" she says.

He sits, looks down at his plate. He holds the jacket, lays it across his lap like a napkin. He shakes his head. A sob is starting low in his chest, dry like a cough. He feels it coming, without tears. He has not cried since he tore a ligament playing school soccer. He has had no reason. Now he is crying, his own voice tearing and breaking through him. Inside him, walls are falling. Interior walls cave like old plaster, fall away to dust. He feels it like the breaking of living bones. In the last cool retreat of his reason, he thinks: I am seeing my own destruction. Then that cool place is invaded too. He feels the violent tide of whatever is in him flooding his last safe ground. He holds himself with both arms; Julie, on her knees beside his chair, holds him. God has done this to him. This is God. Tears drip from his face and trickle down his neck.

Two days later Swain sits alone in his office at the church. He has a sermon to write. Should he tell the congregation what happened to him? His note pad is blank. He has put down his pen. It is an afternoon with all the qualities of a sleepless night: hot, restless, unending. There are no distractions from what he is unable to do. The secretary is holding his calls. The couple who were to come in with marital difficulties cancelled. The window behind his desk is open, he stares out into the shimmery heat and listens to the churning of a lawnmower. He has already been through the literature and found nothing to reassure him.

Son. He keeps coming back to that one word in his mind.

It was not Swain's own father talking. That was clear. His father would never have been so definite, so terse. The elder Dr. Hammond would have interspersed his words, and there would have been more of them, with long moments of musing and probably the discreet small noises of his dyspepsia. He would have asked Swain to consider whether there was indeed 'a truth.' Swain would have considered this, as he was asked. And possibly at some later time they would have discussed it, without conclusion.

Swain, twisting in his chair, resettling his legs, knows he did not create the voice. He did not broadcast that sound out through the pines of his own back yard. He sees again the reddish gold light of the late sun on the bark of those back yard trees. He did not imagine it. His mind does not play tricks.

Though the whole thing seems like a bad trick, a bad dream—divine revelation, coming now. He imagines himself in the pulpit, staring out at the congregation, telling them. He sees the horror waking on their faces, as they understand him. He sees them exchanging glances, glances that cut diagnoally across the pews. He would be out. It would cost him the church. Leaders of the congregation would gradually, lovingly ease him out, help him make 'other arrangements.' He tries to imagine those other arrangements: churches with marquees that tally up the number saved on a Sunday, churches with buses and all-white congregations. Appalling. It makes him shudder.

He turns his chair away from the window, back to his desk. It is too soon. He has nothing to say. Know that there is truth? A half-sentence? He at least needs time to think about it. Then perhaps he can make some sense out of it. Of course he will make 'public confession' finally. He will witness. He has to. "Whoever shall confess me before men, him shall the Son of Man also confess before the angels of God." There is no question. ". . . He that denieth me before men. . . ." It is his mission—to speak. A man could not remain a minister with such a secret.

On Saturday, he has a wedding. He has already put on his robe. His black shoes gleam. He sits at his desk, ready early, signing letters left here in his box by the secretary. Routine business. His sermon for Sunday is written, typed in capital letters. It makes no direct reference to hearing the voice of God.

He does like marrying couples, thinks of it, in fact, as an important part of his ministry. When a couple gets together within the church, it always seems to him a sort of personal victory. As the boy said two weeks ago at the junior high retreat, "Human relations is where it's at."

The pair this afternoon is interesting to him in a more particular way. He has been counseling them since Louise, the bride-to-be, found out she was pregnant. She is 38, roughly his own age. She and Alphonse, a Colombian, have lived together for about three years. They have planned for today a fairly traditional, almost-formal ceremony. She is not yet showing. He remembers her when she was alone. He could see her on Sunday mornings canvassing the congregation with her eyes, picking out the occasional male visitor holding his hymnbook alone. Watching her in those years, he wondered what his own life would be like, without Julie. Whether he would show that same hunger so plainly on his face. He is glad for Louise, pregnant as she is. He caps his pen and stands. It's time to go in.

The feel is different now in the sanctuary, more relaxed than the eleven o'clock. Maybe it's only the afternoon light, filtered as it is by stained glass. He stands at the chancel steps, the ceremony begins. Alphonse comes to stand beside him. They face the aisle where Louise is to enter on the arm of her sister's husband. Swain tests the sound of their names, rehearses them in silence—Louise Elizabeth Berryman, Alphonse Martinez Vasconcellos. The twang and the beat of the Spanish—he has resolved to get it right, not to anglicize. He runs through the name again—and a scene unwinds like a scroll inside him. Gerona.

Louise, coming down the aisle now, slowly, slowly, moves in her long pale dress behind the clear shapes of his sudden unsought memory. He is 20 years old, standing in a stone-walled room in Spain. The straps of his backpack pull at his shoulders. It is quiet here, blocks away from the narrow river and the arched bridges. In this room—he read it in his guidebook—there was a revelation. He stands, with his two friends, in a medieval landmark of the Kabbalah. It is the moment, unplanned, when all three become quiet, when he can only hear the muted traffic from the street. He is looking for something in this room. He lays his hand on the grainy stone of the wall. Standing now in the sanctuary, he feels the damp grit of rock against the fist of his palm. He can't escape it, he can't shake it off. He wears it—this slight tingling pressure—like a glove. A wet glove that clings to his skin. Louise is now at the front before him.

The couple turns to him. They wait. "Dearly beloved," he hears himself say. Faces stretch in a blur to the back of the church. He hears his voice—it must be his—float out to those faces, saying, "We are gathered here today. . . ."

He has told Julie everything, about hearing the voice. Not just the words, but how it felt. He has told her about the intrusion of the scene from Spain at the wedding this afternoon. "That was the last thing I needed," he says. "For that to happen while I'm actually standing at the front." They are sitting at the kitchen table. It's late.

She shrugs. The look on her face is the one he tries to cultivate in counseling. She is not shocked. Yet she does not diminish what happened to him. The look is one of sympathy and respect at once. She does it, he knows, without thinking.

She nods toward the typewriter, his old one, standing in its case near the bookshelves. They both use it for letters, neither one of them has a legible handwriting. "You've always set the margins so narrow," she says. "On yourself, on what's real. You don't give yourself much room."

She waits. He thinks about it.

"True," he says, nodding, looking away from her. "And you give yourself that kind of—'room' you're talking about." He looks at her, her chin propped on one hand, her face pushed slightly out of shape. "But do you actually believe in it," he says, "in what you see and hear, in the things you imagine? You don't. Of course you don't."

She puts her hand down, on the table, away from her face. She takes a breath and holds it a second before she speaks. The look she has had, of authority, is gone. "In a way," she says. She searches his face. "I don't think too much about it. But—yes, in a way, I do."

There is no joy in it. That's what bothers him. He is lying on the living room floor, still thinking about it, though he hasn't mentioned any of it, even to Julie, for almost a week. Maybe silence will make the whole thing go away. Julie is in the armchair reading, her feet in old white tennis shoes, her ankles crossed near his head. He watches her feet move, very slightly, in a rhythm, as if she were listening to music instead of reading. Maybe she hears music and never mentions it. She likes music. Maybe she's hearing Smetana's Moldau, close enough to the orchestra to hear between the movements the creakings of musicians' chairs. She would do this and think nothing of it. She has been patient with his days of silent turmoil.

As a kid, he wanted something like this to happen. Some sign. He did imagine though that it would bring with it pleasure—great happiness, in fact. He had a daydream of how it would be, set in the halls and classrooms of his elementary school, where he first imagined it. A column of warm pink light would pour over him, overpowering him with a sensation so intensely sweet it was unimaginable. He tried and tried to feel how it would feel. The warmth would wrap around his heart inside his chest, like two hands cradling him there. He would be full of happiness, completely at peace. The notion stayed with him past childhood, though, certainly in his earlier years, he didn't talk about it.

But he did what he could to have that experience. Divine revelation. He wanted it. He lay on the floor of his bedroom at home, later his dorm room at Brown, and he waited. He stared at rippling creeks and wind-blown leaves and the deep chalky green of blackboards until his mind was lulled into receptive quiet. The quietness always passed, though, without interruption, at least by anything divine.

The search must have ended finally. Only now does he realize it, lying here with the front door standing open and moths batting against the screen. He doesn't recall any such preoccupation during divinity school, though there was that one thing that happened in his last year. It hardly qualified him as a mystic, though it was reassuring at the time.

He was sitting out on the balcony of his apartment, a second-floor place he shared with two other students. He and Julie, not married then, were in one of their 'off' times. He was feeling bad. The concordance, the notepad had slid off his lap. His legs were sprawled, completely motionless, in front of him, hanging off the end of the butt-sagged recliner. He had lost Julie; he was bone-tired of school; he wouldn't have cared if he died.

He was staring at the scrubby woods behind the apartment complex, behind the parking lot and a weedy patch of mud and three dumpsters. Nothing mattered. Nothing at all. Then while he watched, everything—without motion or shift of light—everything he saw changed. He stared at the painted stripes on the asphalt, at water standing on the yellowish mud. It was all alive. Alive and sharing one life. The parking lot, the bare ground had become the varied skin of one living being. In the stillness, he waited for the huge creature to move, to take a breath. Nothing stirred. Yet he felt the benevolence of the animal, its power, rising off the surface before him like waves of heat.

What he felt then was a lightness, a sort of happiness. This was so important. It was at least a hint of what he had once imagined.

That afternoon he was buoyed. He finished the work he had sat with the whole afternoon. He fried himself a hamburger and ate it and was still hungry. He watched a few minutes of the news. He did not die or think further of dying since that day, other than for the purposes of sermons, counseling, and facing the inevitable facts.

Facts. He is lying on the floor of his living room. Julie is reading in the chair. God has spoken to him, in English, clearly, in an unmistakable voice. He is not glad.

"What would you do, Julie?" he says. He is looking at the ceiling, he does not turn his head. "Would you stand up in that pulpit and tell them, 'I have heard the voice of God'; Would you do it?" He rolls over on his side and looks at her. Her foot has stopped moving. She has put her book down.

"I've been thinking about that," she says.

"What did you decide?"

"Probably," she says. "I think I would." She is not smiling. She looks at him steadily. Her eyes are tired.

"Oh?" he says. There is an edge in his voice. "What else would you say? How would you explain it? Explain to me, if you understand so well." He pauses, waits.

"Say as much as you know," she says.

"What is that? One piece of a sentence: know that there is truth. It isn't enough. I have nothing to say."

"It's your job, isn't it?" she says. "To tell them. Isn't it?" He sees the fear flickering across her face now. She needs to say it, but she's scared. It's the way he would be, standing before his incredulous congregation. Fearing the cost. What could it cost her to say this?

"You're afraid to tell me," he says. His voice is weary, dull.

She nods.

"Why?"

She swallows, looks away from him. "Because I'm saying you need to do something that may turn out bad. It would be the most incredible irony—but it could happen. They might decide you're losing your marbles. They might call it that, when really they don't want a minister who says this kind of stuff—about hearing God. It's not that kind of church. You know?"

He ignores the question. "We could have to move," he says. "We could wind up somewhere we would hate. Is that what you're worried about?"

"Some," she says. "But mostly that you would blame me, if it happened—that you would always feel like I pushed you into it."

"And then the marriage would fall apart," he says.

"Yeah," she says. Her voice shakes. Her mouth has the soft forgotten look it gets when all of her is concentrated elsewhere. In this case, on fear. He is not in the mood to reassure her.

"And what if I don't do it?" he says. "What if I never say a word and you spend the rest of your life thinking I'm a shit —a minister who denies God? What happens to us then?"

She shakes her head. She is close to tears. "I don't think that will happen," she says. It comes out in an uneven whisper.

Swain stands, straightens his pants legs. He looks at her once without sympathy, but her face is averted, she doesn't see. He leaves the room, goes into the kitchen. He gets out a small tub of Haagen Dazs and a spoon, stands near the fridge, eating from the container. There is no sound from her in the other room. Pink light—what a joke. "Suppose ye that I am come to give peace on earth? I tell you, Nay; but rather division." The voice didn't warn him, didn't remind him. He shakes his head. He digs and scrapes at the ice cream.

He is turning his car into the church parking lot when it happens again. He hears God. His window is open. The car is lurched upward onto the incline of the pavement. The radio is on, but low. From the hedge, a few feet from his elbow on the window frame, a sound emerges. It clearly comes from there: a burst, a jumble of phrases, scripture, distortions of scripture: "He that heareth and doeth not . . . for there is nothing hid . . . the word is sown on stony ground . . . why reason ye . . . seeketh his own glory . . . he that hath ears . . . he that hath. . . ." A nightmare. A nightmare after a night of too much reading. A spilling of accusation, reproach. Swain is staring straight ahead. A hot weight presses into him, into the soft vee beneath the joining of his ribs. It hurts, it pins him to the seat. It passes like cramp, leaving only a shadow, a distrust of those muscles.

Another car is waiting behind him, easing toward his fender. He pulls into the parking lot, into a space. He does it automatically. His face feels as hot as the sun-baked plastic car seat. He looks at the hedge, running between the sidewalk and the street. Tear it out—that's what he wants to do. Pull it up, plant by plant, with his hands. He is a pastor. Not a prophet. Not a radio evangelist. He does not believe in gods that quote the King James version out of bushes and trees.

He gets out of the car, goes into the church, into his office. He kicks the door shut behind him. He tosses a new yellow legal pad onto the bare center of his desk. There has to be something in this room to smash. He looks around: at the small panes of the window; at the veneer of the side of his desk; at the cluster of family pictures, framed; at the bud vase Julie gave him, that now holds two wilting daisies and a home-grown rose. Something to break. He grabs the vase by the neck and slings it, overarm, dingy water spilling, into a pillow of the sofa. A soft thump, and the stain of water spreads on the dark upholstery. He looks away from it, looks at the yellow pad on his desk. His career. That's what he'll smash. That ought to be enough. He walks around behind the desk, sits, red-faced, breathing audibly through parted lips. He stares at the lined paper with the pen in his hand. Say as much as you know. He begins to write. Beyond writing it down, he tells himself, he has made no decision.

On the following Sunday, he walks forward into the pulpit. He has received the offering. He has performed the preliminary duties with a detached methodical calm. Now he stands with his hands on the wooden rail, his fingers finding their familiar places along the tiered wood. "Friends," he says. He looks at no one in particular. "I have struggled with what I have to say to you today." They are waiting, with no more than their routine interest. "I have come to say to you that I have heard the voice of God." He says it to the rosette of stained glass at the back of the sanctuary. He cannot look at Julie on the third row. He cannot look at the McDougalls or Sam Bagdikian or Mary Elgar, as he says it. In the ensuing silence, his eyes sweep forward again, from the window back across 300 faces. They are blank, waiting still, mildly interested. No one is alarmed. They have not understood.

He begins again. As much as he knows. "I think you know that I believe in an immanent God. I think you know that I believe in the presence and power of God in all our lives. I have come to tell you today that something has happened to me in recent days which I do not understand.

"A voice has spoken to me. I know that it is God. A voice has spoken to me that was a chorus of voices. I know that they are God." He pauses. "My wife Julie and I were cooking dinner on the grill on our back patio. . . ." The faces grow taut with attention. Sudden stillness falls over the church to the back pews of the balcony. There is no flutter of church bulletins. There are no averted faces. It is not a metaphor, not a parable he is telling. His wife Julie, the back patio—they are listening. He proceeds, with a trembling deep in his gut. He begins with the ladyslipper and voice that came over the hill.

He tells them about the word 'son' and the windbreaker and his own tears. "I asked myself whether I should bring this to you on a Sunday morning," he says. He looks from face to face in the rows in front of him. What are they thinking? It's impossible to tell. The shaking inside him has moved outward, to his hands. He feels them damp against the wood of the pulpit rail. He does not trust his voice.

"I asked myself how you the members of this congregation would react. Would you think that I've—" he tries to say this lightly, with a wry laugh—"that maybe I've been under too much stress lately." The laugh is not convincing. He himself hears its false ring. "But I will tell you," he says, "that that is not what has happened. I have not taken leave of my senses."

He looks at Julie. He can see her wrists, before the back of the pew breaks his vision. He knows her hands are knotted together, moving one against the other. He pulls his eyes away.

"I asked myself whether you would want a pastor who hears voices. Or even whether some of you might come to expect wisdom from me, because of what has happened, that I do not have." He pauses. "I don't know what to expect," he says, "from you or—" he hesitates— "from God. But I will tell you that my heart is now open. I will listen." He steps back, hearing as he does so the first note of the organ, reliable Miss Bateman is playing. The congregation stands, hymnbooks in hands. The service ends without incident. Swain stands as usual at the front steps afterwards to shake hands and greet people. Three of all those who file past him tell him that the Lord works in wondrous ways, or something to that effect. Miss Frances Eastwood squeezes his elbow and tells him to trust. Ed Fitzgerald lays one hand on his shoulder, close to his collar, and says, "I like what you did here today." The rest make no mention of what has occurred. The line moves quickly past him, handshakes, heartiness, veiled eyes.

It is not over, of course. Julie keeps her hand on his knee as he drives home, though they say little. During the afternoon, he receives several phone calls at home, of an encouraging and congratulatory nature. Coming back into the kitchen, where

Julie is cleaning out drawers to keep busy, he says, "It's the ones who don't call, who are calling each other. . . ."

What does occur happens gradually. Swain is given no answer, no sense of having-got-it-over on that Sunday afternoon. First, as he surmises, conversations buzz back and forth, on the telephone, at get-togethers, in chance meetings on the street. People inside and outside the church talk about what happened, about Swain Hammond's sermon.

The night the church operations committee meets, Swain and Julie stay home and play Scrabble. Swain can't concentrate, but Julie protests every time he wants to quit. The call comes at 11:15. It's Joe Morris. "Between you and me," Joe reminds him, "this is all unofficial. . . ."

The upshot of it is that the committee voted five-to-four to privately recommend that Swain get professional help. The chairman Bill Bartholomew, who made the motion, comes to Swain's office to tell him. "Of course," he says, "this is something which is not easy to say. But we all go through times when we need. . . ."

"Thank you for your prayers and concern," Swain says. He is accustomed to assuming a look of gratitude when it is called for. It only fails him in the last minutes of the conversation.

"Are you so sure I'm crazy, Bill?" he says. The two of them are standing now in the office doorway, there is no one in the hall. "Doesn't it seem contradictory?" Swain says. Bill is watching him carefully. "It's okay to believe in God, but only if God is distant. A presence in history. Is that the idea?"

"I'm sure I don't want to debate this with you," Bill says. "It's only the will of the committee—"

"I understand your position," Swain says. He does not seek counseling.

When news of the committee's action leaks, a petition circulates and the members take sides. This time the vote is with Swain. The letter, signed by the majority of the members, affirms that Dr. Swain Hammond is in his right mind and will continue to be welcome as minister. These are not the exact words, but this is the meaning.

Swain mentions this decision from the pulpit, but only as a brief comment among the day's other announcements. "Thank you for your love and support," he says. Unexpectedly, as he says it, he feels a tightness in his throat. He looks from face to face. He won't be leaving. If he thinks about it, he'll lose his composure. He summons a bit of the anger that has sustained him through the last few weeks. It works, he manages to keep the wave of love at bay.

"Besides," he tells Julie later that day, "I don't completely trust it." They are taking a late afternoon walk through the neighborhood around their house. "I feel like all this could change, if the balance shifted just a little. I'm reasonably secure for the moment," he says. "I suppose that will have to do."

She doesn't say anything. She has said her part several times already: that she is proud of him, that she is proud of what he did.

"I'm also disappointed," he says. They stop for a moment to avoid the arc of spray from a sprinkler cutting across the sidewalk. "I thought maybe a few people would be curious about what actually happened. Would want to hear more." He shakes his head. "They don't." It makes him mad to think about it. They've decided to put up with him—that's what they've made of all this. They're being broad-minded and tolerant, that's all.

Swain does hear the voice of God again. This time—last Tuesday morning—it is as a note of music, as he is just waking up. Julie lies beside him asleep. It is early, still twenty minutes before the alarm is set to go off. He knows before it happens that it's coming. He does not move. He waits, while the note emerges from a sound too deep to be heard. Then it is audible, filling the room, humming against his bare stomach, like the live warm touch of a hand. In the same moment, it begins to diminish, a dwindling vibration of piano strings.

Swain lies still. He does not cry this time, or soak the sheets with his sweat. He does not wake Julie, whose breath he can feel on the curve of his shoulder. He looks at the morning light on the far wall, shifting with the shadows of tree branches. He watches the triangles and splinters of light, forming and re-forming, and feels the slow rise and fall of his own chest. Everything is quiet: the room, the yard beneath the window, the street out front. He can see it all in his mind now, one surface, connected, breathing with his same slow breath. What he feels then, flooding the whole space of his being, is joy, undeniably joy, though it has not come as he would have expected. It is not what he looked for at all. ∎

SLIP OF THE TONGUE
Charles Edward Eaton

Certainly one thinks of the remote island,
The rocks deep in guano, the obscene birds—
What is a lady-killer doing here,
With long memories, in tight red loincloth?

The shackled ankles may provide a hint,
The brown body's sprawled, thrown look,
No whip marks, but surely the startled eyes
Wonder if sensation will strike again.

What was the last thing said to the lover?—
Was it a *lapsus linguae* so dreadful
That all the fawning cherubs left the bower
And the woman herself melted like wax?

Sometimes even while they were making love
He could roll over and see the island—
Himself the stripped-down ladrone, the bird mess—
Roll back again and rush the luscious kiss.

It was simply that one night he turned and stuck—
At last she had heard him all too plainly
And with her lips she would not pull him back,
An elastic touch stretched once too often.

Nevertheless, let us taunt sensation,
Make it leak slowly back into the facts:
Why did the lady-killer lose his nerve,
Why did the rushing kiss reverse itself?

I who so love language cannot believe
It alone delivers us to rocks and guano.
Some physical playback jumps the music
And one says what has never been said before.

Ah, lovely flesh—an aesthetic wash
Must roll over it with the passionate kiss—
Two lying at the tropical island's edge:
Just so much tidal thrust, then back again.

Still the eyelid is anchored in nightmare—
Who will be the first to pull, then pull away?—
Sometimes the lucky lie like a lulled ship,
Hung by magic with the deep, plunged iron.

The hot, stifled lungs wanting to be wings,
I wish I could summon Prometheus—
How did the liver grow and live so long,
What was the word the vulture longed to hear?

It is so warm—roll over, and roll back,
An exquisite cradle of creation:
I will stick out my tongue to the black bird—
So much for saying something for a god.

SENTIMENTAL EDUCATION
Charles Edward Eaton

The man and woman went down to the green canoe
To make their fateful incision upon the blue water,
Steadying each other, when they entered, as upon a totally
uncertain concept.

They seemed to be standing upon the vast, illimitable jelly of
their desires—
The quaking of the water had, in fact, a certain comfort in it,
The solidity of their bodies swaying in a soft, primordial
laissez-faire.

Not until she sat down in the bow and he took the oar,
She in a white dress and he in shirtsleeves and straw summer
hat,
Did the luxurious, visceral shimmying reach its partial
diminuendo.

Then they prepared to do, what we all must do—close the
metaphor.
Perhaps they went to an island to picnic from a basket she had
brought,
Perhaps the shadow of a huge tree would pallet their embrace.

He left the seal of his shoe upon the bank, she looked back
somewhat wistfully
As if somewhere there were a room with closely drawn white
curtains, a shaded lamp,
Two contented people doing nothing more demanding than
reading books.

I thought of this fabulous duo just this morning, remembering
How I used to plush my feet in the mud as a child like an
    unfastidious pigmy
To whom the apple-green earth was coated and cored with
    sensual glamor.

The canoe painted with fruit-color slipped into the cove I do
    not know just when,
Nor when the blue water came up voluptuously around my muddy
    ankles
And I invented man and woman to step with some precision on
    the rocking earth.

To this day I cannot dream these powerful, swaying figures
    without frisson,
Wishing even to be a little god-like when I wake upon a dark
    bed of jelly,
Feeling the cool breast of that woman in my brown, seignorial
    hand.

I have encapsulated this vision in many closely shuttered rooms,
Among bibliophiles, chez nous, silently, inwardly shaking with
    inordinate passion,
Letting the keel of the green canoe cut the pages, white, so white,
    then blue.

THE PARROT
Charles Edward Eaton

Thinking in terms of how to solve worldwide malaise,
I watched the parrot in his cage, an old imperialist,
Perched on the swing that goes East and West, languorously
    dividing his predatory ways.

Kept in the kitchen, he remains a mandarin, a Sung,
Proud and dynastic, petulant to servants,
Speaking always in the slightly unreal accent of a foreign
    tongue.

He makes you think of opulence and squalor all together,
Messy with his food, impossible to please,
Arthritically rigid if too many he despises forgather.

Whether you were closed in your drawing room or free outside,
Alone, in the most raucous or diplomatic company,
You would be shaken if informed that he had died.

And why? Because he did not ever fully speak his mind,
Mocking, malapert, and just plain menacing the whole day long
Until he had no right, in death, to be so bland?—

A thing, if you were morbid, you might stuff
To remind you of the worldliness of crime
And how he made you wonder if you had lied enough.

HILLCREST DAYS
Joe Ashby Porter

Marie Tester has killed two people, one quite by accident. Thirty-odd years ago, back when she was still in North Dakota where there were no mountains and no ocean (Marie liked it wide open where you could see forever unless it was snowing), she had her snow chains on so she couldn't have been going at all fast even if she was late to work. It was a stranger who practically jumped into her headlights and another stranger in the stalled Alberta car saw it happen. That was more than thirty years ago, before dawn in January. She worked in a cafe forty miles away glad of the job, nine, ten hours six days for what would be nothing now. She'd have been near twenty. The stranger was dead by the time she got out of the car and the other one testified to her innocence. The cafe let her off for the deposition.

The other person Marie killed was her sister, let's say. It was far slower and more recent. It wasn't murder either. It wasn't manslaughter either. Marie Tester killed her sister with unkindness and her sister was dying anyway. Her older sister who'd followed her to Seattle.

The year is 1976. Marie Tester is short and a bit overweight the way lots of people her age are. When she talks to you and you're a couple of heads taller she mostly looks at whatever she has in her hands or at her empty hands, at her bad nails and then whenever she does look at your face she doesn't tilt hers up, she just raises her eyes and it's like the glance of a dog lying on the floor. She's drinking more than she should these days. Well that's nothing new. More than she used to then and not just in the Sportsman's Lounge (used to be the Tip Top) up the street, but also in her apartment alone with Trixie her blonde Cocker. Trixie's old and overweight too. She doesn't get anything like enough exercise. Pretty soon Marie's going to have Trixie put to sleep and then not get any other animals. You get attached to them and it's not worth it.

Was Seattle the name of a car in the forties? Because it was like one to the Marie of then who'd never been outside North Dakota and still hasn't been east of there or south or north, only west to Seattle. She lives on Capitol Hill in the Hillcrest Apartments. She's been resident manager there going on eight years, with her husband till last year when she threw him out, now alone. The neighborhood was better once. The Hillcrest had different kinds of people in it. Now, well look: Rachel, two couples of gay boys, a forty-year-old woman cabdriver and her mother, the pair of old Lithuanian women in the basement terrified of everything—$60 a month they pay for the two unconnected rooms and a bath they share, they know Marie has no say about the rent and still they lay the politeness on like butter as if that way they could keep the rent from going up. They don't know what they'd do if it went up again. It will, they'll eat less, who knows.

Rachel Padilla is twenty-two, chicana, pretty, independent with a mind of her own. Since all the apartments in the Hillcrest are furnished (except Marie's—she has her own furnishings), pets and children aren't allowed. Yet Rachel has a cat, Joshua. When Marie found out about Joshua and confronted Rachel, Rachel claimed not to have known it was against the rules. "Who made that rule anyway, you? Why don't you change it. Joshua's outside most of the time and when he has to do his business he asks me to let him out. Josh and I are friends, I can't send him down the river."

Marie sputtered in the doorway. "Listen, Rachel. I'm the manager here. I've been managing this building twelve years and you've only been here what is it, two months? You're like a guest in my house here. You'll just have to obey the rules, I mean it Rachel! You signed the rental agreement, it's too bad if you didn't read it, you were supposed to. It says no animals. Take a look at it, you have a copy. I gave you one."

Rachel gave Marie a troublemaker's cool appraising look. "I'll think it over. I guess the owner's name's on my copy of that agreement. Maybe I should get in touch with him. You're not a bad manager but there's probably a lot he doesn't know about. I'll think it over and let you know."

Then for a week Marie was in a dither. At the Group Health Emergency Room—it wasn't just a room, more of a little hospital six blocks from the Hillcrest, Marie worked three nights as a cleaning lady—mopping the corridors she'd bend the other cleaning ladies' ears about Rachel. Afternoons when she and Trixie were out for a walk around the neighborhood she'd be mulling it over, Trixie got more than one earful about Rachel that week and so did Marie's fellow regulars at the Sportsman's. So did a number of Hillcrest tenants, though Marie began more circumspectly with them. From her second floor window she'd see one of them step out of the bus at the corner. She'd light a cigarette and go out into the hallway with an ashtray in her hand, up to the third floor, back along the hallway, timing it. She'd listen for footsteps and then start back, pass the tenant with a preoccupied air ("Oh, hi there Alan") and then turn. "Alan can I speak with you. Has Rachel been saying anything to you boys about me? She's a troublemaker and I think I'm going to have to give her an eviction notice."

The owner of the Hillcrest lives in a suburb on the other side of Lake Washington. He's a retired doctor, a widower with two married children who live far away. He owns another apartment building on Capitol Hill and another in West Seattle. They're much alike. He acquired them all in the late fifties. Marie mails him the rent a little after the first of the month. He came to this country as a boy, from eastern Europe.

He stops by the Hillcrest to look at the damage a spiteful tenant has done one of the apartments. The tenant had a pot of marijuana in his window. Marie wasn't sure but she thought it was, so she asked him, he said yes, she told him to dispose of it. "It's against the law isn't it?" she asked another of the younger tenants. The marijuana grower moved out in the middle of the night (while Marie was at the Emergency Room) with half a month's rent owing. For spite he'd poured a gallon of molasses on the carpet and dumped the dirt from his marijuana pot into it. Marie wanted the owner to see the mess before she rented a rug shampooer. He wanted to look over the building for two reasons he didn't mention to Marie. Because an old woman had died in an apartment house fire the city was starting to enforce fire laws more, and the Hillcrest would probably have to have fire walls and doors built in the corridors. Also the owner was planning to sell the building and he wanted to have a look at some of the apartments to remind himself what they were like. Marie introduced him to one of the gay couples who'd moved in two weeks before. He glanced around. So did Marie. The gay couple didn't seem to have many belongings. They'd rearranged the furniture and taped odd but not dirty pictures on the walls. "By the way, Ms. Tester, when you get a chance could you give us a copy of the rental agreement? Whenever." "Yes, yes," Marie muttered. She was supposed to have given them a copy when they moved in but her typewriter was on the blink. The rental agreement forbade attaching pictures or anything else to the walls. The owner noticed but didn't mention it.

When Marie threw her husband out she threw out everything in the apartment too. Tableware, couch, drapes, rug—she might have sold some of it or the Salvation Army would have been glad of it but Marie threw it in the garbage, left it out for the trash collector. "I'm Irish and I have a temper," she warns you. Both her parents were born in North Dakota and so was she but one of her grandparents was from Ireland and two others had ancestors there.

Rachel sleeps with her jewelry and makeup on. She likes to wear clothes from the forties, from before she was born. She finds them in thrift stores, especially the Goodwill store down in the city market. This year at the market fair live bands played from a rooftop all day Saturday. The weather was hot and perfect. The market complex and the narrow streets were packed with different people having a good time, all different sorts of people, different ages, talking to strangers, sharing food and drink and dope perfectly naturally. Rachel was there. In the afternoon she was dancing in one place with different individuals for more than two hours except for the ten minutes it took her to change from one forties dress (whose seam was splitting) into another. She was stoned and dancing well, sweating like a horse. She was wearing the jewelry she wears when she sleeps—she doesn't even take it off in the shower. One of the bands released fifty red balloons into the blue sky as they played.

When Marie threw her husband out she meant it to be permanent. Divorce seemed right but she had no idea how to go about it or what the laws were. Someone suggested the legal aid society. Its office was down the hill in a mainly black section on a busy street. It turned out to be simpler than she'd expected, and cheaper, so she went through with it. Since then her husband's shown up once or twice at the Hillcrest, always drunk. One afternoon he came banging on the door of her apartment. Marie attached the chain lock and opened the door a crack. Goddamn it let me in, you're my wife, I want in. Marie's dander was up. I'm not your goddamn wife any more and if you don't stop that racket and get the hell out of this building I'll call the police!

Not that they'd come nowadays. Last summer the crowd of young people in the house next door were having some kind of party carousing and playing loud music in the middle of the day when Marie had to sleep. She threw up her window and yelled at them to can the racket or else. They laughed. The police receptionist said she'd pass the complaint on but the party was still going strong when Marie left for work at ten that night.

When somebody threw a brick through the building's glass front door in the middle of the winter Marie wondered if it was one of them, or the tenant who'd poured molasses on the rug or her husband. It happened at night and it was cold. One of the tenants taped dry cleaner's thin plastic over the hole but still the temperature was way down when Marie got back from work and found it. Mrs. Kundrata, one of the Lithuanian women, told Rachel darkly she thought she knew who did it but couldn't say.

The mention of police didn't faze Marie's husband, he was so drunk. Finally she undid the chain lock and let him in. He put his fists to his head and glared. "What've you done?"

"Threw it all out!"

"Oh yeah?" He got a shifty look on his face.

"What the hell do you want anyway?"

He slumped down on the new used sofa.

"What the hell do you want!"

"Come on, Marie."

"Now, now you don't have any business here now!" She got him out after an hour that time. They'd both been yelling mad. He said he wanted to move back in because he'd been kicked out of his rooming house. That was a lie and anyway it was too damn late for that. Marie didn't think he'd hit her now they were divorced and if he'd tried to she could probably have dodged, he has drunk enough. Half the Hillcrest must've heard it though. The woman across the hall—been there going on two years, works nights at Boeing—it woke her up but she didn't complain, in fact she came over and invited Marie back to her place for a double shot of applejack. "It's not right, Marie," she said. "You shouldn't have to put up with that kind of behavior." Marie said, "You're damn right it's not right. I'll tell you this though: even if it was right it wouldn't do me any damn good!"

He stayed away a couple of months. He did get kicked out of his rooming house and lost his job for drinking. He was in real trouble. Marie let him come back and sleep on her sofa for a week till he'd found work again and moved to another rooming house.

Rachel was visiting one of the gay couples and they had a wine bottle on a plate with a candle on it, the bottle covered with wax from earlier candles that had run down the bottle onto the plate. Rachel said, "I like your candle. You know what I was thinking though? I was thinking I'd like to have one and let it run out on the table and down onto the floor."

Marie leafed through a house beautiful magazine under the dryer at La Nae salon up the street. It had an article about weekend vacations in different cities for married couples who'd left their kids home, and one of the four cities happened to be Seattle. The article told what the couple would do Friday evening, Saturday daytime and evening, Sunday daytime. Marie read about Seattle's fascinating blend of diversions—a dinner theater that was a great place to forget little problems, pubs worth poking into, the space needle, colorful survivors from another era in Olde Seattle, unique eateries, atmosphere, marine-oriented attractions, several interesting shops if a bit more browsing seems in order, Pioneer Banque, top jazz performers. . . . Marie wondered if there were people it would sound real to, who'd read it and come to Seattle and have a weekend like the one in the article. The article priced the weekend at $184, broken down into categories. But who in their right mind would pay $40 a night for a hotel room? It seemed like a joke or an insult. Marie looked at the cover of the magazine. It showed a pie and two cakes. She flipped back to the article.

When Marie left North Dakota and came to Seattle of her own accord nobody was holding a gun to her head. She chose to be resident manager of the Hillcrest of her own free will. The soles of her feet are wrinkled white with pumpkin yellow thick callouses—ugly and pathetic, but whose fault is that? Marie could have bettered herself but she didn't. Other people become brain surgeons, stars, chairmen of boards of blue-chip corporations, buy goods and services advertised in magazines Marie's never opened in her life. They become ambassadors and presidents and have incomes in the upper six figures. Nobody with a gun said, "Marie, choose a life with few choices or else." The Who's Who editors didn't send her mother a telegram, "New daughter eliminated. Regrets." Apparently Marie didn't care to be listed in that book. In a sense she even chose her carroty callouses, her basset gaze.

The week after she let her husband sleep on her sofa, when on top of everything else she found $50 missing—money she needed especially then, as will be seen—when she took the teapot out from behind other dishes and found it empty she knew her husband had stolen the money and the first feeling she had was an angry sadness for him that he'd had to stoop so low and that even though he'd never admit it to her or probably anybody the knowledge would add a little to his shame and before he died he'd come to stoop some lower because of it. What Marie felt first off standing there in her kitchen was angrily sorry for him, and no law said she had to find herself in such a pickle.

Let's say the other person Marie killed wasn't her sister. Let's say it was you. Let's say the eyes are dead, moving back and forth, back and forth, moving but dead. How did she do it. Why. Was it quite accidental. Are there extenuating circumstances. Let's say one of the furnishings Marie threw out when she threw out her husband was a metronome. It had never been any use—Marie's not musical, her husband either—

it was just there doing her no good in the world. Let's try that one on for size.

Rachel's mother lives in Tacoma. In Texas when Rachel was growing up she and her mother didn't get along too good. There were certain things her mother didn't want her to do—like having sex with certain individuals—and when she found out she'd beat Rachel. When Rachel got busted for dope her mother had her sent to a reform school. But now Rachel and her mother get along fine, have a good time together. Rachel's father's dead. He was a Mexican without papers to be in this country, a wetback. Rachel thinks he was into dealing drugs of some kind. He'd be away for long times at a time, then show up with money and tequila. Rachel loved him. He'd been gone a long time and Rachel asked her mother when he was coming back—it was the first time she'd ever asked that—and her mother said he was dead, she'd been meaning to tell Rachel. A year or so later Rachel found out he'd committed suicide. It was in a vision she had. He'd got caught with drugs and he was an illegal alien, he was in a dirty little jail and he knew they'd keep him in jail for maybe the rest of his life so he hanged himself, Rachel saw him do it. Marie's parents have both been gone for decades.

Early one morning Marie was having trouble sleeping so she'd got up and was reading the paper in the living room. She heard a whack!, sudden brakes and a yelping. It was the dog from the house next door, those damn irresponsible kids. Marie threw up her window. The dog's owner'd come out of the house, the driver was out of the car explaining how it happened, the dog had run right out in front of the car. The dog was yelping almost without a voice, trying to get on its feet. Marie yelled at the boy. "It's your own damn fault. You let it run loose and don't teach it to stay out of the street. It was bound to happen sooner or later."

If you have a dog you have to take care of it. Any animal. Rachel's cat Joshua. You have to feed it and take care of it, and you have to teach it things. To stay out of the street. Because they don't know, they think cars'll stop for them. You have to teach them, otherwise you shouldn't have them, you might as well put them to sleep right off the bat.

Rachel's Joshua started losing weight and hair this February. Rachel didn't know at first. Insofar as possible she wanted him to have the same rights and privileges as she so she let him go out when he wanted and sometimes he stayed away four, five days. "Who ya been ballin', Josh?" she said when he dragged himself back sick. After a week he was worse and Rachel took him to a vet down on 12th St. The vet said Josh would die unless he had a $45 operation and even then he'd only have a 30% chance. The vet said he'd put him to sleep if he was his. It took Rachel a couple of days to decide. For herself she might have tried herbal medicine but she was in the dark about cat herbs. Marie said, "He's a nice cat, Rachel, I like Joshua. I don't know though if I'd spend the money. Trixie'll have to be put to sleep before long. How're your plants doing?" Finally Josh had the operation. He was sick as a dog for a while but he's pulled through, gained his weight back, grown a new coat and his aura's good as ever.

Marie's sister followed her to Seattle and lived with Marie and Marie's husband at first, then by herself, then with her own husband in Tacoma. The four of them got together sometimes. Marie's sister's husband's been dead almost twenty years now. Ten years back Marie's sister started to get sick. Six goddamn years in a hospital in Tacoma. We all have to die.

This winter there was only one real snow in Seattle, it was two days before Christmas. We had a white Christmas. One of the gay couples—the one in the apartment above Marie's—had a woman staying with them. She was the cousin-in-law of one of them, she'd come all the way from Washington D.C. on a bus. She was French and she'd only been in this country two years. She probably didn't have anybody else to eat Christmas dinner with. She wore shoes with wooden soles. She had a nice face but the shoes were terrible on the stairs and over Marie's head. Marie stood it for a day and then when she heard the wooden shoes coming down the stairs past her doorway she threw open the door and said, "Listen, I can't have you running up and down in those loud shoes. This is supposed to be a quiet building—there are day sleepers here and anyway it's supposed to be quiet: that's why I don't allow children. Tenants aren't even supposed to have overnight guests but I can overlook that if it doesn't happen too often, but I can't have this noise. And another thing: when you're in your apartment tenants normally wear slippers. This building's old and the walls and floors and ceilings aren't at all soundproof." The woman said "Yes?" and nodded like maybe she didn't understand, but one of her hosts was with her and he said "Sorry." That wasn't the end of the story though.

The French woman and her hosts and some of their friends had their dinner and opened presents on Christmas Eve in the gay couple's apartment. They put in the turkey around three. Someone had brought over a record player. It hadn't been on long before they heard Marie clinking on the water pipes. They turned down the volume. After fifteen minutes they heard the clink clink again. It angered them some, but still they turned the volume down more. The dinner went well, they drank a lot of wine, talked and laughed. Around ten they found a note shoved under their door. It said, "I can't sleep because of your loud party. Very inconsiderate." The French woman's cousin-in-law—he was French too—said, "It's anonymous. Why couldn't the person who wrote it just come to the door and tell us?" They tried to be quieter. It was after midnight and they were in the middle of opening presents, many of which were comical, when Marie rapped on the door. "The rental agreement says no guests after ten P.M. and no loud parties. I've had three complaints since I got off work and I'm sure to have more tomorrow. Now this is just intolerable." The French woman's cousin-in-law said, "It's Christmas Eve! We haven't made any noise for three months." Marie shook her head. "People here don't give one goddamn about Christmas Eve. They have to work and they have to sleep whatever damn day it is."

Marie's sick sister started talking garbage about faith and theosophy curing her bones four years back when she first had to stay in the hospital. Later they moved her to a different hospital. Marie hated going to visit Saturdays or Sundays. Her damn husband hadn't once gone with her either. It was four buses and two cabs—Seattle #12 down to the station, Greyhound to Tacoma, cab to the hospital and vice versa but it wasn't that so much, it was more the hospital itself. The building reminded you of the Hillcrest, down-at-heels brick from the same era. And the floors! If Marie let a floor go like that in the Emergency Room she'd get walking papers before the next shift. But mostly it was Marie's sister herself. Her grey broom spread out on the pillow. The weight she'd lost, her bad color. If she was conscious, her mind wandered. It was thirty years ago, they were rich not poor, staying at some kind of lodge in Bismark, Marie was their mother. "Mmm-hmm, mmm-hmm," Marie muttered. Except sometimes she got the feeling her sister knew it wasn't true, it was just a game she had to play and wanted Marie to play along with. When she wasn't wandering it was garbage about theosophy faith, whatever, always cheery as you please (the dope she was on), never chiding Marie for the visits she missed more and more. When she died Marie hadn't seen her in over two years. Marie's shift at the Emergency Room had just started when the call came. Marie knew she must've had terrible bedsores.

Wherever you live your gaze has slipped across the Hillcrest. From a car window in an unlikely neighborhood on your way somewhere else. Of course you've never set foot inside. Or if you have it wasn't to visit a friend or learn anything, unless by a fluke once, you didn't live there certainly or if you did it wasn't for long, not more than a year and it was years and years ago when you were alive, too long to remember. The Lithuanian women in the basement don't read about themselves, the people Marie reads about pay $40 a night for a hotel room. She looks at the cover. Two cakes and a pie. She tosses the magazine aside. Are there non-extenuating circumstances. Back and forth, back and forth.

Rachel dresses up to watch TV in one of her thrift shop outfits including a fur stole and a hat she calls her mouseketeer hat because of its exaggerated black felt bow. She turns her oven on to medium and leaves it open—it's a cold afternoon. The doorbell rings. Sometimes she doesn't answer. She turns the radio in her bedroom on loud enough to hear some of it back in the living room where the TV is. It's a very weird talk show on the TV. Rachel smokes some dope and watches. There's a knock at the door. It's one of the gay guys come to say hello. Rachel offers him some of the dope and some of the chile con carne she's made. They look at her plants and talk. Out her windows the light changes impressively through this late winter afternoon. Once a friend coming to visit Rachel saw her through the window in her stole and mouseketeer hat and assumed she must be about to go out.

There aren't any roaches or ants in the Hillcrest, haven't

been since Marie and her husband started being managers. She keeps the grass against the building cut and makes sure the foundation gets painted regularly with repellent. All the same it's good to have an aerosol can of insecticide handy. Marie kept hers in the cabinet under her bathroom sink.

One night this winter Marie came back from the Emergency Room and saw a fire truck and two police cars stopped at the Hillcrest with their blue lights on and turning, and a small crowd gathered. It was the week she let her husband sleep on her sofa. The aerosol insecticide can had exploded under Marie's bathroom sink, blown the sink off the wall. People in several apartments thought somebody's knocked over a bookcase or something. Marie's husband on the sofa was too drunk for it to register. He didn't even wake up when the police and firemen broke open the door. The people in the apartment under Marie's had called them after they'd rung Marie's doorbell, knocked at her door and tried to telephone her (they were new and didn't know she'd be at work) about the water running through their ceiling. The commotion brought most of the tenants out into the stairwell. Marie's husband was on his feet but he still didn't understand what had happened. "Is there water in your place?" he asked one of the gay boys. "No—we live upstairs and water doesn't run uphill." "I know it doesn't," growled Marie's husband. Trixie was terrified. Rachel leaned over the bannister. She had cherry red toenails and she was wearing a matching silk nightgown and peignoir. "What's going on?" Marie's living room rug she'd just finished paying for was ruined and she had no insurance. One of the gay boys advised her to write the insecticide company. "And who knows, there might be other dangerous cans of it in the area." Marie said, "And think if I'd been getting something out of that cabinet when it happened!"

Rachel got off the #10 bus at the corner. It was one of those beautiful mild Capitol Hill June six o'clocks. Rachel didn't go in right away. She walked a couple of blocks to an intersection where you can see Mt. Rainier if it's visible. That evening it was visible, a flamingo mountain floating in the sky in the southeast, it was beautiful. Rachel leaned against a streetsign pole, her ankles crossed, a posture she'd seen more than one woman assume in a forties movie on television. And in forties pictures, ads for cigarettes or whatever, women lean-ing against a pine tree or a lamppost, gazing at the moon with their ankles crossed just so, platform shoes, some kind of sophistication that was innocent and Rachel loved it. She stood there and smoked a cigarette watching Mt. Rainier change from second to second. Nobody bothered her.

When she came back to the Hillcrest and was going in she met Marie. Marie said, "Oh, hi," as if she didn't remember who Rachel was. She was headed up the street to the twenty-four-hour market whose red and green neon lighted the park-ing lot. Rachel went with Marie and they talked, Rachel knew something was wrong. "I was at the Emergency Room and they called up out of the blue just like that and told me my sister had died. I don't go to church or pray or anything, but this last year I've been wishing she would die if she wasn't going to get any better. She's been in the hospital six years. They didn't warn me though."

At the cash register Marie explained she was buying soap and toothpaste for her sister's niece who'd been called from Portland and had been with her when she died and now would be staying with Marie till the funeral. On an impulse Rachel said, "Here, let me buy it for you." Marie said no but Rachel insisted and the cashier told Marie, "Listen, it don't happen every day of the year, lady."

Marie doesn't go to church or pray or anything like that but this last year she's wished her sister would die if she wasn't going to get well. Marie never remembers her dreams and she hasn't driven since thirty-odd years ago in snowy North Dakota.

This June the gay couple over Marie moved out after a year there. They cleaned the apartment room by room, throwing away some things, giving away others, moving the rest into a corner of the living room and packing it into car-tons to go east by train. They gave Rachel most of their plants and some thrift shop dishes so as to have as little as possible in the car. They'd told Marie when they were leaving but sometimes pulling up stakes takes longer than you'd think and they were eight or nine days late getting off. Marie in-spected the apartment the night before they left. "This is the part I hate. Now you owe me $42 rent for these extra days. I see you've done some work on the oven but I'll have to do it over, it's got to be completely clean. And I'll have to shampoo the rug too. Otherwise you've done a good job. Now the cleaning deposit was $50. What do you say if I take the rent you owe me out of it and keep the rest for the cleaning? You've been good tenants, always paid your rent on time. I'll miss you. I don't know how much longer I'll be here myself. The building's been sold. I've met the new owner and he and I didn't hit it off so good. I think I'll have to look for another building to manage." Workmen dismantled the big For Sale sign in the morning. The Lithuanian women watched out one of their basement windows. ∎

SPREADING FEELERS
Shelby Stephenson

This is life,
and there is
no theory for it:
old man Wash Bird was a midwife:
he was a bitty little man: he'd get on his hands
and knees and
rock directly in front of the woman
in labor
and grunt, saying,
"She'll be here any minute, yessiree!"—the differences
exist in the endless points of view:
across the road
is the old Stephenson cemetery: seventeen
slaves are buried
there without markers, anonymous
as the dirt: where will
I go? I need a lease, anything to hold on to:
"Hand me that maul,"
Uncle Hewell said,
"I'll show
you how
to kill a hog": he put
his feet between two of the boards
on the wall, swung the maul
with his right arm
over the side, backed it farther into a pendulum motion,
directing it toward
the hog's forehead, when the weight
of the curve in the swinging maul
picked his feet

out of the crack
and he pitched over the top
and toppled into the pen
with the hog: it had
been raining and Hewell disappeared in hog manure:
I know
where I am going when I see it coming.

ANTINOUS IN EGYPT
Jeffery Beam

> "I myself felt a kind of terrible joy at the thought
> that that death was a gift. But I was the only one
> to measure how much bitter fermentation there
> is at the bottom of all sweetness, or what degree
> of despair is hidden under abnegation, what hatred
> is mingled with love."   —Marguerite Yourcenar
> *Memoirs of Hadrian*

Falcon. You were not enough.
Protection is a harsh device.
Comes only with the proper tools,
the appropriate sacrifice. You knew
that as well as I.

You served me well. At the end your
hooded sleepy face never betrayed
the wilderness in your blood. The hungry
talons: so like myself in my impetuous love.
Clutching for him took the uncanny
form of physical drowning in a spiritual glove.

All give way. All lights extinguish.
White roses curl their five petals
under Venus's star. My skin oozes
in the honeyed ointment. No struggle
in the Nile. No pain. Just the litany
and the drowsy darkness claiming me.

Hadrian, my master. I am your Genius
speaking to you from the grave.
Know this enchantment binds.

I am your falcon, will follow
every arrow. No spear can harm me.
When the hunted falls, they will
be my prey.

A youthful oddity I am! So few sense
death's power. The sheer curtain
keeping us from it. The blaze, oh,
the blaze! Earthly passions pale before it.

The priests ignite their incense, murmuring
their prayers — supplications to the multitudinous
flower of the spheres. Red poppies flash
their faces at the gate — black throats groaning.

Falcon. You were not enough.
Together we had to go, swelling
the blood-bloom sinew in his chest.

VERMILION
Maudy Benz

for Darryl

Earthen cup of bounty in your hand
you walk in lands I will never know
on dust roads that wind forever over hills
like red threads in the fingers of a child.

A chestnut stallion quivers and beholds
the golden nectar in your palm.
Sucking in hyacinths and tears
he takes his long drink and wonders.

Who is this man wearing one face
in a world of two-headed dragons?
Look! He flys on blue wings of passion
as a butterfly lifts the days.

I am wind shaking the left head from my neck
It falls as a dark plum senses the cold.
I am not afraid. My chosen face prays to
white rivers in the palms of my hands.

DANCING WITH FATHER
Candace Flynt

Even after an absence of three seasons we are recognized as we return to The Homestead, that welcoming resort in the Virginia mountains. "We" meaning my father and me; my husband is making his first trip here. Rusty opens the trunk while Daddy and I alight to proffered hands. My father moves with alacrity, wanting, I'm sure, to appear as he always has: quick, vital, embracing, never daunted by the trials of this existence.

"Welcome back to The Homestead, Miz Vannoppen, Mistah Vannoppen, sir," the doorman says. I recognize his ancient yet unlined black face but cannot recall his name. My father can.

"It's good to be here, Guilford." My father smiles his careful smile. He is hoping, I suspect, that Guilford will not ask him about Mrs. Vannoppen. I know Guilford won't.

Guilford does not have superhuman powers, only a good memory for an unusual last name, and he probably checks the list of expected arrivals every day. Still, until my mother's death, three years ago, we came to The Homestead the first weekend in June for nineteen years, ever since I was four and my sisters, Judith and Louise, were three and one. We probably deserve to be recognized.

We've had a subdued drive up from North Carolina. Although there's been plenty of conversation, the gaiety that always accompanied our trips has been absent. We've talked

117

about our golf games, about the Upper Cascades course, which for the first time my father doesn't want to play ("Too hilly," he comments), about the Lower Cascades course ("Too easy and too buggy"), and about the Homestead course, which we will probably play every day. We did not, as we always had, *ooh* and *ahh* over the castlelike Hotel Roanoke when we passed it, an hour back; nor did we become quiet over the poverty in Clifton Forge, or even gag over the papermill smell in Covington, as, when Mother was here, we had done ritualistically. We didn't want to talk about anything we used to talk about.

"This is a one-time experiment," my father had cautioned, when he called to say he wanted to take the family—minus grandchildren—back to The Homestead. "Not to relive old times," he continued. "Not that. I want to go there as if we've never been there before."

I thought of suggesting another place, perhaps the nearby Greenbrier, where we would not be weighed down by nineteen years of memories, but I did not.

Father has not dated anyone since Mother died, which has not bothered Judith and me though it has Louise. We want him to remarry if he wants to, but in the past year our youngest sister has become passionate about Father's finding a companion. She says he'll suffer less. She says a man like him should not be alone. I have told her that loneliness is sometimes preferable to empty togetherness, but she doesn't believe me. I'm not even sure I'm right. A few months ago I agreed to speak to him about his social life. Louise believes that because I became a lawyer, like Father, I have his ear more than she does.

"We want you to know that if you would like to go out with anyone, it's okay with us," I said to him. We were sitting across from each other in the study where all the conferences I'd ever had with him had taken place. This was the first time *he* had been the subject. "We want you to be happy." He listened with the glimmer of amusement I've seen in the eyes of someone who will listen to you, who will even consider what you're saying, but who believes you don't know what you're talking about.

His answer was quiet but impassioned. "Your mother and I had something extraordinary," he said, his eyes focusing on his folded hands. "You probably know that." I nodded, even though he wasn't watching. "She was a rare, magnificent woman. I could never find her equal. I would never even want to try." Then his tone lightened. "The three of you are enough women for me."

I had always known that my parents were lovers, because of a lifetime of locked doors, but I knew it more, I think, because of how they fought: so passionately, so fearlessly, so frighteningly. You can fight like that only if you are certain of your hold on the other person, if you are unafraid of the consequences of fury.

Father raised his eyes; an unexpected pleasure flooded his face. "You remind me a great deal of her," he said.

I blushed, but because my complexion is olive, he couldn't tell. He had probably said the same thing to Judith and Louise. Even though I couldn't imagine a compliment more exhilarating, I knew I was not the most like Mother. Judith was. Or maybe the truth was this: if the three of us—Judith with Mother's flair, Louise with her irony, and I with her passion, could be one person, we would probably approximate her.

Seven of us will be at The Homestead, since this year all three sisters are married. Judith and Louise live in the D.C. area and are expected to arrive with their husbands late this afternoon. Daddy, Rusty, and I will probably hike the north trail first and then have saunas or massages. Golf begins tomorrow morning, followed by lunch in the garden, mineral baths, salt glows ("Don't shave your legs beforehand," we've reminded each other since we were teenagers), and Scotch hose, the high-pressure massage that washes the salt away. One day we will take a carriage ride—Mother's least favorite activity, because it took us away from the center of things. Even naps are scheduled, from four to five, just as when Mother was in charge. Only now I know that that's when everyone makes love.

Of the entire Homestead experience, though, what we all most look forward to is dancing with Daddy. Will he dance with us? Judith asked me on the telephone last week. I said I could not imagine him not dancing.

"But won't it make him think of Mother?" she said.

"Why shouldn't he think about her?"

"Maybe he'll finally have a chance to eat his dinner."

"Maybe so."

Daddy tips Guilford and walks through the immense screen door that is held graciously for him by a green-coated bellhop. The grand hall glows yellow. The decor is familiar, no wearing of the upholstery and carpeting, but the room has the look of something aged, something comfortable, even though the paint is fresh. Fires blaze in the fireplaces, although by now the sun has finally knocked the chill off the day. We are greeted by older employees who aren't so clever as Guilford yet remember our faces.

Daddy turns from the front desk, holding up our keys as if he has achieved a sort of victory. Perhaps it is a victory for him to walk into this grand hall and not simply turn around and walk out. Perhaps it should be a victory for all of us. But I don't feel sad. I am happy thinking about my mother and all that she taught me.

1957

Daddy stops the car and puts the top down just moments before we arrive at The Homestead. And Mommie turns the heat on high, because everybody in the back seat is so cold. It's June, school's out, but this is the mountains. It's so cold, Daddy says, because we are at a higher elevation. At higher elevations the air is colder because it's thinner. "Why is thin air cold?" I ask, when he leans over me to unzip the plastic window, but he doesn't know the answer.

Daddy says, "This is silly," but Mommie says, "No, it isn't. This is fun. Do you want to look like everyone else?"

Around her neck Mommie wraps a thin white scarf, which trickles behind her in the wind. She tells us to sit up like ladies. We are all huddled on the floor because the wind is so cold. "It's summer," she commands. She cranes her neck over the seat to see us. Her tone suddenly becomes conciliatory, the only tone that we are honor-bound to obey. "If I *ask* you to do something for me," she has told all three of us hundreds of times, "you are required to obey me. If I scream at you in anger, you are entitled to resist. Sit up," she says kindly. "For five minutes. Do it for me."

We sit almost eagerly. At times we each, even the baby, would do anything in our limited power to please her.

We are dressed in dotted swiss. Just before we left home, our shoulder-length hair was barretted back and twisted by Mommie into long curls, her curling iron held the way a teacher holds a ruler. We wear ruffled socks, ruffled panties, and black patent-leather shoes. As a special treat for me, the oldest, Mommie has applied a touch of her rouge to my cheeks. When Judith asked for rouge too, Mommie said rouge was allowed only after you were six. Then, to make Judith feel better, she said: "Katherine's complexion is olive. It needs rouge. You already have rosy cheeks." Judith was not satisfied, and I went to the mirror to look at my olive skin, with which from that moment on, I knew, I would never be happy. Fortunately, though, now I was old enough to color it.

So that we won't miss lunch, Daddy sends our bags up to our adjoining rooms, and we hurry to the garden. Mommie selects a table and sits with Louise in her lap while Daddy takes us to the buffet. Judith heads for the great round dessert table, where a smiling, pudgy woman stands ready to help us build our own chocolate sundaes. In a stern voice Daddy calls Judith back to the vast array of hot and cold foods. She starts down the line without making any selections.

"Judith," I call, angrily. Since I am the oldest, I try to help Daddy. He leans down and whispers in my ear that he will handle her. Mommie would have pinched me. Daddy's sharp fragrance lingers in my head even after he has walked down the line and drawn Judith and her tray back to the beginning.

With guidance we both select a meager amount of food and join Mommie and Louise. We have been away from them for what seems hours, but Mommie shows no sign of irritation. She stands grandly at our arrival, stationing Louise in the grass, helping Judith and me deposit our plates. Daddy returns to the line to fill his own plate, and Mommie instructs us to think carefully about our manners as we eat. "Decide on one particular bad manner that for this meal you won't commit," she says. "If you commit others, that's all right. Just don't commit that one bad one." She smiles an arch,

encompassing smile that always seems to take in the world;
it is caring and yet removed from us, as if to say to anyone
who might be watching that she is more than a mother. Of
course, we know this, Judith and I. We know that our mother
is different from every other mother. But we don't quite
know in what way.

"Enjoy yourselves, little darlings," she says, softly but
with resonance. This means we may start eating. My father
walks up behind her with his plate and leans so that his cheek
is within an inch of her own.

"You *know* you're beautiful, don't you? he whispers. He
often tells us that we are beautiful too, not in front of every-
body, the way he tells Mommie, but privately, as if it's a sec-
cret. I keep my secret but Judith doesn't. She always reports
to me, "Daddy told me *I'm* beautiful," as if only one of us
could be. I think of my olive complexion and how grateful I
am that there is such a thing as rouge. And that Mommie will
let me wear it even though I am only six.

"Do I look smug?" Mommie asks, her face turning dark.

"I was only kidding," he says, taking his chair, which is
close to hers. Her petulance settles over the table. "It was a
new way of saying how beautiful I think you are."

"It *sounds* like a new way to hurt my feelings," she says.

The three of us chew, looking at our plates, waiting for
the moment to either pass or erupt. It passes.

We are not having "supper," Mommie tells Louise; we are
dining in the main ballroom of one of the loveliest resorts in
the world. "Can you say that?"

Louise, long acquainted with mimicry, says, "We are din-
ing in the main ballroom of one of the loveliest resorts in the
world." Since we have been bickering this afternoon about
who is going to sleep on the rollaway, Mommie makes us
draw straws. Judith loses and throws herself onto the rolla-
way. Mommie commands her to get up before she wrinkles
her dress. We are wearing our blue velvet party dresses tonight.
Mommie has put my rouge on carefully, more carefully than
she did for the trip here. The closet doors are faced with mir-
rors, and she lines us up before them, telling us to hold back
our shoulders, which each of us does to the extreme. "Never
mind that," she says. "But do hold up your chins. Just a little

higher than level. That's the prim look a young lady wants at night."

Mommie winds her hair on top of her head, securing it with so many bobby pins that finally Louise begins to complain she's hungry, although we had tea and cookies in the parlor only an hour ago. She is tired of waiting. Mommie pats her hair "finished" and summons Daddy by his name, Max, instead of the usual "darling." His whole name is Maximilian, but I don't think anyone except me thinks of him that way. She gathers us around her like puppies, and we smile even before the approval shows in his eyes. He has on his white dinner jacket, with buttons that glitter like jewels. His black hair is as shiny as the ribbons down the legs of his trousers. He is handsome, handsome. And we are beautiful, though this time he has used the word *exquisite*.

We will learn poise by leading rather than by following, so the three of us are urged down the stairs ahead of our parents. My patent-leather shoes are slick on the carpet, and I take hold of the banister. In single file Judith and Louise do the same. Louise keeps looking to see if Mommie and Daddy are coming, and Mommie keeps admonishing her to look where she is going and to hold up her chin. At the foot of the stairs Mommie gently directs me, "To your left, darling." I remember which is my left hand and move in that direction. Judith moves abreast of me, either unwilling for me to have all the glory or unwilling to walk with the baby.

My father greets the maitre d' and says that he would like the same table we have had in years past—at the center edge of the dance floor.

"Oh, yes," the khaki-skinned man says. Later my father explains to me that there are ways of making people remember you. One of them is to be accompanied by an exquisite wife and three exquisite daughters. But he also tells me about the other way.

After we eat our dinner, Mommie arranges us in a corner of the dance floor, where we sidestep as a threesome while she and Daddy dance. When it is our turn to dance with him, she sits at the table with two of us while Daddy takes the third out on the floor. We watch while she describes how one dances. We are to be supple, not limp in Daddy's arms. "Like spaghetti that's not done," she says. We are to let him lead.

"Step toward him if you feel his hand pulling you forward. Step back if he nudges you that way. To the right or to the left according to the way his palm rocks in the center of your back." But the best part of dancing was something that Mommie never got to do. It was when Daddy picked me up and swung me around so that my legs had no *choice* but to go limp. And when I said Ouch, Daddy, because his rough whiskers scraped my cheek. It was the kind of hurt that I found myself wanting again.

1967

"What a show-off," I say to mother and Louise, as we watch Judith throw back her head in a sort of wild gaiety, revealing the soap-white skin of her long, graceful neck. She is dancing with Father, who has nearly stopped moving in order to applaud her exaggerated rhumba. Of the three of us she most resembles Mother, with her self-aware beauty, her long, perfect legs, her willingness to display herself in those spontaneous poses men seem so to appreciate. Before my comment Mother's eyes were lit with vicarious pleasure, as if she were watching herself in a mirror. She does not keep it a secret that Judith is the one of us whom physically she most enjoys. But she enjoys talking most with me, and she enjoys laughing with Louise.

I would not want to have to follow Judith's act, something Mother has instinctively realized, so she has rearranged the order of the dancing partners. As the oldest, I now dance with Father first, followed by Louise, then Judith, and finally Mother. But perhaps after this year's visit to The Homestead, Mother will dance with Daddy ahead of Judith. By now they have danced so many years together that no room is left for the unexpected. They move as intricately as the cogs of a fine watch: seeing them provides us with pleasure but no thrill.

An entire table of silver-headed pediatricians and pediatricians' wives from Chattanooga, whom we met earlier, turn as Judith leads Daddy off the floor. The wives offer askance looks, as if being wholehearted were somehow wrong, but the doctors smile in appreciation. At various tables around the room sit young men who are also watching us. None of us was asked to dance last night, our first of the holiday, but Daddy has predicted we will hardly have time to eat tonight. Already one of the doctors has danced with our mother. The same man, I notice, has pushed back his chair and will evidently approach our table again. It's time for Mother and Father to dance, I think protectively, trying to send the doctor that message by telepathy. Mother smiles in welcome, always appreciative of the attention of attractive men. This doctor has eyebrows so black that they might be dyed. I wonder if he knows why some of his hair has changed color and some has not. Or even why hair changes color.

The doctor has come not for Mother but for Judith. Daddy fills the awkward moment—Mother has begun to rise—standing so quickly that he is on his feet before she is.

"My beautiful daughter," Mother says graciously, as if Judith were a sort of gift. She is not as embarrassed as Father thought she might be.

"Our beautiful *daughters*," Daddy says. The remark succeeds in encouraging the man to dance eventually with each of us. Judith smiles coolly. She has been noticing a pink-cheeked young man in a not entirely appropriate sports jacket and hopes he will summon the courage to invite her to dance. She does not look at the pediatrician as they step onto the floor, but suddenly, as the band strikes up a fast tune, she comes alive. She has realized, as I could have told her, that she has another perfect opportunity to show off.

When the doctor finally dances with me, I ask him about his eyebrows. Judith made dancing with him look easy, but, unlike Daddy, the doctor has a rather ineffectual lead that keeps me continually off-balance.

"Do you dye your eyebrows?" I say.

"Of course not." He seems insulted by my brashness, although our family brashness is what attracted him in the first place. He proceeds to ask me proper questions about what I am going to do with my life. "Something meaningful, but I'm not sure what" is my answer.

When the doctor finishes dancing with me, he dances one more time with Mother—out of a sense of honor, I suppose. It occurs to me to ask him about age and stamina, because by this time I have finished the glass of wine Mother allows me and I am feeling resentful that he danced with both my sisters before he danced with me.

Now that we are apparently available, the young men descend, and each of us dances until the band packs up its instruments. We know we will not be allowed to remain behind and talk to the young men we have met, although if we were dating at home, we would have been allowed to remain in our den until midnight. Mother believes that the unknown offers more temptation than the known, and what she means by that is the temptation of hotel rooms.

1977

Ironically, we have all married men who do not like to dance. They would like it if they tried, Judith, Louise, and I are all certain, but our husbands are self-made men who were not exposed, as we were, to such things as ballroom dancing. My husband, Rusty, comes closest to being a dancer, because he will at least venture out on the floor, but it is not exactly exhilarating to two-step through a waltz.

"Must all three of us count entirely on Father?" Judith asks, her eyes rolling in what is a teasing mockery of the three husbands, who seem glued to their seats. The band has played two numbers, and none of the men has suggested dancing, although Judith, with her swaying body and her tapping fingers, has certainly announced her inclination. None of us is too timid to suggest a dance, but we would much prefer to be asked. Privately, to me, Judith has promised to ask men at surrounding tables if Jimmy refuses to dance with her. I have asked her, for Father's sake, not to cause a scene. Of the three husbands, Jimmy is the least likely to tolerate having his wife dance with another man. Dancing, we grew up believing, is recreational, not sexual, but none of our husbands views it that way.

Father has not gotten to his feet either, although I believe that it's because he prefers not to overshadow our husbands. Our mother never exhibited such generosity. Each of the men we are married to is attractive in his own way—Rusty, whose large, athletic build and glad face seem so solid; Jimmy, whose face offers a cultivated yet interesting detachment; and Rod, whose baby-blue eyes and boyish face so perfectly match *our* baby, Louise. But none approaches that unusual combination of sensuality and civility, male beauty and style, that has always made Father such an overwhelming presence for all of us, Judith and me in particular. Perhaps our husbands are simply too young. We are not yet our mother either.

"Dance, Daddy?" Judith says.

Before Louise and Judith and their husbands arrived, Father and I hiked the north trail this afternoon, leaving Rusty on the putting green. We talked about my work and his, and about the beauty and staying power of The Homestead. Finally, when he allowed a pause, I asked him if being here made him sad. He said, "Sad and happy."

Although Father does not rise immediately at Judith's invitation—he is actually eating his smoked-salmon hors d'oeuvre —I notice a positive change in his expression. Life goes on, I think, but the idea gives me an unexpectedly dismal feeling. Are any losses insurmountable? Is life always the greatest thing?

"I'll dance with Judith," Rusty says. I have confided my fears about Judith's causing a scene and asked him to try to sidetrack her in any way he can think of. I am a more thorough orchestrator than my mother was. She liked to initiate a scene and let the participants resolve it themselves, while I prefer to control, as much as I can, from beginning to end.

"I really should dance with Katherine," Father says. "She's always first."

I remember the year that the order of dancing with him changed, but how Mother always danced last with Father, never giving Judith that slot even the year I thought she might.

We learned the year of the pediatricians not to rise at an invitation until we were sure who was being asked to dance. Father comes to me now and takes my hand, and I rise like the first princess. I am in love with him in the fierce, pure way one can be in love with something that one can never have. I love my husband, of course, but in a steady, patient way.

We finish the fast dance that the band is playing, and Father signals for a waltz. I am wearing my beautiful tea-length gown—royal blue, to match my eyes. I feel the bristle of his cheek, unusually heavy, I think, against my skin. Father normally shaves twice a day, but perhaps he has given up the extra effort since Mother died. I know that Judith is dancing with Rusty and that perhaps I should find her in order to exchange looks—we are, after all, happily dancing. Father is dancing. We thought he might not even want to, but he is leading me now with such gentle power that I know his heart is in it. Maybe he will grow melancholy only after he dances with Judith, when Mother does not await. Other couples have moved to the edge of the dance floor, allowing Father and me the full circumference we need. When I rise on my tiptoes, my heart rises too. I feel perfect, graceful, exquisite. I feel that all the world is watching and approving. For the first time in my life I know how much like my mother I am. Daddy does not even have to say so.

When he returns me to my seat and takes Louise's arm, I feel such an amazing sense of loss that I have to excuse myself from the table. I am not my mother in love with him. I am not even the last woman with whom he will dance. By the time I return from the ladies' room, my makeup repaired, Daddy has finished dancing with Louise and is leading Judith to the floor. I must admit that they move beautifully together, though never quite as perfectly as he and Mother did. I sit watching with Rusty, Jimmy, Rod, and Louise. I try to remind myself how unimportant dancing actually is in the larger scheme of things, but I yearn to be out there too.

Close by my ear Rusty says, "May I have this dance?" The band has picked up its tempo, playing music that he can shag to. My husband leads me to the floor. Over Judith's sequined shoulder strap my father smiles at me, a vague, wistful, unseeing smile. I am one of his three daughters. ■

PAGE TOWARD A BOOK OF BEGINNINGS
David Cloutier

Silence
eclipsing itself in a whir

a song goes out
in search of a throat

breaking into
light into

circles of opening
a dilation of worlds

sings up an ocean
winged song finned song

sings a man a woman
the slow hum of mountains

and the briefest
of canticles

day flickering
on a leaf

TEAR'S ORE
James Applewhite

Water of the cornea—
Quartz ore sungold veined—
A soprano piano
Chimes your innocence
Icily. Pine green hushes
The cabin, river beyond
Runs time's pig iron.
Raw clay landings
Current her tresses.
A Pamlico matinee
Rises, cinema that sunk her
Like oxide. Roan blood,
You muddy the light. Cypress
Swamps muck your brunette roots.
Antebellum woman
In a wreck underwater, your
Red hair released by the diver
Fans above treasure.
I bubble in my helmet
In the octopus' embrace.
Iron, iron, I taste you in water.
Time drowns ships, their chests
Of silks. Masts, the wheel,
Her floating hair a ghostly shimmer.

FIELD'S CHILD
James Applewhite

Pastures look inhabited,
Like windows. Ponds turn white
As stars on a tin roof, while
Barbed wire limits the isolation.
One scene framed in fenceposts,
Failing as in eyes of an aproned woman,
Is saved by a movement:
The pumpkin hound with pine
Tree brown whose bark
Colors the squirrel's fur
Quicksilver. The small boy follows.
His gun is a stick,
His whistle a star's light.
Moon's fingernail creases his path.
His memory was what
Inhabited the field: warm
Hearth brick, taste of an iron nail
In the well bucket's water. Woodsmoke
Baked into a biscuit. He breaks
Into a trot, doesn't have to whistle his dog.
The pastures where I have not yet seen him
Wait for him, broom sedge holding
Or seeming to hold the sunset
In that rosey straw, that Adam's clay.

SNAIL DARTER
Elizabeth Cox

In the middle of a hollowed-out room, a man leaned to remember being carried somewhere. Not carried on a horse. He didn't remember that. But he remembered being carried in someone's arms and then on a train, though at the time he didn't think of it as being a train. He only knew it now, when he was older and could stand at the train station, waiting. He didn't wait for anything or to go anywhere, but stood, then sat, looking up to the huge space above him. He loved the sooty smell. He loved to hear the steady clacking of wheels when the train came in, see the deep steamy burst of air when it stopped. And he thought of the man who brought him here.

His first trip on the train began one day in the spring forty-seven years ago. He was six and came to this town in Tennessee after recovering from an illness. His body had recovered sufficiently, but his mind stayed locked and he had the stare not of a regular six year old, but of someone who was bored or preoccupied.

He had had a fever. When his mother gave him laudanum to help him sleep, she forgot she gave the first dose and gave him a second. It was enough to put him into a deep, limp sleep that almost took him.

The doctor arrived to see the boy's stillness and ordered a horse to be saddled. He asked for three heavy belts. The mother did as she was told. Doctor Sam Parham was not the only doctor in town, but he was the one everyone trusted the most. He placed the child in front of him on the horse and wrapped two of the large belts around them both, strapping the child to his own chest and waist. The child's head bent downward. They galloped off.

The mother, who had not asked anything until now, called after the doctor "Where are you going?," but they did not go anywhere. They rode back and forth in front of the farmhouse to jog the child awake. The doctor rode hard for hours and even when it began to rain he didn't stop, letting the rain sting their faces. The mother watched from the window. The father was not around.

They ran like that all night. The horse's mouth frothed, but the doctor would not stop or rest, nor did he allow the horse to rest. Toward the end, before morning, the horse's gallop turned measured and slow. So the doctor hit the horse with the other belt, on the high brown haunches, hitting and hitting, because the child had begun to stir, make noises, groans. But the horse was not able to give more running. The doctor's bladed belt pushed down the hooves into the soft earth, then raised them again, the effort giving the effect of speed. But the speed had slowed, so that the child was barely jogged now. When morning broke, the horse died.

And if someone had been watching (the mother at the window slumped asleep, her other children asleep), if someone had been there to see in those furious moments before morning, they would have felt the mindless life of the horse move into the boy, awaken him, giving only one way out of that black hollow where they had spent the night. And they would have heard the doctor shouting, and the horse's hooves steady against the slow earth, and above all, the labored breathing sounds.

The child had already opened his eyes, waking only slightly, never coming all the way back. The doctor carried the boy into the house, the boy as light as shadow. And the families who had given their children laudanum when they were sick no longer kept that medicine in their houses.

The doctor took the boy to live with him, appealing to the courts to allow it. The mother, a thin, furtive woman with a house full of children she couldn't care for, did not protest; but let it happen the way the doctor wanted. The day they left town, the boy carried a satchel as thin as paper, the other children played in the yard, and the mother stood with her back to them as she stirred something boiling on the stove. She waved with the flat of her hand, but the doctor knew when they drove off that she stood again at the window. When the child called for his mother, the doctor patted his knee or his shoulder or kept his hand on the boy's head. He told the child that he was his uncle, and over the years it was an easy lie for the boy to believe.

The spring day they arrived in Sweetwater, Tennessee, a downpour of rain caught them as they walked between the train and the station house. The boy, who loved the rain more than he loved the sunshine, said "Stand, stand," which meant he wanted to stand in the rain. The doctor urged him inside the station house with the promise of candy or a balloon. But he couldn't offer anything as fine as rain.

The doctor enrolled the boy in school and he was promoted through grades along with his age level. Each year the difference became more apparent. Children would ask him his name and when Oliver said "Oliver Brise," it came out garbled and sounded like "Abba." The children laughed and called him Abba all through grade school.

"Abba means 'father' in Hebrew," his uncle told him, trying to cheer him, give him pride in a name the children chose in cruelty. But Oliver liked the name and didn't feel the cruelty, not in that, at least. The cruelty Oliver bore was in the exclusion he felt.

"Abba. Abba has his pants on backwards," one boy yelled during the middle of a history lesson. They were in the ninth grade.

"Abba is fine." The teacher called him Abba too. She knew he had never worn his pants wrong, and the others knew too. The only one who doubted was Oliver who looked down to see if he had done everything right, zipped, buckled, everything. He was never sure.

He knew one girl, Edith Setler. She was not the prettiest girl in school, but she wasn't the ugliest either. Sometimes Edith walked him home, sometimes she sat beside him at lunch so that the other girls began to do the same. The boys started to invite Oliver to join their games. Oliver was never happier than in that ninth grade year. The next year he took a job and didn't see his friends except at the drugstore or around town where they still spoke to him and sometimes asked him to sit down. Oliver joined them, but he knew not to stay long.

The year Edith was a senior, Oliver saw her walking home from school and called to her. She stopped, stood for a moment, as though she couldn't think of his name. Then she said, "Oliver," and they walked along together. He had just taken a job as paperboy. Edith asked him about it.

"It's good." Oliver's head stiffened with the effort to sound normal.

"How's your uncle?"

"He's fine." He looked to the books Edith carried and frowned at the signs and symbols on one.

"Trigonometry," Edith told him. He tried to repeat the word but couldn't. "And it's sure not easy." She rolled her eyes in the way she used to, to indicate difficulty. Oliver laughed.

"Not easy," he said, and took hold of Edith's hand.

Oliver had grown to be six-feet-two-inches tall. He was not good-looking, but didn't have a distorted look. His eyes were particularly large and held that same blankness they had always had. "Edith," he said, not knowing what he would do next, not even knowing what he wanted to do, except that he had wanted for all those years to hold her hand. But now, as he did, a larger impulse swept over him and he pulled her against him, her books hitting against his chest and stomach and her head bumping his chin. She dropped her books and ran from him.

Oliver stood at the corner and saw her move away, her blue dress flying up around her knees and thighs, her arms moving out beside her as if for balance. When she turned and saw he was not chasing her, she stopped and stood for what seemed to Oliver a long while. Then she called to him. Oliver didn't answer. He stooped to pick up her books and looked up once to see if she still stood there. His face was red with an embarrassment he didn't understand. A storekeeper saw the incident and came out, but saw Oliver picking up the books and didn't see anything wrong. Others stood at the windows of shops to watch what Edith would do. She returned to where Oliver was. He handed her books to her, her papers stacked neatly on top.

Before Edith took the books she put her hand on his shoulder, and Oliver's mind went suddenly to the loss of his mother that day and the doctor's touch on his shoulder and knee and head. He felt comforted.

"I'm sorry," said Edith. Oliver nodded and said it was okay. She took the books from him, and told him she'd see him tomorrow.

Oliver continued down the street in the same direction as Edith, knowing that he had moved from a confusion that felt devastating to a confusion that felt good. Edith's blue dress swished as she walked and he showed his gratefulness to her from that time on by merely waving to her from far off. But sometimes when he passed her house, she might come out and they would talk and she would ask how he was.

Oliver couldn't remember the name of the town he was born in. He only knew that Sweetwater was his home, though sometimes he made trips to other towns with his uncle. He knew that this man was his uncle. He knew too, though vaguely, of a ride long ago on a horse and how the horse died as Oliver himself had lived through that night. The spurious courage of that night and of the doctor's decision to take him away from his home. Oliver had been told the story, so that his remembering came more from the telling than from memory. And each time he was told, he knew that the horse's death meant both his own life and his own doom, though he couldn't say how he knew this. And he knew that moving to Sweetwater with his uncle had somehow saved his life.

One year before his uncle died, there was an uproar around Tennessee which involved the building of the Tellico Dam and a small fish, two-and-one-half inches long, called the snail darter. The dam's configuration blocked the fish from reaching the spawning grounds upstream, and unless they were relocated the chance of their becoming extinct was almost assured. It was thought at that time that Sweetwater, Tennessee, was the only place left where the snail darter could survive, and the building of the dam was stopped by order of the

Supreme Court. Oliver's uncle followed the story and told it to Oliver, who loved the idea that people would stop the building of the dam to find a new home for the fish. Biologists came to Tennessee to designate a seventeen-mile stretch of shallow water as a Critical Habitat. But at the same time, there were bands of Cherokee Indians who were also affected by the building of the dam. The water would flood more than twenty of their sacred villages including the village of Tanasi, which had become the name of the state. The doctor crusaded for both the Indians and the snail darter and found an irony in the attention given to the two-and-one-half-inch fish.

Everyone talked about the snail darter and how it stopped the building of the Tellico Dam and the doctor liked to tell Oliver how they, too, had been relocated, brought to Sweetwater, the water they would live in.

When Sam Parham left Rossville, Georgia, he wanted to go anywhere. Sweetwater happened to be the place he chose. He had fallen in love with a married woman in Rossville. She returned his affection, but then one day ran off with a man Sam had never seen nor heard of. Sam was, by then, thirty-seven years old. He had lost hope of having a wife and children and settled into his idea of bachelorhood and reclusiveness with determination, but not much happiness.

The day he saw the boy, Oliver, an instinct rose in him that could not be called anything but paternal. As the boy recovered, the instinct increased, and the doctor grew to love him. He felt two things: that if he lost this part of himself that was able to care for the boy, he might lose his capacity to love anyone, and more important, there was the danger that the mother might again give the boy an overdose. He appealed to the court, saying that the boy was brain-damaged and as a doctor he could give better care as it was needed. Since the mother didn't protest, but remained wordless, agreeing to the court with nods and shrugs, the court gave the boy to the doctor.

But from the beginning the doctor saw how difficult it would be to take care of the child, so he hired a housekeeper, someone to be with Oliver when the doctor wasn't home. The woman he found had been a nurse and though she didn't mention why she was no longer in that profession, she seemed capable enough. He hired her.

Oliver was almost seven when Mrs. Constant came to work for them. She had no trouble with the boy and was able even to control him when he flew into one of his tantrums.

"Constant," he yelled, "bring Abba a comb." But Mrs. Constant would not do everything Oliver wanted.

"You can get the comb yourself, Oliver dear," she would say and after a stubborn silent refusal or else a demanding Indianlike yell, Oliver got up to get the comb himself. Sometimes he threw it at her, sometimes he combed his hair in front of the mirror then messed it up with his hands, pulling it straight up so that he looked as if he were floating underwater. Mrs. Constant would take the comb and fix his hair, neatly parting and smoothing down the sides. She ignored him when he ran his fingers through it to undo what she had done. The doctor praised her patience, her ability to hold her temper.

Once when Oliver threw the comb, he was standing very close to Mrs. Constant, so that the comb hit hard on the side of her nose. She reached and slapped his cheek, and though this did not surprise Oliver, the doctor had to leave the room to keep from interfering. He noted the next day that there was still a faint patch of red on the boy's cheek, but the boy seemed to have forgotten.

The way Oliver remembered that block of time—the year or two when he stayed his nonschool hours with Mrs. Constant—was this: he remembered her large body which seemed to him like some huge rock, and he remembered when she had to stay with him at night because the doctor would be gone. He remembered how she screamed at him when he couldn't sleep, or if he woke with a nightmare and called out. He could still see, sometimes at night, her big, stocky, fat-legged figure bursting into his room, so that he knew he must have cried out or made some noise or shout that brought her, because she came at him appearing suddenly. And she seemed to be in flight, a huge bird that hung over him. He could even hear from her small birdlike sounds that came not from her mouth but from her throat as she filled the night with her consternations. And it seemed to Oliver at those times that there were more people there, more than just this bird woman who descended and hovered above him whenever he cried out and woke her from sleep.

"I'll teach you," she cried. Her voice had the quality of a hissing goose. "You broke my sleep." Her red hair flew in all directions, her breath rank with a smell Oliver couldn't identify. She hit Oliver. Her fists, at first, lay closed and hard against his head, then her fingers opened to scratch him, make him bleed. Sometimes she lifted something from the floor and used it. If the thing she chose was heavy, Oliver would be knocked unconscious. Oliver didn't know why she came in to him during those nights, but thought, as children do, that it was surely his fault and that he would be glad when the hitting stopped as it always did.

Oliver's mind wanted only to fall asleep, quiet and sleep. When she left and he watched her go back down the hallway, a lassitude settled on him, made him unable even to cover himself. Rarely did she come back twice in one night. Some nights, though, she would not come in at all and when Oliver woke and saw the dawn he knew he had slept through and had not suffered her hands. And he always believed on those mornings that these terrible nights were over.

It was a January night that it ended. His uncle arrived home earlier than expected. Oliver heard the car drive up and tried to mention it to Mrs. Constant.

But Contant yelled her drunken talk, saying much that made no sense to anyone but herself. And Oliver was always surprised how the next morning she would be sitting at the kitchen table with toast and jelly, offering to fix eggs any way he wanted. But at night all he saw was her stoutness coming toward him against the hall light. Her fists ready.

His uncle was in the room by the time she had hit him twice. He threw her against the far wall, startling her into a fit of short rage, then crying, then pleading.

Oliver watched dumbly. He watched his uncle, or the man he now called his uncle, yell at this woman to get out, get *out, get out.* His face raged in the same way hers had, only this time not at him. Oliver, relieved to have the protection, had not expected it or even thought to ask for it.

Constant left. They never saw her again. The doctor looked over Oliver's body to find bruises, cuts the woman had made. Some of them were already healed. He stayed near the boy until sunup, not sleeping, but staying to cradle Oliver. The boy slept, though fitfully. And when he woke with his inevitable nightmares, the doctor was there to say, "It's okay. Okay, Oliver," saying it over and over again, like a cant. "Go back to sleep. I'm here. I'm here." And he would brush the boy's hair from his forehead with one hand.

It was past sunup when the doctor himself went to sleep.

There was a space of about ten years when Oliver wore a blue serge suit. He wore it both summer and winter, though in winter he wore a heavy coat over it. The suit grew shiny and people began to mention to his uncle that he should have a new one. But Oliver didn't want new clothes. Finally, someone gave him a soldier's coat, medals still on it, captain's bars intact. They gave him two pair of gray pants to go with it. For a while Oliver wore only the pants and the jacket he had worn before. But his uncle saw him try on the coat in front of the long hall mirror, walking back and forth, saluting. Then one day he wore it into town. He saluted everyone, making the gesture a little high with finger pointing upward as the British do. No one corrected him, but returned the salute and began to call him Soldier. He liked the name.

Soldier ran all his years in Sweetwater, ran as smooth as he could. He took jobs his uncle found for him and when his uncle died, he took from the town. Now his face grows rounded and more aged, not aging as quickly as his body. His eyes stay young, though, and so does the way he walks or rides his bike.

Some days he sits at the train station, and watches the one train come and go. He sits on the steps of the trains parked in their stalls, but mostly he sits inside the station house. People think he remembers his early train ride and that that longing brings him here, but he isn't reminded of anything exactly, he only returns to sit at a familiar place.

But there are moments when he seems to remember, when his body moves into a position. He turns his head as though he has heard something and just been caught in a snapshot. And at those times, when he listens, gives all his attention, his back sits straight, not slumped. He is a picture already taken, his head held with an abrupt dignity, like that of a servant who feels proud in his work.

But all the while something works inside him. He sees his mother at the stove, lifting only the flat of her hand when he left, and Soldier holds his two hands together.

He spends his life marveling (without knowing he has marveled) at what he has lost. He wonders where his life is, feeling at some point it was shifted. He wants to be carried somewhere. So he leans into the dark smell of the station house and finds comfort in the high-ceilinged room, the black glint of long narrow track. He finds comfort in strangers who speak or nod. But he could no more say what that comfort was than he could say what makes him feel lonely or tired.

Sometimes he says out loud, not to anyone, but out loud, "Please, don't make me remember that." ∎

GLOSSARY
Heather Tosteson

i

I don't know what they do—Feverfew, Motherwort, Rue—
but I can imagine, as I can't imagine the use of elecampane.
I write it down. Writing is a technology, or so say priests
and linguists. I sound the cymbals I have made.
El-e-cam-pane. I sound another sequence
of syllables—chamomile—another—lungwort—and feel
the gray bag inside me billow, flatten, billow.

ii

Comfrey.

On a grass-stained pad of graph paper, my son slowly
copies down the word. He yawns uncontrollably.
He always does when he tries to read or write. The symbols
themselves give him difficulty. He can't see the difference
between a W or M, a P or 9. *Wormswood*
he writes, checking it twice against the sign.

iii

Sky. Is. Fall.
These words written were my weapons
and I shot them nightly from my arced tongue.

For terror, in my seventh year, was substantial,
an animal.

With a tread regular as my own pulse, it stalked
a house so still it felt like there was no one left
inside it breathing. Except for me.

I knew the animal was insatiable as me.

And I knew, unlike me, it could groan and die
and come right back
to life.

iv

YOU LET ME BE he screams at night, mastering
a line from his first reader.
Seven, he makes his weapons out of cardboard
or warped plywood. On reels of brown paper
we've tacked to the walls, he draws diagrams,
then quietly studies the anatomy of his dreams.

Clary he writes now and hands me the notebook
to copy *Scolopendrium.*

v

Now read me, he demands, what we've written.
Comfrey, wormswood, feverfew, rue,
motherwort—

Three times he headed out, three times he stopped—
hearing what? The shirr of wheels on damp
asphalt? The screech of a rusted axle?
When at last he reached the far curb,
he looked up, saw me at the window, waved,
and, with a little hop, disappeared around the corner.

Go on, he says, shaking the paper.
You haven't finished the reading yet.
Scolopendrium and *chamomile. Lungwort.*

This morning, waving to him, closing
the window, I kept saying his Christian
name over and over under
my breath.

vi

Lying in bed last night, he drew a supine monster big
and fat and grinning like a Cheshire cat. It has a little
hole above its left clavicle where the air comes in and
fills a big balloon. When the balloon is full, it jostles
a little man who jostles a little octopus. The octopus
lets loose some dark chemicals that the man collects in
his hands and puts back into the balloon. When the balloon
collapses, the man edges away from the octopus; the

octopus stretches its tenacles, yawns, and goes back to
sleep. This process, he assures me, is not the way his
nice monster speaks. It speaks by twanging rubber bands.

vii

Look, he says, breaking
a branch from a flowering bush, crushing
the needles inside his palm holding
them to his face, breathing—

"They forgot
to give this one a sign."

On days like this I can't
touch him—my
elecampane.

SLEEPING IN FRONT OF THE FIRE
Sam McMillan

Build fire to take the rainy chill
away, hardly notice the bright
light leap up, I poke the poker
into the coals, think of Moses &
his Pharoah, how he popped
the brightest burning light into his mouth
rather than a diamond, how ever after
Aaron spoke for him; the biblical
simplicity & beauty of that act.
So I stare into glowing coals
a long time, wondering when
my life will ever be biblical
simple or beautiful; I amuse myself
with a memory of my father
explaining why his cousin did time
in the state pen: He just never
knew when to quit. Neither
do I, I know, I know, while I fuss
with the fire continually, throw another
chunking log thudding into the chimney,
it sends a shower of sparks spinning
up the flue like small quick secrets
the night sky snuffs out and forgets
while the fatter embers flare & fade
spit, pop, hiss and speak
to the dark room in a tongue of fire.
Next morning ashes heap cold and gray
as a granite New England tombstone
that faintly says: As I once was
So you Shall be, Prepare for

Death, and Follow me.
So Moses owns an indelible knowledge,
his thick tongue swollen coiled
like a rope in his mouth, so glib
Aaron speaks like a god, gets all the good
lines, so all life burns away
and the scent you smell clinging
to your clothes, your hair, your hands
is only the smoke of desire, is
all that remains after the ashes are lost
scattered in the next strong wind.

SONG OF SARAH
Bill Toole

In her bedroom far away Sarah looks at the many-colored mirror. Is it that old woman? The sound comes again. No, it is not her. Now Sarah knows. The bluebird has come back to flutter against the window in the kitchen. The window that lets the late afternoon sun spread itself like soft fuzzy butter on the breakfast table. Sarah has heard this bird-sound before and knows what it means. This sound like soft green branches played by a strong wind. Sarah moves from her downstairs bedroom to the doorway of the kitchen. "Jason," she says. Then she begins her skat. "Whisst then an teebessh window sst and o Jason," she says, concluding happily on that word which is as clear to her heart as the sunshine is on the table. Sarah's hair is snow white. Once, not long ago, it was blue-gray. But Sarah does not remember this. "More blue than gray," Jason said once; "Clara's tryin' to make Momma a Yankee." Sarah remembers this. She remembers many things about Jason. But she does not remember what it meant. She remembers that Jason was funny. Funny Jason made her laugh. But Jason is gone.

Sarah is wearing red-and-white flowered pajamas and her smile is as thin and bright as the early March sun. She hurries to the window, anxious. The bluebird has gone and there is only the rustling althea bush and the swishing branches of the dogwood that play with the sunlight before tossing it through the window. She is sure that the bluebird which sometimes flutters against the window is Jason trying to get in. She has not seen the bird. She has only heard it. But she knows that she will see it. She knows that it is Jason's trick. The smile she wears is to tell him he is welcome. "Shh whist Jason not Albert zzt seo in," she says to the window just in case the bluebird is close enough to hear. Then she stamps the floor with her bare foot in anger. Because Jason is not there. And because of the way the skat darkens her talk. None of them seem to realize that she is not always happy with what she says. But she is happy to be able to say. And she always smiles or giggles when she skats because she is afraid of something worse than skat. She doesn't know what it is she fears, something dark inside her she cannot see. Something that will take her away. Put her outside so that she will not be here. Not be home when Jason comes.

Sometimes when she skats she forgets and thinks she is talking bright. It is when they smile and pat her "good girl" and shake seriousness behind her look thinking she does not see that she remembers. She knows why she skats, Sarah does. Sarah is clever. She is not easily fooled. It is the white-haired woman who looks back at her in meanness from the mirror. Who sometimes shakes a fist at her. It is that old woman who has taken her talk. And wants more. Sarah knows. And she cannot make them understand. She has dark hair, pretty Sarah has. Jason loved her long dark hair. She has tried to tell them, but they do not understand. Walker's wife thinks she understands. Walker's wife brings her food and smiles bright as the sun on the breakfast table to be good to her. When Sarah stamps the floor with her bare feet, Walker's wife turns on the radio and dances with her. Then Sarah laughs and giggles and Walker calls her "good girl." But Sarah knows that if she does not do this they will think she is not a good girl and the old woman who wants to take her place will. The something dark will happen. Sarah will be outside like Jason. She will never find Jason outside.

Walker has covered all of the mirrors in the house to help her. But they do not understand that the woman is still there. When Sarah is alone in the house, she senses her presence, waiting behind the many-colored afghan that hangs over the large dresser mirror in her bedroom; waiting behind the tape that imprisons the bathroom mirrors; waiting. Cover does no good. Tape does no good. She is always there. Sarah knows. Once Sarah walked backwards into her bedroom. To fool the old woman she walked backward slowly skatting toward Albert who had fallen asleep at the kitchen table. But when she pulled the afghan quickly away, she was there. She can move like lightning through the house from mirror to mirror, that old woman. And Sarah cannot trick her. That old white-haired woman will not let Sarah see herself. See the long dark hair Jason once loved to watch her comb. Now that old woman comes between her and herself just as her words skat from what she tries to think or say.

Jason would understand, but Jason is outside. Jason has made Albert angry many times, but this time he has made Albert so angry that Albert will not let him in the house. Until he gives back something he has taken. What is it that Jason has taken? Albert takes too. It is not fair. Something inside her cries out when she thinks of what Albert has done. Or of what Jason has done. But what is it? Something whispers things to her she cannot hear but make her hurt. But sometimes the voice whispers clear. Whispers things, tricks. Whispers bad girl. She is not afraid of this voice which is part of her, rooted deep within her. The whisper-voice is sometimes clear as an icicle, sometimes points her to the den where Albert sits beside his gun collection and eats his supper in front of the television. Points her where once she served Albert his supper every night.

In the den there is the head of a deer suspended over the television set. As though it had leaped through air and part way through wall and come to rest caught high in the room to brood over it with hard-soft brown eyes and bare November branches soaring from its head. Sarah sometimes slips behind the television and reaches high to stroke the beautiful coarse gray-brown hair of the deer's head. She is careful not to look at the eyes which remind her of Jason who shot the deer to make Albert proud.

The voice brings her to this room and she knows what it wants. She envies the voice because it says so clearly what it wants except when it tricks her with a whisper that hurts below her thought. The voice reaches her when it wants to be heard. It does not have to skat back and forth between what it thinks and what it says. The voice is stronger than Sarah. When Walker's wife found the pretty silver knives and forks and spoons Sarah hid behind the radiator cover in the living room, she had said "bad girl" and Walker had said "bad girl." She tries to make them understand that it is the voice, not her. But she can no longer reach out with her thoughts into the minds of others as the voice reaches into her mind. So she cannot make them understand, just as she cannot make them understand that they cannot remove by covering the mirrors the old woman who hides there and threatens her. So when they shake their seriousness at her and waggle bad girl she giggles and dances. Dances with Walker's wife because dancing makes Walker's wife so happy. She giggles and laughs and turns her head and makes Walker's wife who has long dark hair her mirror. Once she knew Walker's wife's name, but it has left her and will not come back though Albert and Walker sometimes say it to her. When she tries to say it, it skats. It has gone for good. Taken by the old woman who hides in mirrors waiting to shake her fist at Sarah. Waiting to take Sarah's place. She has put on Sarah's clothes, waiting. Sarah knows.

Everything. That old woman wants everything. Well, she can have Walker's wife's name, but she will not get the voice which is not afraid of the old woman or of anything. The voice is more than person. The voice comes from somewhere deep in time and is as dark and crafty as her bad girl heart. Sarah is not able to think this but she knows it.

As Sarah walks around the den she comes to the door of the small half-bath and looks at the mirror which tapes her face. Once, before Walker taped the old woman in the mirror, she had sneaked up behind Albert who had foamed half his face white. To boo him and make him laugh. But that old woman had peered with a crafty look over Albert's shoulder and then turned her eyes angry. Sarah stamped her foot because Albert stayed in the bathroom with that old woman who wanted Albert too. Then she rushed away. Albert did not come to her bedroom to say sorry. Albert was too strong to ever say sorry.

Now the voice speaks clear. There are dark, bad-girl things to do because they have to be done. Things that will skat with time. Things dark as a whisper that hurts. Albert is dark and crafty too. She knows, Sarah does, that some of the silver

Walker's wife found Albert has hidden. For himself. To use sometimes in the den. Keeping there for himself. Albert always has kept for himself. He is a good hider, Albert is. Albert has always had a bad boy's heart. Sometimes when she misses Jason most she thinks she sees him hiding in Albert. A sad Jason. Is Albert hiding Jason to hurt her? No. Jason is being punished, not Sarah. But why does she hurt so much? What is underneath the whisper she cannot hear? Dancing does no good. Giggling and smiling good girl does no good. That hurt that hangs beneath her thought and skats her talk stops only when the bad-girl voice points her like an icicle to take.

Once they told her—was it long ago? she is not sure. Once they told her Jason was in a long dark box. And she believed them. But then the voice came to her as she sat in the folding chair under the green tent in front of roses. Sat there straight as an icicle while Albert cried. (Little boy Albert who had never cried, was he sorry he wanted his golden gun back?) Sat there looking beyond and above the long black drawer at November trees whose bare branches scratched at the lazy back of the sky which did not look cold but was. Did she see far off a bird fly through those sad bare branches? It was then the voice told her what she suspected.

Jason is a trickster too. Once in the woods "Jason!" she had cried. Everyone had cried "Jason! Where is Jason?" Her heart then spoke through her eyes and running everything came together—trees, bushes, pine needles thick and soft on damp ground. She, they, all stumbled through, crying "Jason!" But when they went to search the water, she came back to the cabin and sat on the floor, her long dark hair down over her face, alone except for Walker who was still hiding inside her. Then a sound. Was it a fluttering sound? Yes. She looked up and there in front of her was Jason's two-year-old crafty smile which he had been hiding behind the blue shower curtain. Bad baby Jason.

There under the tent like the tent over the bed in which she and Albert had hidden late one night and made Jason. There she knew the trick. Did Albert and Walker know? She had tried to ask them but the skat got in the way of her talk. Walker and Walker's wife would shush and pat and "good girl" her Jason skat, but Albert would turn his back and sometimes slam his head into the den because he knew she would not follow him there to sit under the brown eyes of the deer Jason had hurt himself to kill.

Now she knows Albert had been too clever for her again. She cannot find his silver. But the voice is more clever than Albert. Beside the chair across from the television there are hunting boots, one on each side with their wrinkled tongues askew like tired beagles. Sad boots. Tired boots. Filled with glee, Sarah moves across the room and follows the will of the silent voice which is stronger than she, stronger than Albert, and stronger than the terrible old woman who moves through mirrors. She picks up one of the boots by its twisted tongue and dangles it from her right hand, watching it twirl with pleasure. "Albert slippet top and zzweat," she croons. What is it she has in her hand? She knows what it is, but it will not come to the top of her mind where she can see and say it. The old woman would know, but Sarah knows better than to ask her. What if she comes out of the mirror to answer in Sarah's clothes? What would happen to pretty Sarah? Sarah is not sure.

As she stands holding the boot and thinking these things alone in the house, she hears a train whistle. The whistle means her daddy will be home soon, the railroad man, black lunch-pail in hand, and she and her brothers and sisters waiting excited for his tar-blown wind-swept freshness mingled with the strong-sweet taint of gin breath. She is his favorite. After the red shoes because of the way he hurt. Even more than the pretty red shoes had hurt. But there is no way now she can tell this as she told Jason and Walker once. Now she can say none of this except to the voice. Or is it the voice who says it to her? She cannot be sure. There is so much of which she cannot be sure.

Her daddy is sure of Albert. He says, "He's a good boy; he'll go through fire for you, little Sarah. Be good to him. You've made a good match." Yes. Be good to Albert, her father's sweet thick voice says when she stands frightened in front of him with tears in her eyes and a pretty beaded purse which hides her nightgown. So secret and sweet that midnight ride in the rumble seat and the sleepy-eyed old man in the silver spectacles with gray nightshirt stuffed into silver-striped pants and his soft-eyed wife who cries as she and Albert stand there scared happy in the parlor with the flowered bowl of light on the piano. Cries as she presses a white rose—saying "for you, sweetheart, and happiness"—into her hand as they leave. But then she is scared of Albert who is as sweet and fierce as the wind around the rumble seat. She must see her daddy. First before going to the great stone house with Albert she says. But she has changed her mind, Sarah has. She does not want to go with Albert who paces in the blackness outside, his excitement pressing agaist the small white house where she stands in front of her daddy. She is excited too. But frightened of the house to which Albert wants her to go. Her father says be a good girl to Albert and she has. This now is not what the voice inside her says.

But she will not entirely bad-girl Albert. Before slipping furtively from the room, she stoops and pats the boot on the floor, lifts its lagging tongue and folds it gently back into the heel corner so that it can rest straight and comfortable. "Now," she says emphatically, firming her jaw. She does not look at the empty space in the gun collection on the wall beside the chair.

Oh, now, she knows what to do and she swims in the comfort of certainty and sureness as she moves swiftly up the stairs to Jason's room which sits in stillness, waiting for Jason, the only movement behind the door she opens is the motes of dust floating in the beam of sun that flashes through one broken slat of the blinds over the window. She opens an empty bureau drawer, the bottom one. Why should Jason have taken all his clothes? Why should they be gone? Was it Walker who had taken them? Why should Walker take them away? Something deeper than mind turns at the roots of her being and the dark pain which flashes like lightning pierces her eyes so that for a moment she cannot see. What is it that coils and flashes inside her? She tries to think-see, but it is gone. No use. It frightens her, this sudden movement of something which surges across the blackness of her mind and reaches down to grip her heart, this whatever. It frightens her and she wants desperately to know but instead remains poised, hovering between knowing and not knowing, like a swimmer lost in darkness stretching for something solid, something sensed but not seen.

The voice knows what to do. So Sarah pats the boot into the drawer and closes it gently. "Shh," she whispers to the room, two fingers sealing her lips gently as she backs toward the door and catches the knob behind her with her hand. Then Small Jesus sees the trick. Wearing a long purple robe, Small Jesus stands in the square frame over Jason's bed surrounded by curly lambs. They make her think of Clara. Clara's lambs, she wonders? This makes her giggle. "I'm the devil," she says. Sarah is playing funny girl. But Small Jesus does not think she is a funny girl. His kind eyes speak lightning. Sarah is timid but the voice is strong. She backs through the door, pulling it toward her until only her head is in the room. Now she is like the deer in the den downstairs. But her dark eyes move and she can speak. "Whisst she he sisst Jason meetee you," she skats to the Lord. Fixing her eyes directly on those of Small Jesus, she puts two fingers to her lips and invites Him to sweet conspiracy. "Shh," she whispers. "Shh." Then her head slides out to join the rest of her and she thinks happily of Small Jesus watching over the secret something of Albert in Jason's drawer.

Now Sarah's white hair floats in the dusk of evening down the lavender carpeted stairs which warm her feet shining in their bareness almost as whitely as her hair. Little Sarah has pretty feet. Once the train whistled her daddy off with an armload of shoes in long boxes. Hers red and pretty hurt so she kicked them off. Bad girl Sarah was whipped by her daddy. Hard. Too hard. He came to her in the night with tears in his voice, picked her close, and swore never to whip little Sarah again. Sarah thinks this now pondering her pretty bare feet in the kitchen because it is nice to think clear. And some of this long ago is so much brighter than now and what comes between. That same nice husky voice of love in the night floated her from his small house with pride to the stone house where now she stands in the kitchen.

"Be good to Albert. Albert's a good boy. You'll have a better life now, little Sarah." Pretty Sarah has done well and so she goes, hiding in her beaded purse the white nightgown which Albert will not let her wear. Bad boy Albert. Who sleeps upstairs by himself and takes pills to stay awake. Who put Jason outside and tried to make her think he sleeps cold under grass. She remembers the rose she took from the long dark drawer in which they said he slept. "For you, sweetheart, always." Did she say this and hide the rose where no one, not even Walker's wife, can find it? Or was this the soft-eyed lady who spoke with sleep in her voice as Albert crooned her back to the car while their friends—who were their misty faces? While they, whoever, rumbled her roughly home under the moon-flecked dark to be encircled by the pride of her father; to meet Albert's mother and father tall and straight, armless as icicles; to slide into the secret warmth of the bed upstairs where Albert now sleeps alone, the ruffled canopy which covered them like a tent long since gone.

Sarah begins to move about the kitchen, back and forth like a beagle onto the scent of something but confused by conflicting signals. Her eyes dart about the room as though she thinks someone may be hiding from her. From time to time she makes a soft sound—something between a hiss and a whistle. "Whisst." It is a nice sound which she makes to keep her company in the empty house. To tell herself she is there and not outside. To let the woman who hides in mirrors know not to step out. The sound is like a soft wind moving across autumn leaves.

The voice straightens her path. Her face lights up. She moves to the cupboard and plucks out a box of cookies. Albert likes cookies. She looks around; no one is watching. She backs out of the kitchen, across the hall that leads to the garage, backs into her downstairs bedroom. She makes sure that the old woman has not pushed some of the many colors aside to spy on her so that she can tell Albert secretly in his bathroom. She knows there is nothing that old woman will not do. Once the box is under the bed she is safe. "He seetee be Jason ssh whisst," she says. Jason will understand. Walker's wife cannot understand what she says, but Jason will. He is not there but her thoughts will hang in the room, wait for him to know. The cookies are for him. Jason likes cookies. She hangs her laughter there too for him to share, sweet and conspiratorial. Jason and she have secrets that Albert will never know.

A car rustles the garage. There is the quick slap of horn. An old signal to which she no longer responds. Once it meant: Pour the coffee, pull the warm plate out of the oven, take the tray to the den. But she does not do this anymore. Once it meant: Make sure everything is right! Rush! Hurry! Some of this feeling slips across her mind but she remains still, listening. Secret in her bedroom she feels as safe as the lambs that Small

Jesus keeps behind his purple robe. No one knows what she has done but Small Jesus, and even if he is angry or sad he is good and will not tell. Sarah hears the heaviness move down the hall past her bedroom door and across into the kitchen. She waits, then moves softly to the kitchen door. Albert is sitting at the table by the window where the bluebird fluttered. Now there is no sunlight on the table. Albert has put his head in his hands. He is wearing a plaid hunting shirt which hangs down loose over dark pants and there is so much sadness rumpled into his shape that Sarah's heart cries inside her. But she stands mute in the doorway. When she skats, Albert becomes upset. "What is she saying? What in the hell is she saying?" he cries and Walker's wife, if she is there, will explain. Walker's wife thinks she understands, but Sarah does not understand what Walker's wife says she says except that it is nice. That is why she plays and dances with Walker's wife even when she does not feel like it. Once she did not like Walker's wife—she does not remember why—but that was before the old woman crept into her mirror. Walker's wife who has long dark hair is her friend. Sarah needs friends.

Albert is still unaware of her presence. His hair is dark too except for some gray streaks. Sarah is sure he has told his hair not to get old. Albert does not like old. When Albert says he means. He is strong and sometimes angry. He is not the Albert who rode with her once in the hum of night and promised her everything. He is tired and if he does not take his pill soon he will fall asleep. She must always put his pills beside his plate on the tray in front of the television. But now she doesn't. Is that the flutter of wings? This time against the window over the sink. This time far away Sarah is near but in the gathering darkness cannot see. She moves to the sink-window anxiously.

"Sarah!" Albert's voice strikes the startled room. Albert's voice hurts. He has lifted his head with some effort. Sarah moves her head back and forth scanning the yard outside. Is there something beside the white oak tree? She pays no attention to Albert's voice. His right hand moves slowly across his face from top to bottom as though he is wiping sleepiness off him. Or pulling down the shade of something else. He speaks again. He struggles to be gentle.

"Sarah." Still there is no answer. "I guess," he goes on,

"that now you've forgotten how to make coffee. You could at least do that last week. I guess now I'll have to make my own coffee at night. It's not enough I have to eat out or cook for myself." He has begun to reach out for anger but, with an effort, pulls himself back. "What's the use? First Jason, now you." When he turns his eyes toward her, Sarah is still looking out the window. Albert shakes his head turning his eyes away. At the head of the breakfast table he sits by himself, looking straight ahead. Then Sarah turns to look at him and her eyes smile softly close to tears. Albert is right. She does not understand his words, all of them. They hang there in the kitchen. She wishes she could pull them down and carry them away to secret places.

She understands his voice. It stirs something inside her. "Whisst." She moves to the lower drawers of the long panelled cabinet that runs along one side of the kitchen adjacent to the stove. She moves purposefully making her happy half-whistling sound. She is there. There are things she can do when she has a mind to. She will be a good girl for Albert, make him proud of her, maybe. This evening she did not have a mind to make Albert's coffee but now the voice responding to Albert's voice has given her mind. She knows that Albert is at the table. If she knows that he has lifted his head hopefully at the familiar clatter of pot and skillet on the stove, she does not show it. If she knows that his eyes are following her hopefully as she moves to the refrigerator to take out eggs and bacon, she does not show it.

"Maybe you can still do something even if you can't understand anything," Albert says. Albert's voice is strained but gentle, encouraging. It is meant to be inspirational, but if she understands she does not show it. She is caught up in a backwater eddy of experience, the rhythm of a past ritual. As she floats easily in the swirl of knowing, Albert begins to speak again, more softly. "You see, it's easy. You can handle anything if you put your mind to it."

Something in his voice makes her turn to look at him and she is caught breathless. Is Jason there?

No. It is the light's trick. Leaving the bacon and eggs on the stove, she slips over beside Albert moving as silently as the dust that dances along the sword of light the broken slat lets into Jason's room. She is sad because her sudden hope is broken. Jason is not there. She is sad but she ruffles Albert's hair with affection and giggles. Makes a mock fist as though to threaten him, playing the old woman in the mirror. Playing funny girl. Saying, "Knock, knock," gently against the side of his head with her imitation old white-haired woman's fist. Saying, "Knock, knock," and answering, "I'm the devil." But Albert doesn't like her funny girl. He turns wearily to her and then looks away. Does Albert have tears in his eyes? Poor Albert. She played funny girl to make him laugh, but his talk does not laugh when it starts again as she moves back to the stove.

"First Jason doing what he did to himself, now you, what you've done to yourself and me. No one knows what it's like to live with a wall, a walking wall." Something makes her turn around and she is transfixed. Jason *is* there! This time she is sure. He is standing there misty beside Albert. Albert has been hiding Jason. The secret is out. Bad Albert. Has he had Jason all the time? Bad boy Jason to hide so long. She smiles love at him. Albert's voice pretends Jason is not there, but he cannot fool her now. "Maybe it's my fault I didn't start with him soon enough, let you spoil him. When he was born you thought he was everything, couldn't see anything or anyone else but him, and I let you have him. Maybe it's my fault but he never seemed interested in anything I did anyway." Albert's voice has withered to a whisper and his head slumps down onto his arms on the table.

Sarah glides across the room to stand beside him and look at misty Jason who has slipped into the window. The Jason she sees she cannot touch. She knows this but does not care. This is all she asks—to think-see. "Whisst pills she he be forgot," she says in a whisper of sweet conspiracy to Jason. She pats Albert's sleeping head affectionately, then makes a mock fist, bracing her jaw comically aslant like Popeye the Sailor Man. "I'll hit sisst you watch shh see them." She taps her fist gently on his head. When she looks up she can see Jason's misty smile. Jason thinks she is a funny girl. But she must shake seriousness at him too.

"Mirro," she begins and what comes out is all skat until she stops and lets the voice inside her reach Jason's mind. Jason's mind is not misty. He understands. Then suddenly he is gone and she is afraid. But ᵗhe whisper is clear. Sarah feels warm and good. She has stolen Jason from Albert while he sleeps. And she will not tell him.

At the stove she moves quietly and efficiently. The skillet is on the stove. The bacon is stretched neatly across the skillet. Poor sad bacon. Water is poured into the coffee pot. Brown good smelling grains of coffee from her hand are spread into the water. Who is doing these things? It must be pretty Sarah. She marvels at herself. The voice floats through her with silent telling. "Jason," she says happily. "Cookies whisst." She looks over her shoulder quickly. Albert is still asleep. He has not heard. "Shh," she smiles. She continues fixing breakfast early in the dusk of evening. She breaks two eggs over the raw bacon which is spread in the skillet on the cold burner. She drops shells and all onto the bacon. "Now!" she says with satisfaction. She goes back to the table where Albert still sleeps. "Knock, knock," she says cheerfully. Albert does not stir. "I'm the devil," she giggles. But he continues to sleep. Bad-girl Sarah skats on barefeet out of the kitchen. She pauses in the hall to look back over her shoulder at Albert. "Whisst," she says. Her face is radiant. ∎

BLESSING
Rebecca McClanahan Devet

Like kisses these petals
you leave in my lap,
torn sweet from the
branch, tender.

And as my grandmother
lives on in the mirror
of certain blue plates,
so this moment.

Say my name
and a child is born
somewhere
in a flood of amen.

Touch me
and vapor rises
healing the air
around us.

Our fathers laugh
with open mouths
and for once do not
count the change.

Here our mothers
are young again,
their backs straight
and lovely in the light,

their waists only a sash
of blue, like river
or something a shy man
once painted in a dream.

ALL HALLOWS EVE
Kathryn Stripling Byer

I go by taper of cornstalk,
the last light of fields wreathed in woodsmoke,
to count the hens left in the chickenhouse
raided by wild dogs and foxes.
Our rooster crows far up the hillside
where three piles of rocks mark the graves
of nobody I ever knew.
Let their ghosts eat him!
Each year they grow hungrier,
wanting the squash run to seed in our garden,
the tough spikes of okra. Tonight while the moon
lays her face on the river and begs
for a lovesong, they'll come down the mountain
to steal the last apples I've gathered.

They'll stand at the window and ask us
for whom is that buttermilk set on the table?
That platter of cold beans?
They know we will pay them no heed.
It's the wind, we will say,
watching smoke sidle out of the fireplace,
or hearing the cellar door rattle.

No wonder they go away
always complaining how little we living
have learned, on our knees
every night asking God for a clean heart,
a pure spirit. Spirit? They kick
up the leaves round the silent house.
What good is spirit without hands for walnut

to stain, without ears for the river
to fill up with promises? What good,
they whisper, returning to nothing, what good
without tongue to cry out to the moon,
"Thou hast ravished my heart, O my sister!"

THE INSULATING PROPERTIES OF TREES
Ralph Earle

Three white ducks waddle among
pine trees and picnic tables.

Nearby a family celebrates, mother and girls
gathered around a vase with a red rose.

We expect the baby will start to scream.
Thanks to the insulating properties of trees
it will bother no one but us
and even that is beginning to blur.
He screams. Ann's face falls.
I take him against my shoulder
and follow the ducks toward the sound
of the rushing spillway.

          Behind a tree
where we can't see his mother eating
we play this game: Sorry, Ann,
I put him down on the water a moment,
like Moses, you know,
to see what would happen and he just
floated away.

        This is why
some people put babies up for sale
or hang them in trees all day long,
like the Indians used to, in pine trees.

NOTHING TO DO WITH US
Julie Suk

An owl hoots from a nearby tree.
A siren floats off down the street.
Lying here covered by the warm night,
I don't want to think about torn flesh.

Once while we slept,
your fingers dug into my thigh.
I was bruised for days.

So tender are we to touch,
the body reacts without knowledge,
not because of it,
mumbling along even as we die,
the way an animal brought down
continues to kick
while a spasm of guts spirals out.

Relentless—the telephone ring
that breaks into sleep
to trample our lives.

Don't tell me that old wives' tale
about the owl call,
not now,
the moon resting like a benediction
on the bed where we sprawl
exhausted by love.

BLUE SNOW
Kathy May

In the kitchen the kettle puffs
small clouds of steam
that hover in the air
like your breath outside
where you are shoveling snow.
I'm thinking how we've drawn closer
moving to this place
and suffer not from loneliness or cold
but from the city's crowded bleakness
as I watch you clear a path
down toward the street.

Snow sifts through trees and telephone lines,
shrouds buildings, houses, battered cars,
small heaps of strewn garbage
I used to mistake for animals
dead on the side of the road.
Starlings scavenge in the yard,
their mite-infested, iridescent heads
mechanically bobbing.

When the sun sets behind
a false horizon of banked clouds,
the neighborhood begins to shimmer.
Scattered patches of sky
reflect watercolor blue
in the microscopic crystals of the snow.

It's not illusion
but a quality of light
that's been there all the time,
that I suddenly understand
when you come into the room
and your cold lips touch mine.

TABLE LEGS
Paul Lyons

"What you wanna do, young blood?" Table Legs said from the other end of the table. "You wanna shoot pool or just stand there like the fool you is?"

"I'm shooting pool," I said. "When I miss you can shoot."

"Then shoot, chump."

"Quit if you don't like my speed."

"A man'd have to be a lunatic to quit an all-day-long sucker like you."

"And you ain't a lunatic?"

"The kydd," someone said. "You tell him kydd, shoot strong, shoot strong."

Yeah, I told myself, shoot strong. Concentrate on matters at hand. You missed the silly dinner. You made your play, go through with it.

But I kept seeing my sister blushing under my father's gaze: "Maybe he just went for a walk somewhere for chrissake," and my brother picking at the crisp duck skin, and my mother, straight-backed, who would never have doubted my absence from the moment the miniature jeweled watch about her neck millimetered past seven, who would have sat on the pillowed couch in the living room sipping Apricot brandy while the courses burned or got cold, looking at the little jeweled watch of hers. And I saw my father folding his hands

169

on the table and lowering his head: "Rub a dub dub, thanks for the grub, dig in."

Dig in, I told myself. The nine ball is sitting dead on and it will be a tricky bit of thinking and doing to play position behind the thirteen. Put english upper right and stroke the object ball strong left and the cue will carry off the rail at a radical angle. The ball only needs action.

So their meal would be strained, I thought, it would be strained if I was there anyway. Too bad. But not one of the great tragedies of the universe. It was a pity to put a strain on my father. He worked hard all day and deserved better. That was the worst of it. And for a moment when I thought of him I considered running home and making up some story about a triple overtime game in Riverside Park. Something about it getting so dark that no one could see the hoop, especially when the street lights went out. Of course no one would believe me to the letter, but they'd appreciate my hustling back, my wanting to make things go smoothly. I'd bound up the stairs with my sweat smell from having run the ten blocks and wash the crescent of blue-black chalk-dust off my hands.

I steadied on the nine ball, straightened my bridge fingers. I stroked the nine ball and it went smack in and the cue ball snapped in a delayed reaction as if popping out of a stupor and continued around the table. Not perfect. But enough. I could see my way clear and ran the rest out.

Legs lay his cue stick on the table. It had green and orange decorations up by the joint. A Palmer. "You shoot like Godzilla hisself for a funky two dollars," he said, "but I ain't got time for no two dollar action, let's shoot pool, baby."

"I'm shooting pool," I said.

"Two dollar pool, the hell you is. I don't do nothing for two dollars. I don't drink ice-water for two dollars."

"What do you wanna play for," I said.

"My grandmother don't roll for less than ten."

"Let's play for ten then," I said.

Of course I shouldn't have started playing Legs at all. He was too tough at the table to control. I had to shoot full strength to win and he could bust me even if I did. If I'd played a tropical I could have set a win or lose time limit for quarter to seven and relieved the lemon of ten or so dollars and made it home for dinner. Smooth. Later in the week the lemon would want to get even and I'd squeeze him again. I'd make him my tropical. He'd never know my game and would always lose and I wouldn't bring in too much line at one time. I'd keep him in my back pocket and educate him slowly.

But there wasn't much in that sort of thing. I could only do that for so long before I became like Gonzalez, standing against the wall in his two hats though it must have been eighty degrees in the place. He wore those two hats all day long, summer or winter, from one year to the next. And it didn't make the slightest difference to him that people laughed and told him to get a new pair of hats. He worked all week in a kitchen nearby washing dishes and let his roll ride every six months or so. In the meantime he'd play fish, beat them up, and his game would get soft.

Or I could get like Andre the Great, a performer between acts—short Spanish man in a neat three piece suit with his hair slicked back. When the action slowed up and everyone was sitting around Andre would take out two balls and shine them ceremoniously and set them up in some crazy position for an eight-rail bank on the center table. He'd clean the table with a brush and chalk his cue for twenty minutes not looking at anyone. Then he'd shoot the shot maybe fifty times, slowly, deliberating over it, and never make it. He'd talk to the balls under his breath and do calculations in the air and brush the table again. The shot could be made. So what. When he made the shot once every six months there would be a great cheer for "Andre the Great, Andre the Great" and Andre would smile humbly as though he hadn't known anybody was watching him and was embarrassed at his mastery. The rest of the time he sat around and people shook hands with him.

No, a player had to play live players. A player needed action. Needed to feel the action a live, restless thing in his gut. The thrill was playing tough games, the ones that turned into battles that you didn't know about, where you had to get harder or get beat, where the action was electric and every slip cost, one dollar, ten dollars, two hot raisin bagels at the corner shop and the *New York Post*, until you didn't have money for the phone.

Table Legs was a rough game. He'd been around and played big pool on the road and wasn't supposed to lose to me. His game wasn't as sharp as it had once been but he knew the moves, the angles. He'd beat me flat sometimes. I didn't mind losing to him. I liked his chatter. We'd insult each other. To him my money was peanuts. He controlled a few pimps and always walked around loaded, betting a thousand dollars on hitting a ten in a crap game. Crazy. What did it matter to him.

We played back and forth for the tens. It got to be eight, then nine. People bet on the side and I liked being watched, talking with old-timers between shots. I bet extra on myself. I bet with four people I'd never seen. I made some good shots, enjoying the evening. Two or three losses in a row could wipe me out with all the side action but no one knew that. That was the thrill of it. And when I was down on my last dollar and sharp and felt the pool juice pumping into my nerve endings I felt I could beat anyone. I told them I had money and put a twenty dollar bill around a roll of old singles and dropped it where everyone could see it as though it were an accident so they thought I grew money. I told them: "I don't leave home without it, I don't get out of bed without it, I always carry it." They liked my action. We'd bet on everything, on whether it was going to rain. I'd listen to stories about Jersey Red and String Bean when he was young and could shoot. Now people called him Bean String and he rubbed his large shoulders against the wall like a cat.

Legs started to wear me down. I'd make a few great billiard shots where the ball came around the table almost kissing the still cue ball to win but he'd come back and win the next two games. I started to play slow and try to hold onto something, to think out each shot. I thought if I played slow he'd let up. But I missed a key shot and he ran out. "When in doubt, run out," he said. Some of the guys who were betting on me cursed and made cracks about how dumb it was to bet on a baby half in the cradle. Another called: "Shoot back at him baby, shoot baby: I'll put ten on the baby, who wants some of it?"

I was racking the balls and when I looked up I saw my father. I turned and he was standing by a neighboring table. I don't know how long he'd been there. Killer the old boxer was trying to get him to play eight-ball. He was mumbling all sorts of things which my father could never understand. Killer had been hit in the throat too many times as a club middle-weight and his voice was all one slur. He'd shown me his scrapbook once. A Star of David hung over his wide chest.

I thought I was going to be hit. I mean I didn't know what to think. I was startled. It was a minute before I could breathe right. I thought he'd come up there to hit me or drag me out. But my father didn't move. He just stood there like he didn't know what to do or what was supposed to happen, like may-be he'd come there to do or say something but had forgotten what. He just looked at me and then at Killer who kept mumbling propositions at him and then at me.

I had to say something. So I said: "Hi Dad, what are you doing in a place like this?"

The words stumbled out but he heard me.

"Got restless," he said, "decided to take a walk."

"Up here," I said.

"Why not," he said.

"Why the hell not?" Legs said. "You shoot pool too daddy, you want in, we could play three handed? You know. All three of us."

"You didn't have to worry, Dad," I said stupidly—and then, "How's everything at home?"

"It's a zoo back home."

"I was just getting ready to leave," I said, "to go home."

"Sure you were," my father said.

I had about twenty dollars left and we had upped the bet to twenty and I figured there was no way I could let my father watch me get busted and have to owe the house money for time. It was bad enough already. It was terrible.

"That's right, baby," Legs said, "get with your daddy and get your funky ass out of here, go back to the zoo with the other animals and get your whooping like you deserves."

"Let's see you shoot," my father said. "I don't get out of the house much in the evenings."

"I couldn't, Dad," I said.

"Get on out with daddy, then," Legs said, "we don't need no terrified zoo babies that doesn't want to be their own man in here."

I started to gather the balls and put them on the plastic

rack. My father walked out from behind the other table and took me by the arm. I mean he really gripped me. Seized me. He looked ridiculous in the smokey room with his tie and suit and shined leather shoes. He'd probably had them shined in the subway that morning.

"Don't whoop him up here, now," Legs said, "have mercy, don't whoop him in a place like this, Lord have mercy, it'd break my heart to hear the baby cry."

"Can you beat this guy?" my father asked.

"He doesn't mean anything with all that talk, Dad," I said, "he's just having his fun. He likes to talk. He's just talking."

"I asked you whether you could beat the guy."

"Maybe I can beat him," I said.

"Hell no you can't never whoop my butt." Legs had seated himself on the table between us and was shining the cue ball on his black satin shirt. His shirt caught and played with the light. "A no-shooting-all-day-long sucker like you can't never beat a player like me," he said.

"I'd like to see you shoot," my father said. "If you spend all your time here you ought at least to be able to shoot."

"I don't spend all my time here, Dad," I said.

"You spend enough time here."

"I don't want you to see me the way I am here."

"The way you is," Legs said, "the way you is is you ain't got no heart at all." He shook his head and walked toward the cue rack to get his carrying case. "Lord have mercy you shoots pretty straight when you ain't so scary but your heart ain't no bigger than a little green pea."

"Play him," my father said.

I said to myself: What the hell. Maybe losing in front of my father is supposed to be some kind of lesson. I don't need a lesson but what the hell. Things can't get worse. I just let go. I said to Legs: "Rack the balls, sucker."

Legs rubbed his hands together and stood behind the table. He put the balls on the table and placed them one by one in the wood rack. Then he moved them back and forward along the table talking to me. "Baby don't wanna go home and get your whooping, well you doesn't have to, you can get your whooping right here if ya wants to. Come and get your whooping baby, I'm gonna give it to ya."

"Take care behind when I break," I said, motioning him out from behind the table with my stick.

I broke too hard and Legs ran a few. Then he played safe. I wanted to beat him quick and erase the scene, but with my father watching I couldn't shoot a lick. It was like my cue ball had stones in it like loaded dice and my stick was crooked. It was a mistake because I lost either way. I should've paid my bill and left. It was bad enough without my father having to see me lose to some joke like Legs.

And I lost without putting up much of a fight. I slipped Legs the twenty and sat down next to my father on a bench near the powder rack and shrugged. I tossed my stick back and forth between my hands. My head throbbed.

"What's that game you're playing," my father said, "I've never seen that one before. That some kind of trick game?"

"It's one-pocket," I said, "we each take a pocket and the first to make eight balls in his pocket wins. It's lots of defense. You have to keep the balls away from the other guy's pocket. You have to move them to your own pocket. Think ahead. It's a thinking game."

"Thinking game." My father laughed.

"Anyway," I said, "I'm all through."

"I just got here," my father said.

"I'm broke," I said. "Let's get out of here."

"That's all you holding, you all through already?" Legs said disgustedly. "Lord have mercy that's a shame."

"What were you playing for?" my father asked.

"Twenties."

"Twenties?"

"Twenty dollars a game."

"That's a piece of money," my father said.

"I'm sorry," I said, "I know it is, let's go."

"Twenty dollars is a lot of money? You call that money?" Legs said to my father. His straightened black hair rose in a wave. "Twenty god-damned dollars. I spend that much on cab-fare every day. Twenty dollars. I don't walk nowhere. You come in here with a tie and jacket and funky suit and call twenty dollars a piece of money. Do you know where you is? This is New York City, man, this ain't no West Turkey or Tennessee. This ain't no Mars. Where do you think you is?"

"That's about enough," I said to Legs.

"What you gonna do, sucker?"

"Ease up Legs," I said.

"Ease up hell, twenty dollars. I wipe my ass with a lousy twenty dollars. You want your lousy twenty dollars. I wouldn't want you white folks to starve without your twenty dollars."

"Beat this guy," my father said to me. "I'll put up the money. You shoot your one pocket or whatever the hell it is."

"It's not important, Dad, he's just mouthing off."

"Do you shoot pool or not?"

"I shoot a little," I said.

"You shoot a very little," Legs said. "A very very very little. You shoot a little when you ain't so scary. But you ain't got the slightest bit of heart. You got a heart half the size of a pea."

"Okay," my father said, taking his wallet out.

"You gonna shoot me yourself, sir, daddy. You gonna shoot against the great Table Legs?"

"No, he's shooting," my father said, pointing to me, "I'm betting on him and paying if he loses."

"I'll play now, sir," Legs said, "but good sir, I won't play for no twenty dollars. Twenty dollars is an insult to decent folk. It's a disgrace. A bad shame. You wanna shoot with the great Table Legs you gonna have to play like a gentleman, you gonna have to come up with some real money."

"Is fifty dollars a game all right?" my father said.

"It will be all right for a start," Table Legs said.

I stood by the large window at the end of the poolroom looking out over Broadway. On the corner of 79th street men were unloading fresh bales of news from the *Daily News* truck. Night porters piled the day's waste from restaurants along the avenue in the streets. It was cooler by the window. I tried to phase out everything that didn't matter, everything except me and the shot to be made so that it was just me and the universe and the cue ball and the object ball. I tried to get back to where it was me in a white room with nothing but a pool table and the cue ball and the object ball. The perfect table and the cue ball and the object ball. The perfect table, well-weighted stick, no second chances. Stroke smooth and easy as apple-butter.

I walked through the empty tables in the back of the large room to the bathroom and washed my face in the cold water and stood there for a minute breathing heavily. The room stunk wretchedly and I breathed in deep until I felt like I was going to throw up. Then I spat in the sink and went out to where Legs and my father and a half-dozen men stood around the one lighted table. I didn't look at my father. I racked the balls for Legs back and forth, pressed with the knuckles, lifted the rack.

"Shoot Legs," I said.

He shot. It went back and forth. I played well but Legs upped his speed and kept his mouth shut and put a little extra into each shot. The balls got pushed back to the far end of the table and every ball had to be banked and played safe so the games took a long time. I won a game and he won one and then we each won another. I went and got a black cherry soda. The clock above the soda machine said one.

"Let's make it two-hundred a game," Legs said.

My father nodded at me. I nodded back at him. I didn't wonder whether he had two-hundred dollars in his pocket or what he would be doing with two-hundred dollars in his pocket if he did. He never had that much in his pocket.

It went slower still. I did not make any mistakes. I safed when I could have taken long shots that I ordinarily would have taken and picked off points when Legs made mistakes. I beat him the first game and he paid. My father held the money in his fist. I beat Legs the second game and he paid. I started to feel lighter. Like my game was coming together. Like I only had to be patient and not get happy and apply steady pressure and he would break before I would. The way it is when you get a guy's arm in a wrist-wrestle and he's got to give. It was like we were both underwater and I had more air left in my tank than he did and I only had to wait for him to burst to the surface. I was willing to wait. All night. All tomorrow. Until Christmas. Now that we were here, playing the game the way it was meant to be played.

He started taking chances. He'd try tough combinations and then I'd pick off a few balls and safe him down to the end of the table. He made a few great shots but he paid when he missed. I made him pay. He'd bank and slow roll the ball toward the pocket and I'd move it again. Kill the cue ball. Dead stop with draw. Leave him long. I beat him a third game. My father held the money. I didn't want to touch it. I didn't want to touch anything but the cue stick.

Legs went into the bathroom for a few minutes. He liked to smoke a joint or blow some coke when he got stuck and that was fine with me. Go junk yourself up, I thought. Fill yourself with junk. Don't worry about me. It won't bother me if we wait three hours. It won't throw my rhythm. When you come back all junked up I'm still going to beat you. I'm going to be sitting here waiting to ambush you and whoop you worse than you ever dreamed of being whooped.

Legs came out. He had tucked his leather pants up behind his leather boots and walked with a bounce. "You want something for the head?" he asked me.

"No thanks," I said.

"Your daddy want any?"

"My father doesn't want any," I said.

I broke. Legs got control early and I had to play straight defense for ten shots without any hope of turning it around. He made several fabulous cut shots, turning the cue ball loose like you must on such shots and lucking the position. It happened like that sometimes when you took chances. More often not. I banked a few home. He banked two. We safed back and forth. He cut another one in. Played safe. Then there was only one ball left on the table and whoever made it won.

Legs banked it for his pocket and hung it. I came in behind with right hand english and kicked it loose and back down to the safe end of the table. He banked it toward his pocket again, controlling the speed so that if he missed I would not have a return cross bank. We shot at the ball for half an hour. At least. He kept sending it for his pocket. I kept knocking it away.

Then he left the ball a foot too far from the pocket so that it was possible for me to bank the ball eight rails around the table and put him back on defense. Andre's shot. I went over to the powder rack and rubbed some of the fine powder between my bridge fingers. I stood over the ball for a minute, figuring the english, trying to remember the last time Andre made it, steadying my hands. I looked over at my father and at Andre who was standing next to him. Andre smiled and made a fist. My fingers closed around the stick. I stroked the ball cleanly and hard. It raced around the table twice and headed back toward my pocket. It seemed in line. It seemed like it was dead in line but maybe, yes surely, not hard enough. Like if I had really pounded it it might have carried on through and sliced the axis of the pocket. Andre shifted a little by the wall and strained to watch the ball. My father moved a little next to Andre. Gonzalez with his two hats opened his eyes when he felt Andre move. The ball kept rolling. About half-way across the table now, seemingly in line. But about to stop. My father took a step toward the table. I stood back and bent my body at the ball in the direction of the table, pulling it along. Andre moved next to my father, his lips parted slightly.

The ball rolled and rolled like it would die any moment, like it was gravely wounded and would skid to a stop any moment, but it kept rolling for the hole. I thought: roll ball, roll like a jelly roll, roll like a jelly roll with a thousand legs. I thought: roll on ball and I rolled with it and pushed it with all the force of my will and the ball kept skidding like the table was greased, like it was slipping down the buttered throat of the table or being pulled by something stronger than the laws that governed pool balls, because it was just moving too slowly and there was no earthly way it wouldn't stop and then it did go dead and wobbled and had nothing in it, no energy or force at all, and leaned over and gave a last little stretch or a pull from somewhere within and fell into the pocket with the softest plop.

"Sweet Lord Jesus, sweet mother of Jesus," Table Legs moaned, letting his breath out between his teeth in a little whistle, "sweet mother of Jesus and Lord have mercy on me that was a player shot, dear Lord Jesus that was a player shot."

I sat down on a wood bench against the wall beneath the sign that said "Positively No Gambling." I put my head in my hands.

"That's all," Legs called to the house. "Take it on down." He was still standing by the pocket where the ball had dropped, staring at its absence and shaking his head. He took out a box of toothpicks and started working between the gold of his teeth.

"You quit," I said.

"Yeah," he said, shaking his head, "I quit your funky Godzilla ass."

"Okay," I said.

His dark face was all wrinkled and glinting like light on black tin foil. His whole face was smiling.

"All right," I said.

"Here's your money," Legs said, stripping four fifties off a fat roll and squeezing the roll back into a leather pouch on his belt. "You done got more of my money than you supposed to."

I just nodded.

"Keep your white ass out of trouble now," he said.

"I will."

Legs went over to the cue rack and picked up his carrying case and snapped it around his cue. He dusted off his hands and turned toward the phone. "Take it light daddy," he said to my father.

My father was leaning against the powder rack next to Andre. There was not a hair out of place on Andre's head. Gonzalez looked like he was sleeping on his feet but his eyes were open beneath his two hats. My father was holding six-hundred dollars loosely in his hands.

"Take it light now," Legs said to him.

My father looked at him and nodded. He had loosened his tie and taken his white shirt out of his pants.

"That's it," Legs said. "Had enough of this action; time to get myself a woman to make things right."

I went up to the table and took up the four fifties and stuffed them into my pocket. Killer the ex-boxer came over and mumbled that he'd brought me luck and I ought to give him a buck or two to eat with so I took out some singles and gave them to him. I said: "Thanks for the luck."

I collected the balls and brought them up front to the houseman. I gave the houseman money for time and an extra twenty.

He said: "You got him good, eh Chipmunk."

"Yeah, I got him," I said.

My father followed me down the stairs. They were sticky with spilled liquor and cold because someone had put a hole through the glass door with a pool ball.

Out in the street we started walking without going any-where. I felt I should say something but I couldn't think of anything to say so we just walked. We walked about ten blocks toward Lincoln Center and then turned and walked up

Amsterdam and back down to Broadway.

"You want to go somewhere?" I said.

"Okay," he said. "Let's go to breakfast."

"Okay," I said.

We sat in a little Hungarian restaurant. Flies played around the cracks of the window. The waiter came and we both ordered honeydew melons, an omelet, hashbrowns, and extra toast. We sat there without saying anything. My father went right through his melon and eggs and mopped up the grease on his plate with the extra toast. I nodded that he could have my extra toast too and the waiter brought a few slabs of soft butter. I finished my food, though I wasn't much hungry. I didn't feel the food going into my stomach. I ate from the memory of hunger. Every few minutes the waiter came by to ask if everything was all right and we both nodded and the waiter filled my father's cup with coffee.

When my father finished eating the toast he balled up his napkin and put it on his plate and began to cry. Not hard, but the tears traced lines down his face. I had never seen him cry before. He looked old and tired. I reached out and took his hand and said it was all right. I did not think it was funny to be holding his hand in the restaurant. All sorts of things happen at night in Hungarian restaurants. I said it was all right, that it was going to be all right. He wouldn't have to worry about me anymore. He didn't move his hand from under mine. He said he didn't worry about me and that I shot a beautiful game of pool and he went on crying. The tears streamed along his cheeks and I thought how he would ride the subway to work in maybe an hour because the streets were grey outside. I figured we would sit there for an hour or so until it was time for him to go to the office. I could see an old man out the window on a traffic island rubbing his hands. I was still holding my father's hand. ∎

FINDING
William Harmon

I found a quarter in the parking lot
this morning. (It would have been a penny
in North Carolina, where I used to live,
but this is Texas, longhorn land of exaggeration.)

I found a quarter and put it into my pocket
and felt—in spite of debts and deficits
that threaten to put me in the old poorhouse—
that I was ahead. The greatest poverty

is not to live in a fiscal world, I'll tell you that.
I'm saving up to buy an Orange Crush
for reasons purely atavistic and totemic:
the first real bear I ever saw (circa 1940)

was chained to a tailgate on the shoulder
of the road between Charlotte and Concord,
grunting, growling, drinking an Orange Crush
in the old corrugated brown bottle. Likewise,

the first Orange Crush I ever saw was being drunk
by a chained bear there, and, ever since,
there's been this nexus or plexus, so to speak,
embracing bears and Orange Crush in the brown bottle

and a brotherhood of avatars—Arthur, Beowulf,
Medvedev (the Russian "honey-knower"),
the bow-tie-sporting teddy bear I gave you
which you gave my name to in your dear sweetness.

If I can find or make another quarter
I'll try to find an Orange Crush, probably canned
nowadays. The beautiful bear-brown bottle of my boyhood
would be too much to think of asking for.

(untitled)
William Harmon

oceanoceanocean

oceancanoeocean

oceanoceanocean

DETAIL DISSOLVES DESIGN
William Harmon

There being something wrong with everything,
let the perfectly austere utterances
come down willynilly from on high
like rain or Agamemnon's farewell bath
or what water the salt that was Lot's wife
draws from the moonshine perniciosa of the plain cities.

The highschool folklore turns out to be right:
wardrobe, complexion, personality
are all that matter, and mine, all three, are bad.

This house has state-of-the-art skylights
wherein convex tics lurk
like clocks in a dark workshop
clearing their throats of frogs
and making their smirking remarks
about dillers and dollars

while the nondescript anonymous rain
hits like Maris and Mantle in their great year.

Vulgar as all are in willed solitude
I turn up the volume on Wagner
which the convexities exaggerate
as presbyopia caricatures literacy:
footballs echo in the memory.
Being clean alone resembles being dirty.

I say, since so little is known or knowable,
I'll settle for knowing the price of everything
and the value of nothing. That would suit me.
I can't see the forest for the trees? Good.

selections from
A DANCE IN ARMOUR
Angela Davis-Gardner

1.

The osage orange tree hung over the tennis court. It was an enormous tree for its kind, perhaps fifty feet tall, and had a muscular trunk and limbs with bark of a greenish tinge. Its smaller limbs were pinked with forbidding thorns that kept others out and made the tree Beryl's fortress. Years ago her father Jack had built her a treehouse there; though this was nothing more than a platform bolted into the crotch of the largest, smoothest limbs, he liked to refer to it as The Second House That Jack Built (the first being the eccentric family dwelling he had designed, and which was known throughout Marshall County, North Carolina, as Fontaine's Folly).

In its first year, Beryl's refuge had been threatened when her brother Stevie, riding their pony Pegasus out of control beneath the osage orange tree, had been badly scratched by its thorns; he still bore a lightning-shaped scar above one eye where 18 stitches had been taken. Their mother Mem had declared the hazardous tree must come down, but Jack had silenced her arguments by simply lopping off its lower branches. Beryl remembered Jack's boasting to Mem that even if a full-grown centaur were to come cantering through the yard, not so much as a hair of its beard would be grazed by the now-decorous tree. About the oaks and maples in the yard,

186

most of them a-dangle with her consarned bird feeders, Jack could make no promises, but he had sure God taken proper prophylactic action against the tree of thorns.

Pruning seemed to have encouraged the osage orange, however; over the years its lower branches had grown back thicker and spinier than ever. Though this no longer presented a real danger to Stevie—the pony being long departed—it did make the upward route to Beryl's treehouse more perilous, but she was glad for that. It kept intruders out. And she knew the ritual for an unscathed ascension. This is how it went: Keep to the right on the first three steps (segments of sawed-off broom handle, these were no more than toe holds), shift to the left up the next six, inch sideways across the top step—keeping salamander-flat here, and whispering a word-potion (her current favorite being Nil illegitimi carborundum, or Don't let the bastards get you down, an expression that Jack, an irreverent professor of classics, had taught her). From this point on, it was an easy, thornless climb of two limbs to the right, one to the left (from which the outer line of the tennis court was in excellent spitting range) and once around the tree's circumference on a spiral staircase of branches and she was there, on the platform, inviolate in her lofty green sanctuary.

In late summer the osage orange tree produced its char-treuse, brain-shaped fruits; when ripe, the osage orange plopped into the long grass under the tree or fell onto the tennis court where they split and bled a thick, milky liquid. To Mem, the family's chief tennis enthusiast, this was one more strike against the tree, and each year, in the season of falling fruit, she launched another campaign to have the tree cut down, a barrage of arguments lobbed into the depths of Jack's invincible silence. What Jack did not say out loud—and thus made of it a more powerful statement—was that he was protecting Beryl's rights. Mem charged that Beryl clung to the tree just to spite her; though Beryl fumed against this, in her heart she knew that Mem's opposition to the odd tree increased her loyalty to it. By the time of her adolescence, Beryl had taken up residence in the osage orange as if she were its inhabitant nymph and her very existence depended upon its staying intact.

To her osage orange sanctuary in the summer of her fourteenth year, Beryl daily took her journal, the lavender, gold-nibbed fountain pen she had inherited from her grandmother, and a bottle of Skrip ink. In the journal she recorded the weekly list of Top Ten Tunes (with asterisks by all of Elvis Presley's hits); odes to the osage orange tree and to Pup Dog (P.D. for short), her black and white flop-eared companion who occasionally suffered being hauled up to the treehouse in Jack's army knapsack; and lyric descriptions of the pasture and pond behind the house and of the woods beyond. But that year it was what Beryl did not write in her journal that mattered most. Into the odes and descriptions, even into the rococo calligraphy with which she inscribed the Top Ten Tunes, she poured a passion deflected from elsewhere.

She did not, for instance, write down what she observed from her hideaway that summer.

When Beryl stretched out on her platform, she was all but invisible from below, her overhanging head as difficult to pick out, she imagined, as one of the hidden images in a puzzle drawing, yet she could see everything that happened on the tennis court and in the back yard. For years she had engaged in casual espionage, just because it was fun. One event she witnessed—it was the year Jack had built the treehouse—had even turned out to be profitable. She had spied her brother Stevie peeing against the trunk of her osage orange, which not only gave her a view of a penis, but it was an act for which she was still successfully blackmailing him. Whenever Stevie threatened to tell on Beryl (as last spring, when he found out that she was secretly meeting Zeke at Eunice's house) she needed only to say, "You do, and I'll tell about the time you peed on the osage orange." That he was silenced surely had less to do with the actual content of her sentence—at nine, he could have reasoned that this was not the heinous crime his sister made it out to be—than with the menacing quality of her voice, which, with its confident edge of superior years and experience, had given the threat an incantatory power.

Until this spring, Stevie had been the main object of her surveillance. Wearing the red satin superman cape Mem had made him, and wielding the fireplace poker, Stevie often stalked invisible enemies across the yard. When he got one cornered he called "En Garde!" (a term he'd learned from Jack, who had fenced in college) and began feinting and jousting with the air. Periodically he attacked the lilac bush, gripping the poker with both hands, flailing at the leaves and crying "Cha! Cha!" Though this made Beryl rock with muffled laughter, there was something sweet and sad in his bravado, and the back of his neck beneath the long, brush-cut hair looked vulnerable and forlorn, reminding her of the way his skin smelled: sad. And reminded her of the times he'd tried to follow her to the woods, or to Eunice's house, or up into the treehouse, and she'd shouted him back till he stood defeated, silent, his brown eyes huge and brimming with tears. There was more unalloyed pleasure in spying on Stevie when his friend J. T. came to play and they wrestled or hid behind the lilac bush with the book of nude photographs Mem thought she had successfully hidden behind the top row of books in her bedroom. Then Beryl watched with pure glee and a sense of power that reached its zenith when she one day spied Stevie and J. T. on the roof of the house and sent them scuttling back to the opened skylight by crying—her voice in the leaves disembodied and godlike—"Get back inside, you two!"

Then, one afternoon in early June, just after school was out for the year and Beryl had retreated to the osage orange tree to escape the boring party Mem and Jack were having inside the house, she heard a strange noise. Her first thought was that it was a cat in distress. But she looked down and saw Mackey Tull, Jack's pretty colleague in the classics department, crying by the chimney. In fact she held two fists against her eyes, rubbing them up and down in a way that was somehow reminiscent of a cat washing its face. Then around the corner came Jack. He rushed up to Mackey Tull and took her in his arms. It was like a movie, or a book. It was not anything Jack ever did with Mem. So this was what Mem had meant, Beryl realized with a shock that made her hold her breath, by her recent confidence that Jack was treacherous.

Jack took out his handkerchief—a big, wrinkled, pockety-smelling thing he always seemed to have, Beryl knew it well—and patted at Mackey Tull's face. Then he pulled her head to his chest—and she willingly submitted, her two paw-like hands against his shirt—and he stroked her blond hair. Beryl knew how his plaid-shirted chest smelled too, of soft clean cotton and pipe tobacco and apples, a mixture of odors that always reminded her of the long-ago mornings when she and Jack went together to feed Pegasus, just the two of them together, and afterwards he would sit her on the top rail of the fence and point out the beauties of the day. When she and Jack had gone back to the house those mornings, Mem had looked angry, her expression the same, Beryl now realized, as when she had lately called Jack treacherous. As Beryl looked at Mackey Tull's head against Jack's chest and for a moment imagined telling Mem, she knew she would not. So along with shock, and fear (that Jack might leave) and a jumble of other emotions Beryl would not have been able to describe, she also felt a certain amount of complicity that added to the fervor with which she watched—after that June day—the scene below her.

Beryl watched Mem's furious absorption in the geometry of bricks (she was building a patio by the back steps that summer), observing the ruthless efficiency with which she handled trowel and mortar, and the grim satisfaction she took in cementing down the bricks, as though sealing over the grave of something unspeakable. She watched Jack as he moved about the yard, digging, transplanting, pruning. A slender, ginger-haired man, his body was constantly in motion, but his closed face was hard to read. Poker face, Mem called it. Beryl had occasional glimpses of what she thought must be his true feelings when he walked about the yard on a tour of his shrubs; there was often a gentle smile upon his lips as he made his survey, picking off a brown leaf here or there, cupping a new bud in one palm. Occasionally he ran his hand along the underside of a fresh green branch with a sort of fluffing-out motion; then Beryl felt sure he was thinking of blond hair. As always, he sang when he worked, but instead of "I Wish That I Could Shimmy Like My Sister Kate" or "The Tatooed Lady" his songs were now of love. "It had to be you-u-u, wonderful you-u-u. . . ." On the high notes he sometimes broke into a harmonic trill that sounded magical, as though he, like one of the mortals in his beloved *Metamorphoses*, had suddenly been transformed into a paradisical bird.

Beryl paid particularly close attention to all activity on the tennis court, where the weekend matches seemed to have taken on significances that went far beyond tennis. The mixed doubles competitions seemed especially charged; unlike the games Mem played with her women friends, these were deadly serious. There was rarely any conversation, only the angry *thwock* of the ball as it traveled from racket to racket, and, between points, in a tone of simulated disinterest, a voice stating advantage: "Fifteen, love; thirty, love."

On the rare occasions that Mem and Jack teamed up together there was an iron silence between them, occasionally broken by an outburst from Mem such as *"Damn* it, Jack, that was my shot," when he rushed up to net, where Mem already was, and chopped the ball out of bounds. Jack didn't respond with words; instead, he would first wipe his forehead with his wristband—very very deliberately, and then, his jaw as rigid as though he were grinding down on a bit, he would take a ball from his pocket and bounce it slowly against the court. Mem would fume, but silently, chastened by the message of his posture: that he was communing with the inner source that gave him the strength to tolerate this woman.

Jack never played with Mackey Tull—the Southern belle type, she often watched from the sidelines, beneath a wide straw hat—but usually had as his partner one or another of his more athletic female students, whom he would compliment on a particularly good shot by calling out, "A *plus*, sweetie, A *plus*." That made Mem glower. Jack had several names for her, none of them anything like sweetie. It was he who had christened her Mem (short for Mem Sahib). He also called her Meddie (short for Medusa—in fun of course), and S. B. for Straw Boss, or, when he was angry, with ice in his voice, her real name, Kristin.

Mem's most frequent tennis partners were Dr. Kistler, chairman of her comparative literature department, a doddering old gentleman who had a habit of nervously hitching up his shorts between points, and Bernie Hoffman, a bearded sculptor who had just become artist-in-residence at Millbrook, the college where Mem and Jack both taught.

Mem and Bernie, both strong players, usually won as a team; when Jack and his partner did win, he cried out, in mock agony, "One more such victory, and I am lost!" Beryl understood the allusion, for Jack had explained when reading *The Iliad* aloud to her what a pyrrhic victory was, but she couldn't understand what Jack meant by being lost. Did he really love Mem after all, and not want her to be mad at him?

Bernie was the most puzzling factor in all this. Mother

sometimes flirted with him—very awkwardly, Beryl thought, even Eunice could have done better—calling out, "Way to go, handsome!" after a good shot, or simpering at him in a wholly uncharacteristic way, but only, it seemed, in retaliation for Jack's more debonair attentions to Mackey Tull. Yet Jack seemed affected by Mem's unsubtle attentions to Bernie. Jack was Bernie's friend and mentor—they had long, bourbon-laced conversations in which Jack advised Bernie, a self-described neo-classical sculptor, on the Greek mind and spirit. But behind Bernie's back Jack now called him the madras rabbit—with reference to the fabric of his shorts (everyone else wore regulation white on the court) and to his slightly buck teeth. And during the tennis matches Jack sometimes seemed to aim the ball right at Bernie, making him execute a quick, two-footed jump to one side, like the red-hots step in jump rope.

However, Mem seemed to grow angrier as the summer progressed, leading Beryl to conclude that the strategy of making Jack jealous wasn't working. One Sunday afternoon in mid-August Beryl watched from her leafy hideaway as Mem practiced her shots against the tennis court backboard. Mem was a tall, powerful woman with black and silver streaked hair—skunk hair, she said scornfully, whenever complimented on it. Stern-faced even in repose, Mem was always formidable, but never more so than when her eye was on the ball. Today, practicing, thinking herself unobserved, Mem's face simmered with inner vengeance, reminding Beryl of the Japanese Noh mask of the demon woman that hung above her mother's desk. As she socked the ball against the backboard without once letting it bounce—bam, bam, bam—Beryl could imagine the poor skin of Jack nailed there, flattened on the green scaling paint by the power of Mem's wrath.

Mem finally missed—a high backhand, her weakest shot. She stood glaring at the backboard as though to drill holes in it with her eyes, then suddenly slumped, letting her racket hang at her side; Beryl thought she was going to collapse into tears. Instead she began to walk in a circle, using the racket pressed against the court as a pivot. Around she went, faster and faster, and then—this ritual apparently having given her fresh strength—picked up a ball and served it into the opposite court, winding up and uncoiling with such force that the ball singed the net and pocked into the Har Tru surface of the court like a fired bullet. Grinning, Mem scuttled sideways, as though triumphantly positioning herself for a return she wouldn't have to make—for that serve would have aced any opponent—and, as she did, tripped on an osage orange lying at the edge of the court. She pitched forward, landed on a hand and one foot and was frozen there a moment, like an off-balance runner at the starting line.

Then Mem leapt up and kicked the offending osage orange, hissing "Son of a BITCH," with such venom that Beryl, like a turtle into its shell, drew back her head and lay very still on the platform. There was an ominous silence below—Beryl could sense Mem looking upward, her eyes piercing the cover of leaves—and then "Ber-yl. Ber-yl Fon-taine." To keep back the sound of what Mem would shout next, Beryl listened to the rustle of leaves about her and to the gentle, pendulum-like sway of osage oranges on their stems. So fiercely did she concentrate on the tree that instead of her own heartbeat it seemed she could hear the coursing of sap through the trunk to the very tips of the thorny branches, and when Mem called, "Beryl, get down here and pick up this trash off the court. I've warned you a hundred times. . . ." the voice seemed to travel from a great distance, faint and insubstantial, as from a remembered dream.

2.

Beryl's first journal—a ledger book she bought at Woolworth's after Zeke made his astonishing appearance in her life two years ago—had begun as a record of actual events and people. The first entry in her diary, as in Eunice's, was an account of that historic Friday night trip to the State Fair in Raleigh when they met Zeke and Wayne on the ferris wheel. The boys had thrown popcorn from the rocking chair just behind them, and when that ride was over—Eunice's mother Roxanne having gone off to look at the prize heifers and gilts —they had paired into couples for the next go-round. Eunice had later read Beryl her entry about Wayne, how he'd tickled her palm with one finger and asked if she'd ever "done anything." Zeke had been too gentlemanly for any such behavior, but when they stopped, swaying, at the very apex of the ferris wheel, he'd looked at Beryl in a serious way and said "Where y'all from?" Beryl had recorded that electric moment, and added a paragraph on the mysteries of fate: here they had gone all the way to Raleigh, and had met two darling older boys (both with drivers' licenses!) who lived just on the other side of their town, Marshall. Beryl had read Eunice that segment of her diary, but not the next (entitled "Full Moon Magic") about the first kiss, which had been consummated in the woods behind Eunice's house when Beryl was supposedly there just to spend the night with Eunice.

Eunice continued to read Beryl everything in her diary. This included all the vulgar expressions she knew, like "Boy Howdy, is that stud hung!" (this picked up from her mother, when a bull came to service her cows), and cheers. Eunice was a cheerleader in their county junior high, which didn't amount to much, as hardly anyone attended the games, but her ambition was to be a "big time cheerleader," that is, at Marshall High School. Beryl was often forced to watch Eunice practice as they held their woods conversations, Eunice gyrating her small hips as she shuffled back and forth across the pine straw, and muttering beneath her breath—interspersed with talk about Wayne, or clothes, or her favorite movie, *Gidget Goes Hawaiian*, starring Sandra Dee—"Whassa matter, can't ya take it, can't ya Carolina shake it, can't ya boogie to the left, can't ya boogie to the right, can't ya boogie to the center and FIGHT, FIGHT, FIGHT!"

Eunice's diary also featured a listing of hers and Beryl's good and bad points. Eunice's good list (naturally wavy blond hair, long eyelashes, peaches 'n cream complexion, short, looks like Sandra Dee) was much longer than her bad (nose a little crooked, boobs small but growing daily); her reckoning of Beryl's debits, on the other hand (skinny, tall, braces, eyelashes short and pale, zits, straight hair), far outweighed the assets (small feet, hair color ok if you like red).

In retaliation, Beryl composed her own evaluations of herself and Eunice. It was hard to come up with flaws for Eunice —she *was* maddeningly Sandra-Dee-like—beyond "talks too loud, pigeon-toed, legs too thick." "They are *not*," Eunice said of this last criticism, and bent over, hands at her waist, to inspect her sturdy, tanned legs. "Well, look at *mine.*" Beryl held out óne of her own legs, with the pointed-toe grace she'd picked up in Miss Sturgill's ballet class. "Miss Sturgill says I have very good ankles." In the positive assessment of herself, Beryl included (but did not read to Eunice, who would have scoffed) "intelligent, kind, thoughtful, fine sense of humor, hair *auburn*, not red, and has potential for being not just *cute*, but a *real beauty.*" (This last an extrapolation from Miss Sturgill's pronouncement that Beryl might be very pretty some day, when she grew out of that complexion, if only she would not *slouch* so.)

Beryl continued her journal in a realistic fashion for several months. There was a catalogue of Zeke's charms: hypnotic blue eyes, peroxided hair cut in a ducktail, large arm muscles, and a complete collection of Elvis Presley records. The records he played for her over the telephone, murmuring before each song, like some moon-struck disk jockey, "This one's for *you*, Sugar Lips," or "Honey, don't be crool." Beryl also wrote long jeremiads against Mem and Jack, who did not approve of Zeke. Jack characterized her suitor as "the chain gang swain"; Mem wanted to know if he spoke English. Beryl set down their words verbatim, and her own angry (though unspoken) responses.

But over time her journal had become partly a work of transformation, with certain important autobiographical details omitted or carefully disguised. There were several reasons for this. One was that Beryl suspected Stevie of being a snoop, since he had once shouted up into her tree, "Time for dinner, *sugar lips!*" and run away laughing maniacally. As there was no extension telephone to listen in on, there was no way Stevie could have known Zeke's pet name for her other than finding it in her journal—unless he had spied on them in Eunice's woods, which she wouldn't quite put past him either. At dinner, Beryl had accused Stevie of reading her journal. "Why do you think *that?*" Stevie had said with a sly grin. *He* knew she couldn't come out with the evidence—"sugar lips"— because Jack would be so furious Beryl wouldn't even be allowed to talk to Zeke on the phone again, much less see him. But Beryl had said, "I just *know*," in a convincing enough tone that Jack proceeded to give Stevie a lecture on privacy.

Beryl devised a booby trap of strategically placed scotch tape and hair pins to determine whether her journal, hidden in her underwear drawer, suffered any further violations. But even without Stevie to worry about, Beryl's journal would still have become less personal, for intimacy with Zeke began to involve her in acts too shameful to record. She had allowed him, more than once, to inch his trembling fingers beneath her shirt and her brassiere, arousing sensations that she relived at night beneath her covers, after which she fell into a heavy, guilt-drugged sleep. Unlike Eunice, Beryl found such incidents too sordid for admission, either in conversation or on paper.

Eunice even wrote about the time Wayne came in his pants on a Friday night date at the drive-in movie (a place strictly off limits to Beryl). "Come, Cum, Kum," Eunice and Beryl had written on the dirt floor of Eunice's woods, figuring out how to spell it for her diary entry.

One day later that fall, when Eunice was helping Beryl pick up osage oranges from the tennis court, Eunice whispered that the juice of the fruits felt and smelled just like Kum. This set the girls into such a paroxysm of giggles that Mem, who was on the other side of the court readying the Ball Boy for Stevie's practice lobs, narrowed her eyes at them suspiciously and told Eunice it was time for her to go home.

Later Mem told Beryl "I don't like that Eunice" (Mem always called her That Eunice as though Eunice were her middle name). "I think she's a sneak and a slut. I wish you'd find some better friends."

"Like who?" Beryl retorted. "There isn't anybody else, out here in the sticks."

Mem could only shrug: it was the truth. "Your father insists on living in this absurd place," she said, locking Beryl's eyes to her own by the formaldehyde of her gaze, an expression compounded of a beseeching woefulness and rage.

Another important factor in the evolution of Beryl's writing style was Jack's gift to her, last Christmas, of a new journal. A leather-bound volume with water-marked pages, it was too beautiful for recording any but the noblest thoughts. Beryl had continued to include The Top Ten Tunes, but with such elaborate borders of flowers, hearts and faces around each list that they resembled pages of an illuminated manuscript. Otherwise, the content became more determinedly elevated. That summer of her intense surveillance of Mem and Jack the few entries dealt in a general way with the tragic nature of life or described (often in rhymed couplets) the glories of nature.

Then, on August 17, 1957, this entry:
"Dearest, dearest Diary,
Ah, Love! Oh eyes of Michaelangelo! I am yours, forever and a day!"

The unchronicled event was this: Beryl had been summoned from her treehouse for dinner—none too patiently—by Mem. She had descended, fuming, and on the fourth step from the bottom had leapt, turning in mid-air—a feat she had executed many times with no ill consequence. Usually she landed bent-kneed, two-footed, in the grass. But this time she lost her balance and fell on her back. There was a moment of terror when she could not breathe, or cry out. Then Bernie was kneeling beside her, holding her wrist. "You're all right, you've just had the breath knocked out of you, but you'll be all right. Lovely girl, lovely girl." He stroked her arm. Beryl gasped and sat up. "See? You've returned to the element of air. You *are* a dryad, aren't you?" Bernie rocked back on his haunches, bouncing on his sneaker-clad feet, and grinned at her. His eyes, at once warm and piercing, made Beryl feel *seen*, a phenomenon that rendered her again nearly breathless.

"You dryads breathe some other aether than we mortals do—isn't that right?—and you just forgot. Here—may I help you up, lovely dryad? Or is it maenad? You could also pass for a sylphid, you know." He reached down to take her hands. Beryl had never felt so graceful before, as when she sprang toward him; it was like the beginning of a dance, a pas de deux. Then he dropped her hands and bent to pick up her journal. For a moment she feared he might open it, or make some comment, but he merely handed it to her—in such a *respectful* way, Beryl mused in her later replayings of this scene—and said, "Have you ever modeled? For an artist, I mean. I'm doing some little bronzes—a dryad would be a lovely subject."

Beryl still could not speak, but Bernie did not seem to mind. They walked in silence to the house, every fiber of

Beryl's being tingling with his approval. At dinner, the spaghetti tasted like manna. He smiled at her—twice—and once winked.

Afterwards she went to her room and looked up dryad in the dictionary. Although fairly certain of the definition, she wanted to hear Webster's authoritative judgment: "A maiden of the woods," she read, "A sylvan beauty."

Beryl leaned across her dressing table and gazed into the mirror. "Sylvan beauty," she whispered. In the dusk of her room, with the imperfections of her skin smoothed away, and her eyes glowing back at her, it seemed almost true.

A few days later—it was the morning of Labor Day, before school began on Tuesday—Bernie appeared as Beryl was clearing the tennis court of a windfall of osage oranges. Though she grumbled about it, this was a task Beryl secretly enjoyed: relishing the odor and pimply texture of each fruit as she gathered it, tossing each orange to the wheelbarrow up on the grass, and then trundling them to her grotto in the corner woods lot, where they made a fine acrid stench, rotting in a heap.

"Good morning, dryad. The mortals have you at work, I see." Bernie plucked an osage orange from the wheelbarrow and tossed it in his hand. He was dressed for tennis, in the usual madras shorts, t-shirt, woolly socks and dirty white tennis shoes. "This is such a peculiar tree you inhabit. What is the name the earthlings have given it?"

"Macluara pomifera. Osage orange. Native to the Southern U.S. Makes a handsome screen."

"Where did you learn all that, dryad? Quite the scholar, aren't you?"

Bernie gave her that close look again, quickening her breath. She was surprised to hear herself go on in a steady voice, "The fruits are actually useful, even if my mother doesn't think so. The Indians ate them—so could we, if there's ever another Depression. And the wood makes excellent wheels and bows. Maybe even sculpture," she added, trying out a coy tone.

"Hmm." He glanced up into the tree, then back at Beryl, with a grin that made her face go hot. "But you wouldn't want a limb cut, would you, dryad?"

"Maybe for *you*," Beryl said, walking brazenly to stand beside him. When he looked down at her and she didn't know what to do with her eyes or hands, she stooped to pick up an osage orange from the court and sniffed it. "I like the smell, don't you?"

Bernie bent to smell the fruit in her hand, not the one in his; his closeness made Beryl's heart thump so loud she was afraid he must hear it. "Strange," he mused, straightening, scratching one forefinger deep in his beard. "Strange, but familiar."

"Yes," Beryl managed to whisper, suddenly remembering Eunice's comparison, and so that he would not see her face aflame, bounded up the tennis court steps, grabbed the handles of the half-filled wheelbarrow and raced it toward the woods lot.

"Capricious, these little goddesses," Bernie's teasing voice lilted after her. "Beyond the ken of we mere mortals."

Beryl moved in a sensual glow all that day. The air did seem aether, and her limbs warm and graceful, as though not blood but ichor flowed in her veins.

That evening there was a Labor Day picnic in the Fontaines' yard. Eunice came over before supper with a sack full of her mother's make-up (it being Eunice's intention to improve Beryl's appearance for high school). As the two girls sat crowded together on Beryl's dressing table seat, drawing on lips and brows and painting mauve crescents above their eyes, Beryl, compelled by passion to speak of Him in any context, told Eunice about Bernie's reaction to the odor of the osage orange.

"Strange but familiar!" Eunice yelped, then doubled over with laughter. Beryl began to laugh too, spurring Eunice on to greater merriment. As they continued to laugh, looking at each other in the mirror, they became swept into one of those laughing fits that nothing—not even a glare from the Pentecostal Holiness preacher, whose church Beryl had once attended with Eunice and her parents—could stop before it ran its natural course. In Beryl's laughter was excitement and release; but Eunice's hysteria, Beryl realized as she began to sober, had something mean in it. "Strange but familiar," Eunice gurgled. "I guess he's such a queer, like Mama says, that he's hardly ever smelt any."

"He's not a queer." Beryl jumped up. "I've got to go help my mother."

"Mama says half the people who hang around here are queers and commies," Eunice said as she followed Beryl down the stairs. "And how do you know *he's* not a queer. Heh heh."

"Shut up, Eunice. You've got a filthy mouth, just like my mother says."

They went separate ways, Beryl to the kitchen to make potato salad, Eunice outside to sulk. But Eunice was not one to hold grudges, and when they all sat down to supper on the patio—the adults at the picnic table and the girls, Stevie and J. T. at a nearby card table—she behaved as though nothing had happened.

All through the fried chicken, corn on the cob and potato salad, Eunice chattered about the new outfits her mother had bought her for school, and her quandary about which to wear for cheerleader tryouts. Beryl, eyes on her plate, barely attended to Eunice or to Stevie and J. T. (who, having earlier filled up on cookies, were now spitting watermelon seeds at each other and the girls), for she was listening to the carillon of voices at the next table.

Mackey Tull had a soprano voice and a fake-sounding laugh that was inevitably set off by Jack's short, deep-toned comments. Mem talked in a tired monotone, sounding as though she pushed her comments along without much interest or belief in them. The pair of anthropologists, male and female, ursine in appearance, also sounded like bears, Beryl decided. But the voice she listened for was Bernie's. When he spoke, she stopped chewing, stopped breathing: yes, it was a tenor voice, with more variations up and down scale than Jack's, but distinctly, decidedly male.

There was no communication between the two tables until dessert, when Eunice took a huge bite of coconut cake and cried, "Yum *yum*! Strange but familiar!"

Beryl kicked Eunice under the table and looked at Bernie to see if he had heard. He had: his glance was quizzical—and, Beryl thought, hurt. But he looked away and unconcernedly poured himself more wine. Oh God, Beryl cried inwardly, he thinks I am a *child*!

Eunice was laughing now, splattering cake. Mem fixed a

glare on Eunice, then Beryl.

"Beryl Fontaine, what's that junk on your face? You look like a clown. You go wash it off right after you finish, you hear?"

Beryl aimed a parting kick at Eunice and missed—Stevie yelled—flung back her chair, ran upstairs to her room, and took out her journal. For want of moveable heavy furniture (the room was designed so that all the main pieces were built in) she barricaded the door with her own body, and wrote, "Eunice is a stinky slut and our friendship is over, over, OVER."

Then, wincing at the exposure of such a raw sentiment, Beryl inked it out, going over and over the words with her pen. The resulting long black bar—and its ghostly stain on the next page, otherwise left blank—marked an important transition in her journal. What followed was fiction. ∎

AN ESSAY IN POLITICAL SCIENCE
Paul Jones

All day the ibis stalk in eel grass,
their legs gauging moon's pull
on the marsh. Even if we wished,
we could not force them
to gather. They disperse
more evenly than their prey.
Occasionally, fish pool
just beneath one of them
or a nest of turtles boils
open with young. Still they honor
territory. If they compete
they do so warily, without
gaggle of gull or dive of hawk.
The tilt of one's beak conforms to the weave
of grasses. Another seems wingless
as it stands like a strange knot
of tufted reed. When they rise,
each choosing its own time,
light softens as if rough gauze
drapes the sky. Now the dark
condenses them. The mangrove lump
which in daylight confused our view
whitens as they disguise the branches.
The entire marsh appears reduced
to a solitary ibis at low tide.
Here by the rookery, I want to turn to you
and talk about the value of nations,
but already the ibis are only vaguely luminous.

As their voices quiet,
we hear a meek quaver
tremble through the reeds
with the restless hesitation
of an old woman alone at night.

FRAGGING SAN JUAN
Ronald H. Bayes

Vendig Street's well named
with ten bucks for a quickie
& daylight muggings.

&
Taking flight Christmas Eve, the drunken host
off. . . . off . . . & away off the top
of his condominium
on a skate board
from the 14th floor
spoilt the party at Isla Verde.
"No Rudolpheven,"
the dude from DC said, "caught him
on a fly-by."

& about two hours later, or could it have been
simultaneous souls taking flight (?),
the art critic stabbed to death,
El Mirador (also Condado area).
Body found at 10 a.m., Christmas Day.
God rest ye, Villa Del Mare Oeste (Oreste!).

Three robbings & a fake bomb
in a gaily
wrapped parcel. And, Don,
another unwise man, near noon, carrying jewels,
shot dead
by two other unwise men who
sold them to him
then used the retrieval methods (*supra*).
"Gold I bring, Frank."

O Ponce, when you were Guv
did such things go on?
Did you?
You who finally got it like Harold
of The Saxons
with an arrow
with an arrow went your fountain
of youth dripdrip

& most of us fools in that pursuit.
All, I dare say,
of the above and the
undersigned too, one way or
another
like the arrow to.

A DREAM OF LIONS
Chuck Sullivan

When a lion stalked about the moonlit
dark of their kraal the warriors
of the Masai were amazed at the tawny nerve
of the beast they would never fear
until magic skilled him to roast his own meat
and so the bright-belled warriors would burst
for dawn to break so that they might
charm the sun to lighten their chase
to teach the King of the Jungle his place

Pointless warriors the new law has made
to chase in place
hunters now in only heart and name
These still are the primal legions of leaping
bodies ever one with the earth they leave
These are the chosen noble of the tribe
their flesh red with ochre
and a dazzle of rainbow beads
These are the honor-keepers of war
in peace wed unto death to the checked
gleam of their weapon-feathered spears
These are the young watchmen of the lost
ways of lion hunts and cattle raids
These are the anointed beast-starved boys
linked in shining leonine pairs proud
comrades bound in ritual arms guarding
the lamb within each other hunting
girls and games only able to dream of lions
praying the old prayer saying:

God, bird of prey, guide me
On this hunt
For if I am not killed
I will kill
And You with hungry wings
Will fall from heaven always
Having one of us to feed upon

As in the feast of El Salvador's
ritually gunned-down nuns
their flesh habits of grace riddled
with the peace-keeping force
of the State in that split land claimed
for the Savior from which still comes
yet another torn eyewitness account of a mother
calling to account the day when the sun sunk
faceless as a flaming victim bobbing between
the power lines behind the dying tourist
hotels where suddenly she found herself
Prey to a stark green camoflauge pride
of young combat-booted lions stalking
her as she knelt to pray beside her carrion
son the meat of his face roasted skillfully
to the bone his Confirmation cross of gold
snapped from his neck and dangling
from the trigger of the first rifle
that struck her face as the beastly
boys with fangs and claws toyed
with her prayers and teased her screams
saying:
                "Touch him! He's still warm, Mama!"

Taunting as they pawed and tore her black
well-worn dress butted her breasts

and fell to making mad passionate love
to her in front and back
of God and everyone spearing her one
by one first with the sweating points
of their featherless warrior selves
and then with the gleaming
barrels of their unpaid for American guns

(untilted)
Steven Lautermilch

I have been thinking of that sweater, your body. The barbaric luxury
of your hair, the curls and tight rings of yellow brown lit by the sun behind
your head, even the fine hairs at the edges of your ears are always lit and
taking fire from the wash of the day. I swear even now I can see the smooth
skin of your neck, rippling where it branches down and out into the small ridges
and hills of your shoulders, the valleys and caves of your throat, your collar
bone.

These mornings of early winter the sheerest of fogs spread over the creek
and creek banks beyond my apartment, this two-story townhouse of two bedrooms,
one livingroom, and the room I keep for writing and meditation. When I wake,
the water that is the frozen ground, the flowing creek, and the mist around the
pine trees is a floating shimmer of muslin so fine it is as soft and permeable
with lights as the air.

And it lifts, like the air, with the sun, as I make my prayers, make my
breakfast, make my bed.

My friend, I cannot decide which image of you I know best. The tendons of
your upper arms, your forearms, rippling as you move to the plate, warming up,
swinging the two or three warclubs. Or the weightlessness of your legs,
your back, your wrist and outstretched glove as you float at the top of your jump,
snagging the long fly deep into center field.

Or this old, cotton warm-up shirt that hangs to one side of my closet, the
three-quarter-length sleeves black against the white body, limp, a fall of loose
folds.

RACE WAR
Charles Fort

We are carnal sinners blown about forever
like Hell proper's *Paolo* and *Francesca*.
We are face to face. We are reaching out
but we are not alive anymore, nothing like love
here tonight between races that moan, rocks that rise,
and a kindness that wounds and aches and whimpers.
This is a moment in history that refuses
to sit still, and our hands become great serpents
in a battle without victory. In this southern town
we exchange blows on our shapeless faces
until our eyes meet like playmates in a meadow.
We are children of circumstance, slave ships and reckless stars,
and there are few hours left in this world that *we may rise*
on stepping stones taking our dead selves to higher things.
We lead each other away from each other
odd and sightless creatures.
This moment is against us. Ripe and cunning,
earth is not sufficient and earth is our only companion.

*lines 15 (we may rise) and 16 (on stepping) from Tennyson's *In Memoriam*

BLACK AND WHITE
Mary Kratt

The preacher who urged risktaking
isn't with me the day
I walk the empty hall
to the art center darkroom,
find the black man
timing his prints in the developing tray.
I am a white woman who thinks she has
so much to lose, who was warned
so early she cannot remember.
And he is very tall there tilting trays,
moving a picture back and forth in liquid.
I am a moment without defenses
like a woman unpinning her hair.
By the dim safelight I begin,
hoping it is
safe to share this close, shadowy room,
conjuring images lured outside
into cameras, our curious, handheld eye.

Like an answer,
her face slowly rises
from chemical paper,
old woman looking all possible kindness,
shapeless dress,
armchair in front of a stove.
The calendar on her wall finally reads April.

All these buoyant pictures,
lines of noses, hands, leaves, the Hotpoint
stove behind his grandmother,
she in the room with us floating,
her eyes.

CULPEPPER CONTEMPLATES ART
J. W. Rivers

Lounging in a wheelbarrow,
he studies photographs
of Moorish architecture,
spies Alberta beneath an ogival arch.
Her face is veiled, her arms
are outstretched toward him.

He opens a book of love poems
translated from the Chinese,
finds illustrations of Alberta
entertaining a war lord.

On a fresco from Minoan Crete
she pets a he-goat.

Naked on a stamp from Knossos
she stands flanked by lions.

On a terracotta medallion from Athens
she holds a whip and poses with a stag.

On a vase fragment from Samothrace
she performs a dance with bulls.

        *   *   *   *   *   *   *

Like a surreal image,
with an armful of collected vines,
Alberta comes out of the swamp.

How svelte, he thinks
as she plods toward him through mud;
how nubile, how much like a sylph.

She stops beside him,
grabs a shaft,
dumps him into manure.
Depositing her vines in the wheelbarrow,
she wanders off like the Muse.

THE POST OFFICE
Robert Fromberg

Sunday evening, late June. Two cars pass with suitcases strapped to the top, one with a canoe—people coming home from a weekend at the beach. He sees a red cloud ahead. He presumes the sun is behind it, just below the horizon, but that seems wrong, since he is certain he is heading east, not west.

He is driving to the post office with a letter that he thinks may need more than one stamp. He will need to weigh it, and to get the stamps out of the machine. When he is finished at the post office, he will go home and make his lunch for work the next day.

He does not mind work—he would just as soon spend his days there as anywhere. The company is called Public Research Associates. His work is codifying charters and ordinances. He also has been looking through old letters and newspaper clippings, gathering information for a history of the state's Municipalities Coalition. He enjoys the work, organizing, cataloguing, and especially the old letters. One said:

"My purpose in writing is to inquire if the body is a live organization. It seems to me that there is a present necessity for calling its possibilities into activity, and it seems to me that a meeting should be called at no distant day; and that there should be enough interest in the matter to command a large attendance . . ."

This is one of his favorite letters, though there are many

other facts and stories he likes. For instance, Friday he discovered that many years ago the general counsel of the Municipalities Coalition resigned "to temporarily leave the legal profession and tour the country with a musical comedy nightclub band." That was an interesting event to uncover, though he doubted it would fit very well into the history.

At the post office he finds the stamp machine is out of order. This has happened to him before; once he wrote a note which he hung on the knob: Why Does This Machine Never Work When You Need It? Now he is not in as angry a mood. He gets back in his car and starts for the post office in the nearest town—eight miles away.

Driving, he finds himself paying closer attention than usual to many things. The red cloud. The cars and luggage. At a fork in the road he sees an exit sign whose arrow always pointed right now is pointing left. He hears himself say, as though to someone sitting beside him, "Notice that sign."

He studies the other cars on the highway—their color, size, bumper stickers, license plates. One car passes him moving very quickly. He speeds up in order to see it better. It is an orange Volkswagen with a bumper sticker that says: Peace With Christ. Its license plate is XXP 222.

He is beginning to feel excited, looking at so many things, and he thinks about a way to stop it. He turns on the radio, adjusts the knob to find a station, and tries to pay attention to that.

The letter he is going to mail is to a girl he had known several years ago in another city. One year the letters on her license plate were ACE. The next year they were NUM. He used to talk to her about that, but she was never very interested. Sometimes he would put notes on her windshield addressed to NUM or ACE.

He hasn't seen her since he moved, but she surprised him by writing regularly, and he always writes back, afraid that if he doesn't, she won't write again. He is always dissatisfied with his letters. They seem cool, matter-of-fact, just telling a bit about work, a bit about movies or television. His letters feel awkward and insubstantial.

Her letters sound as though she is in pain. She talks about her feelings that week or month—insecurities, problems with her husband or her friends. Along with these letters, to cover everyday events, she sends one and two page sketches with titles like: "Janet Walks In The Park," "Janet Writes A Poem," "At The Psychologist's Office," "Janet Turns Thirty." She always starts with the general title, "Adventures With Janet." These are simple, plain, confident descriptions of events and encounters. In the last letter, though, she did not send any of these stories. Instead, it seemed she had tried to include one in the text of the letter. She told of a visit to a fortune teller. It was a beautiful description, he thought, a little shaky, a little unsure. She mentioned a color television set playing in one corner of the room, then said, no, that a television was there, but it wasn't on and she didn't know whether it was color or black and white. She wrote that on a table beside her were pieces of Asian pottery, but again corrected herself, saying she knew nothing about pottery, so why was she saying these pieces were Asian? The fortune teller said she would have a short period of misfortune, then a period of contentment. She wrote: "I must have looked like I couldn't take very much bad news."

He finds it impossible to imagine anything in the future. For instance, when he is driving to work in the morning he cannot imagine that the day will end. He can't even imagine getting to work. He can only see the driving he is doing at that moment.

However, he recalls the past easily, plays it through his mind. This afternoon he watched a baseball game: the Atlanta Braves and the Cincinnati Reds. He enjoys the specificity of baseball—"a game of inches" the announcers always say, and it is true. An inch can mean a foul ball or a game-winning triple down the right field line, a strike on the outside corner or ball four. And the umpires' decisions are always definite, irrevocable.

This afternoon the Braves' pitcher was Pete Falcone. He has a good curve ball and slider, but often has trouble controlling his pitches. It is a problem of concentration, the announcers say; he has to keep the ball lower in the strike zone. He looks like a serious, but nervous man. Usually he works very slowly, always pausing to walk a few steps and wipe his face between pitches.

Today he had good control: he kept the ball low and worked much more quickly. In a full nine innings he gave up only five hits and no runs. It was his third good outing in a row, but he did not look any more confident while pitching.

He enjoyed watching that game, and now finds himself looking forward to reading about it in the newspaper. And after work tomorrow there will be another game to watch.

He works in a room with an older woman and a girl about his age. On Friday afternoon they ran out of work. Penny, the girl, said she wanted to go to the beach that weekend, rent a cabin and swim, but she didn't have the money. "Give me some of your paycheck, Ann," she said to the woman.

"I got doctor bills and hospital bills to pay," Ann said, "and no money left for you."

Ann pushed her chair away from the desk and got out a novel—what she called her sex book. Penny opened the paper to the want ads. She studied that for a while, every so often interrupting Ann when she found a business she thought they should buy—a small restaurant or a group of cottages.

Earlier in the day Ann had received a phone call, then whispered to Penny to come with her into the hall. They talked there for several minutes, and the rest of the morning rarely spoke above an undertone. Once he heard Penny say, "Now don't start worrying until you're absolutely sure." Later Ann said, "You know she's all I've got." In the afternoon they stopped whispering, and Ann seemed less frightened. He assumed the problem was resolved.

A half hour before the end of the day Ann put down her book and asked Penny how her grandmother was doing.

"Okay," she said. "The operation went fine."

"Good."

"She was funny last night, though. She kept asking Mom and me to get her checkbook for her. When we finally did, she wrote Mom a check for a thousand dollars and me one for five hundred. She kept saying that she was going to die and she wanted us to have some money. But she said, 'Don't cash those until I get home and move some money into my checking account.'"

The last time he and Janet were together was at a museum. He was excited, fascinated by a group of abstract paintings. Janet said she didn't like them, and he talked and gestured, trying to bring her around to his point of view. He was hungry and his legs were tired, but he didn't want to leave the museum. Janet, blinking her eyes quickly and biting her lower lip, asked if they could go. "There's no air in here," she said.

"Yes, of course." He understood her reaction, because it would normally be his. He dislikes things that interest him or excite him. He prefers entertainment that is slow, steady—like golf or baseball on television.

They drove through many blocks looking for a nice place to sit and have a drink or snack. She described her house, the area where she lived—places he had never been. He listened closely, but seemed to forget the details as soon as he heard them. Was the house one story or two? Brick, redwood? Her husband?

He is reading the signs as he passes businesses on the out-skirts of the town. One advertises "Tire Trueing." He has never heard that phrase and is not sure he likes it. A sign he appreciates more is bright red, in the shape of a sink, and is still lit though the shop is closed. The name on the sign is "Blau Sudden Service Plumbing."

He looks forward to seeing the post office again. It is a small, old, brick building across the street from a shopping center. The building is so small that he imagines every inch of space is needed and used. He wishes his apartment was that way, but no matter what he brings home, there always seems to be extra space—especially around the TV, which sits on a small table in the center of the living room.

Now he remembers the announcers on the TV this after-noon during the game. They spent time telling funny stories about when they were both working for radio stations. One announcer said, "John, do you suppose anyone in the world has as much fun as you and I do?"

At work, Penny uses many words and phrases he is un-
familiar with, among them "kingfish" and "Hollyrock." King-
fish, he decided after a week or so, was like "top dog" or
"big gun." He had some difficulty deciding about Hollyrock.
She would say "Miss Hollyrock" instead of "Miss America."
Or, "Bill, you drive your new Hollyrock car today?" Finally
he asked, and she explained. On a cartoon set in the stone age
called The Flintstones, the name used for Hollywood is Holly-
rock. So when Penny wants to refer to something that is high
class but not particularly substantial, she says Hollyrock. He
asked her if she made that up—he had never heard anyone
else use it—and she said that she guessed so. He told her he
was impressed.

Penny also tells many stories. On Friday after the story
about her grandmother, she told about the funeral of one of
her uncles. Penny cried all during the service, and was still try-
ing to control herself as everyone got into cars for the proces-
sion to the cemetery. In front of her, in an expensive yellow
dress, was a loud, pompous aunt whom she hated. The aunt
got into the car, and Penny watched as she shut the door on
her dress, leaving the hem to drag through the mud and along
the highway all the way to the cemetery. Penny began laugh-
ing and couldn't stop until the procession was over.

After that story they were all quiet for a while. He leaned
his head back and closed his eyes, something he had been do-
ing off and on all day.

"Tired?" Penny said.

"I didn't get enough sleep. All night I was dreaming that I
was a shortstop. I kept telling myself that I had to wake up
or I wouldn't be able to make the plays. Then I woke up and
couldn't get back to sleep."

Penny asked, "Did you ever play baseball?"

"No."

"Then I wonder why you like it so much."

"I don't know."

At the post office he weighs the letter, sees that it needs

two stamps, and gets them from the machine. He is still thinking about the last time he and Janet saw each other, about stopping for a drink after they left the museum. He was trying to explain the advantages of having both his parents dead. "It's like having a clean slate," he said, "like all the terrible things you've done to them have disappeared."

She looked down at her glass. In a moment she said, "You're an awful person." She glanced up. "No. No, you're not. But other people might think you are."

Before putting the letter in the slot, he pauses, remembering what he wrote. Though it is a long letter, he is not satisfied. He wishes there was more feeling in it. In her last letter, Janet complained about not being able to accept praise, not believing compliments. He walks to a table where a pen is attached with a chain, and turns the envelope over to its blank side. He writes: "Heartfelt praise enclosed." Now satisfied, he puts the letter through the slot. ■

LADDER
Del Marie Rogers

A ladder is lying on its side in wet grass.
The sun's arrow, it leads into the earth.

It rests, calm as a hospital patient,
paint peeling from its skin:

the man has surrendered to night,
his eyes drift out the window.

I am no longer here, I watch the sun,
it moves along stripped wood.

Come with me, get a good grip, use both hands,
you are climbing downward—

when you reach the last step you will be near
the door to a room under our world of surfaces.

Birds light on the cloud-grey steps,
they leave their shadows fluttering on empty footholds.

THE SPIRIT LAUGHING
James Gurley

Like a whale with his mouth locked open,
I swallow more and more—
first I draw a line, a universe,
a language recovered
with charcoal. I make the canvas
a laughing man, the beauty
of a model's thigh,
a necktie and a scarf tossed
carelessly on a sofa.
Nothing is lost: not the chain
around a woman's neck,
it's a live thing—a gesture
of her dress billowed in wind.
I swallow the beautiful street,
the houses and windows opening,
the sky stretching down
enveloping me: a model
and the canvas blossoms
with sun into the glimpse
of a body under loose fabric,
a couple embracing,
I go on all day like this
with my impatient line
remembering the syllables of the body,
the power of a whale churning
unfathomed waves.

feet to dance
Will Inman

for Lloyd, with thanks

he stood in my face and spoke quietly
said i was making too narrow a path
that we in america need to expose ourselves
to all cultures, to widen ourselves, to dilate

then he put his cassette playing
a quiet jazz number   with strings
some unshrill horns   a low bucking run, a shifting
of earth
            even under feet too stiff to dance
asked me if that music drained me i said yes
he cut it off i was relieved but sad i needed his
self-assertion
                more than i needed not to be drained
i can fill up soon enough my silence sings
                                    but he
has so much room in him this quiet between us
cannot still his eyes his space
can hold even my narrowness he knows in his hands
what reaches over and beyond

i do not force myself to like what i don't like
but what moves in him i can't hear does not wait
for my knees to bend or my ears
to widen to and something deep in me
dances laughing to that

MARIGOLDS, WAR AND THERMA ANN
Ruth Moose

I have argued with that woman, and argued with that woman, but when she gets Shasta Daisies planted in her brain, there's no uprooting them.

"They fall over," I told her. Little spindly things. Nothing to them but a stem and blotch of yellow fuzz. She won't hear it.

"Therma Ann," I said, "You're going to split the garden club right down the middle. You're going to turn friend against friend, neighbor against neighbor and preacher against preacher." She won't hear it. Goes traipsing around to the Lion's Club, the Wednesday Night Men's Fish Supper and who knows what all with her little rolled-up drawings. Loves for them to say what a wonderful job the ladies in this town are doing to make it a better place to live. Acts like she thought of it all by herself and is doing it single-handed. That garden club has been selling Chocolate Nut Crumbles and Pecan Pralines-in-a-Can for the last six months. Fronnie Everlaid is so mad she's not speaking to half the members. Said they knew when they voted that she had never been able to resist chocolate in any way, shape or form. They made her drop Weight Watchers. Said they saw she was losing and couldn't stand it. I said the rest of them could have sold candy . . . she didn't have to. Nobody held her arms and made her. I tried to get them to order stationery. It's harder to sell, but not impossible.

They said it wasn't something people had to have and there wouldn't be repeat orders, and besides, nobody in this town wrote letters anyway. I said, well, why don't we just close down the post office, too, but nobody heard me.

This town is dead enough as it is. We don't need any more empty buildings to sit and run down. If it wasn't for the bank, drugstore, hardware and Baptist Church, we could close up shop. Strike Eddysville off the map . . . if it's on any. I'm the only business still open on my side of the street and it's awful. Those empty stores attract mice and who knows what all slips in from the back alley?

I remember when this town had four hardwares, an FCX and six churches. There was a dress store in every block, three dime stores and more shoe stores than you could get into on a Saturday . . . if you tried on a pair each place. I have known Saturdays when you had to park a mile from the square. When you saw *everybody* . . . neighbors, cousins, preachers . . . people you hadn't seen since the last funeral.

The shopping center will ruin a county I've always heard. They put in a chain department store, drug store and hamburger drive in, run the local businesses out. Joe's Grill had been on the lot behind the jail for twenty-five years. Wasn't big enough to stump your toe in, but Joe could cook with his eyes closed. He made the best fried egg sandwiches in town.

I ate one every day of my life as long as he was in business, except Sundays, and then when I had a funeral. Ten o'clock sharp, Joe would send whoever happened to be passing, around with my order and throw in a fried pie. I don't know how that man stayed in business. Sometimes I don't know how any of us does, with the way people in this town like to take their business elsewhere. Not to the one who is your neighbor and best friend and does the job best at the cheapest price, but for no reason. Whim. Fickle. I have had to face the truth that people will listen to somebody talk a fast streak and smile a lot even if she is wearing a five year old 100% polyester dress most of us threw out years ago. Mine was made from the same pattern, Simplicity #6066, but I pushed it to the back of the closet and forgot it. Some people don't keep up . . . won't keep up, whether it's clothes or other things. I say if they don't *see* fashion, how can they *see* something as complicated as landscape design. That's what this boils down to . . . landscape design.

Not many towns this size have two entrances and one exit. You have to keep that in mind. Marigolds, I said. You can depend on marigolds. Nothing touches them. Not dry weather, not rot, not mildew, not mealey bugs. I've worked in flowers half my life and I know my Abelia, my Pittosporum, my hollies, and my Buxus from a name on the page. Why can't people trust a trained eye? I know daisies and design. I *see* them. And trouble.

Every year I take two days off, close my shop and go to Convention. No telling how much business I lose. Don't anybody die the second week in July, I tell people. Because Lallah Carpenter won't be here to help you out. I gas my station wagon, run up motel bills you wouldn't believe and come back with it loaded to the rims.

I see to it personally that people in this town hold up their heads with the best of them when it comes to weddings and funerals. I was the first to go with artificial flowers . . . nobody called them that but those of us in the floral industry . . . and they almost took over. Silk flowers? When they started, I filled my shelves with every color rose and carnation made, blue, black and orange if they wanted them. I was the first to make bridal bouquets in silk flowers "for keeping" and I've looked the other way when some have been used twice.

I know how to put on a wedding. People give me credit for that. Women who wouldn't speak to you if you ran over them in the street, will come calling when their Janey or Susan or Mona Rae starts thinking wedding. Asking what dates I have open. I got lace cloths and secret wedding punch recipes nobody can touch. And I have sugar flowers put on my wedding cakes. Those little bride and grooms are overdone, I tell my people. Flowers are my middle name. Sometimes I dream them all night long. Arrange them in my sleep, take orders and deliver. It's not a business you can let go at the end of a day.

Especially the funeral part. After the preacher, I'm the next to know. And I do a good job. Nobody has ever said they didn't get their money's worth on a neighborhood wreath. There are families in this town who won't let a permanent arrangement in their door. And those who welcome them for every holiday in the year. People appreciate your knowing things like that.

My sweet daddy-in-law was the one who got me into this business. I always had a way with plants. What I couldn't grow, nobody could. After my first husband left, I had nothing but little Tommy to look after, my daddy-in-law and a yard full of flowers. Plus every house plant you could name.

"You could start a business," he said one morning making his way to the breakfast table. We always drank coffee together. That was one thing he taught me. I'd never touched a drop in my life until I married Tom Dickinson and he brought his daddy to live with us. Now I can't do without it. Can't find one hand with the other until I have my first cup. So Daddy Bell was the one who started me off. And the business has been running, nights, days and weekends since.

Everybody in the garden club said I was the one with the natural green thumb. For awhile I thought of calling myself that, but it sounded too much like plants and shrubs and nursery. So I ended up with "Budding Beauty" because I could see the B's with two big loops.

I can *see* things, that's what I tried to tell the garden club after their civic beautification committee came calling . . . after they'd asked Therma Ann to draw up their plans. If they'd come to me first I could have saved a lot of heart ache and heart break. But no, they go to Therma Ann. Let her make some little chicken scratches on paper, put color over them and get everybody excited.

For somebody who has never had a single art lesson in her life, she does draw a straight line. With a ruler. And the brick entranceway with "Welcome to Eddysville" looked good when you realized how bare that place was, Highway #701 is not your heavily traveled road. Thank goodness, I say. But it is two-laned and paved and we have a stop light.

There wasn't an evergreen in the plan, but did I point that out? I did not. I was the soul of sweetness. They said bricks had been donated and Therma's husband offered to lay them free. I said be sure he works on a day when he's . . . ah . . . feeling well. I did not mention his drinking habits which everyone knows, but if they don't watch him every minute . . . stand right out there . . . they'll get a wall crooked as that bend in the road to the river.

And little gas lamps? Donated too. And weren't they tickled? I asked if anyone had considered electricity? Something not quite so eternal, but could be turned on and off. They have lights burning all the time and while it may look friendly and welcome-to-our-townish, somebody will complain, cry taxpayers money, even if it's not.

Too late to change their minds, I could see that. All them acting like hens on a nest of Easter eggs. Jelly beans, I started to say, but didn't. Wasn't going to shoot off my mouth to anybody who would listen. Those things come home to sit on your mantel and roost. Therma Ann ought to know.

She was the one calling the baby premature when it came two months too soon. Nine pounds? All along I said it didn't matter if things were hurried up. Of course I wanted, and expected Tommy Lee to finish school before marriage, maybe take a course in mechanics if he wanted too, but I have learned with children what you want and what you get, aren't always the same things. I said boys will be boys . . . especially if girls let them. Make the best of it, I said when they told me. You weren't the first and you won't be the last. It's nothing new, since Adam and Eve and nothing to be ashamed of.

I was the one who insisted on a church wedding though. Every girl needs a memory like that in the back of her life, I told Rita. It will mean more to you as time passes. And Tommy Lee agreed when I mentioned the showers for Rita and bachelor party for him. He didn't mind waiting a few weeks until we could get things in the works. I think he'd still be waiting if it was up to him. But he's like me. We make the best of things. And more.

I mean how many mothers of the groom do you know who plan, direct and pay for the whole wedding? While Therma Ann is in the background the whole time pushing them to go across the state line to Cheraw so she can fudge the date a little if she has to. And she did. She was scared to death Rita would show walking down that aisle. She wouldn't have been the first. I expect to see bridal gowns in the maternity shops any day now. It wasn't anything the town didn't already know. Out in the open, I've always said. The way I've been. The only way to be.

When my first husband up and left, little Tommy not but two, I told it. Good riddance I said. If he ever sets foot in this door again, I'll shoot it off. Then when Charlie Flaggle was dying with his trouble, I told it. We didn't keep it to ourselves even if trade did fall off at the barber shop. Picked up some afterwards and stayed steady until he couldn't hold the trimmers and got to nicking too many ears. Nobody cut hair like him. Three generations in the same barbershop. I even thought maybe Tommy Lee might take it up, but it's too much indoors all the time for him. Gilda made the best beauty shop . . . those mirrors down one wall and the old pole out front. She cuts men and women. Only store open in that whole block. "We're in the same boat," I tell her. "And no beautification project is going to change a thing."

But try telling that to Therma Ann. I would if it wouldn't mean breaking my word not to speak to her again. Six weeks next Sunday. I said it and slammed the door. Billy is her grandson, same as mine. Or more. If you go back and look at some things. I never let my son go swinging his hips up and down the streets of this town with cut-off jeans so short they showed what they were supposed to cover. Little terry top no bigger than a washcloth with everything spilling out. Advertising. I never claimed my son was any stronger, or weaker than a regular man. Make the most, I said, but it was a marriage he was caught into. Trapped. At least he hasn't gone running home every time somebody turns their face upside down at him.

"Make your bed," I said, "You sleep in it." And he has. He's been the only one to make it. Rita wouldn't know how. If her mama had been home showing and telling her a thing or two, not out running around from club to club, she might be holding her end of a marriage up.

Park benches. That's what Therma wants now. For the vacant lot where Miller's Drugstore stood for fifty years. She's got them drawn into her plan. That's one thing I agree with her about. If she's bound and determined to plant the lot, then I'll help her with them. If people are sitting, they can't be parading around, showing all they've got. I give her credit where credit is due.

But I will fight her until the fourth of July on Shasta daisies. I know my flowers.

As my sweet daddy-in-law used to say, "Lallah, you got more wheels in the road than anybody I know." And I don't intend to let somebody in a five-year-old polyester dress with Shasta Daisies on the brain run the show. ∎

DRIVING HOME
David Hopes

Out of the night's crush and solitude, out of rage and
time and the dark and walled city, accelerating
up Pisgah Highway, a tic in the torment of days,
flame-eyes of my Ford juggernauting dim townlands down,
I find, unaccountable, at bend of the mountain,
calm animal eyes: farm cat
stalking topaz; heron;
opossums foraging in gleam
and shuttering of jewels;
marsh compassionate with lights,
void but for black and fire.
I see my road is the highway of the wayfare moon,
that beasts, moon-praising, night-studding, link their steps to some
majestic partner buck-dancing on the floor of lights.
Deers' ruby low on the slopes.
Opal of hunting owl.
Fillet on Pisgah of the
nighthawk's flying, hem of
the she-bear circling lonely
all the velvet ramparts.
Beast glance lanterns from the dark. Catamount aflame. Sky
mirrored in the spider's multiplicity of gaze.
Dance of the mountain Ladies in their glow-worm baubles.
It is the hour I transfigure from my fury to
be one of them. My lights give them light. My car becomes
moon's dragon blazing the road,
benediction torch-eyed
in the abysses, splendor blasting into
splendor all that watches, hungers, moves, that scatters to
join by morning behind Pisgah in a sphere of praise.

AUNT LORETTA'S PHOTOGRAPH, 1958
Debra Kaufman

in silence
on white carpeting

her children are arranged
sad mannikins

the boy's too soft
the girl's too plain

they earn only their mother's
disdain   her affection's

chilled like a perfect martini
just a kiss of vermouth

her skin like the gardenia
pinned to her dress

her lips red patina
the way she smokes a cigarette

even her cough seems glamorous
a man glides into the room

casts a lean shadow   drapes
his head in black

Loretta rearranges the fresh gladiolas
tugs at her son's cashmere suit

the man is impatient
threatens to shoot

"children this homely
deserve a nice . . ."

she says as light
bursts from the camera

the boy is caught looking
down at his shoes

the girl's jaw is set
like a stubborn Dutch farmer's

Loretta with hair tossed back
teeth bared resembles

her father's palomino
trapped in its stall

the night lightning
set fire to the barn

OCTOBER SONG
Karen Osborn

The moon uncurls in the woods.
Soon nightshade will dance
and tear open the ground,
for the old woman, unable to turn in her sleep,
has water in her lungs
and the air turns blue with frost.

There is no way out of the forest
when the old woman stops opening her mouth
for breath. We should wrap her in an overcoat
and pull on her clumsy boots.
We should carry her to the edge of the forest
where the field begins.

In the dark wood stems turn, berries split open.
Lonely shoes know the dance of death.
The old woman touches us with swollen hands
as leaves bury the path.
Hurry. Her hair is like smoke.
Her face turns moon-colored with frost.

THE WAY BACK
Janice Townley Moore

The mountains are barren
in the season
you would have been born,

their useless bellies push
against Christmas sky.

It is the month of children
like those on the doctor's
bulletin board
in the room where he put me,

the one time I lay in that room,

his affirmation attached
to my long night
of losing.

A difficult way to daylight
it seems. I find it months later,
kneading dough for a seasonal bread,
the first I have ever made,
awaiting its rise in the oven.

THE QUEEN OF DEER CREEK
Jeff Rackham

She punched Marvin Mifflin with the knuckle of her first finger. "How old you think I am? Go on, how old you think I am?"

The neon Coors sign over the bar painted her face green then blue then red. "I don't want you to lie now. Just tell me how old you think I am." She had played the game before. "You think I'm thirty? Or maybe sixty?"

She ate a handful of peanuts from the bowl on the bar, grinding and munching and popping. "I was Queen of Deer Creek when I was twenty-two only everybody swore I was fifteen." She winked at him. "That's a clue, ha, ha." She said, "Ha, ha," like a cartoon figure speaking in a balloon above her head.

Marvin Mifflin held a Schlitz in front of him on the linoleum bar. He was forty-one and starting to bald. He no longer liked himself. He wore a turtle-neck sweater to hide his Adam's apple. His Adam's apple seemed obscene. He had never been aware of it as a boy, or even as a young man, but now his Adam's apple seemed to puncture his throat. His Adam's apple poked, bobbled, gulped.

She kept punching him and asking questions. She could have been his age only in the swirling lights she might have been sixty and who could say.

"Don't tell a fib now. I ain't going to suicide myself if you miss." Her face was not hard, not overly lined, except around the eyes that were sunken and puffy. She wore heavy makeup, the kind you see on middle-aged women behind counters of small-time loan companies called Easy Finance. The hair was poofed up high and stiff, like Jackie Kennedy's in 1962.

"You got me lady," Marvin Mifflin said. He just wanted to drink his Schlitz.

"Shirley told me the other day I was a lady. You're the second person this week tells me I'm a lady, so I guess I must be."

He took a long cool swipe at his beer, letting foam float over his tongue and feeling the bob of his Adam's apple as he swallowed. The juke was playing a cowboy song. *How many times have you done this before? How many times have you walked out the door?*

"Shirley and me come here on a lark." She pushed the peanuts at him across the bar. "We was just closing up and I was planning to go straight home to a warm hot bath, and Shirley says, let's drive to Green River. She's just like that, just as much fun as can be, always full of jokes, only she's a lot younger than me. And it was just snowing to beat the band but I said, well, why not."

Marvin Mifflin hadn't noticed any Shirley. He hadn't seen anyone when he came in the bar except the barmaid. The barmaid was about twenty-three and wearing a little cowgirl skirt with fringe that swayed against her thighs as she walked. He had sat on a swivel stool with a leather seat and surveyed the barmaid's thighs. Cool slim thighs that went right up under the fringe. She looked bored. He was trying to find courage to score when the Queen of Deer Creek hopped over from some back table with her beer and peanuts and silver lame purse and pop-up cigarette case and jangley bracelets. The barmaid retreated into the darkness at the end of the bar. He could see her in the shadows feeding coins into the juke. If the Queen of Deer Creek hadn't shown up, he would have found the courage. He would have said, "Can I buy you one?" and the barmaid would have laughed and leaned over the bar to talk to him. Her eyes would have watched his mouth.

"Well? What do you think?" The Queen punched him with her knuckle.

"About what?"

"Ha, ha. You give up?"

"I guess I do."

"Ha, ha." She lit a long slim cigarette with a Cricket lighter. The bar felt warm after driving all day in the snow. Above the mirror several moose heads stared morosely into the past. Dusty paintings of old time cowboys hung on the walls. Real oil paintings, not reproductions. Marvin knew she was watching him. He tried to get interested in one of the painted cowboys with long white hair who was probably Buffalo Bill or somebody gazing off into the sunset.

"Pike and me drove down to the Grand Canyon for the Fourth of July." She blew a curl of smoke past his ear. "He just called me up when I was locking my desk and thinking of heading home for a cool cold bath and he says, why don't we have a time of it down at the Grand Canyon? Well, now I've been there before with Homer Richards and I don't think Pike is near the looker Homer was, but he's just as pleasant to be around as they come, and at first I was going to say no, but then I thought, if you start turning down invites pretty soon people won't ask you, so I said well why not."

Marvin nodded. He was wishing the barmaid would come back. He would give some kind of signal so they would both laugh silently with their eyes and maybe he would go over to the juke and pretend to read the selections. She would come up behind him and her breast would swing lightly against his arm. They'd both bend down to read song titles. She'd whisper she liked men with little hairs on the back of their neck.

"Pike is such a jokester, you know what I mean? He never lets up, just one after another. We were riding those mules down into the Grand Canyon. You ever been there? And Pike suddenly hollers. I dropped my teeth, and you know it's a thousand feet straight down. I laughed so I about fell off my mule, and Pike he calls out, don't fall off your ass, he meant the mule of course, that's just the way he is, always a real pleasure to be around. He's a lot older than me. I don't want you to think I got false teeth, ha, ha."

Two live cowboys came in the bar. One of them wore a white hat. The neon Coors sign made the hat glow. The cowboys sat at a back table. In the darkened mirror he watched the fringed little skirt of the barmaid float over to them.

The Queen of Deer Creek was popping peanuts in one

hand and smoking in the other. "They say this is the last cowboy town in the west. Only those that say it ain't never been to the Grand Canyon."

The shadowy mirror image of the barmaid bent over the cowboy's table. Small fringe on her skirt quivered. Marvin felt a sort of weight in his chest and he felt it in his groin, too, only faint and distant, like a memory.

"My name's Lou," she said.

He felt tired and in the dark mirror behind the bar he could see the bald spot on his forehead shining red then green then blue.

"Actually my name's Virginia Louisiana Frances Junkin. And you know they couldn't hardly call me Virgin for short could they? Ha, ha. So they called me Louise for long, that's just the way I say it, sort of to make it rhyme, you see. After Baker divorced me I just let it become Lou and I liked it better. A lot of people think I'm named after Lou Grant on the old Mary Tyler Moore show. He's got another show now."

Marvin finished his Schlitz and motioned to the barmaid. She came up with bright swaying breasts under a cotton top. She was looking past him. She thought he and the Queen deserved each other. He could tell. His hand went instinctively to his Adam's apple to hide it.

"You bring us two Lucky Lager, honey, and we want 'em on tap, none of your bottled stuff." The Queen punched him with her knuckle. "You don't tell 'em they really dump the cheats on you, you know what I mean?"

He gave in and tried some of the peanuts she was holding out to him. "Shirley's just the funnest thing, just full of life and spunk and lots of charm. Everybody says she's a charmer. I've been told that myself a few times, only Shirley has this way about her. We stopped at a Conoco station outside Morgan and the boy says, what'll you have, and right off Shirley says in this Alabama accent of hers—of course she's never been to Alabama in her life—well, she looks up at him standing there with the snow blowing around his head, you know what kind of storm it was this afternoon. She says in this Alabama accent, I'll have it anyway you can give it to me, and this boy, he couldn't believe what he heard, and I was laughing so I almost fell out of the car. That's just the way Shirley is."

The juke was playing. *It's been so long, it's been so long, since my heart was in song. Who can show me the way?*

The barmaid sat down with the cowboys at the back table.

"So where's Shirley?" Marvin Mifflin said. "If she's gone to the john.you'd better check because something must be wrong." It was a poor joke. He was never any good at small talk. It horrified him. He took himself much too serious for small talk.

"Oh you're a corker," Lou said. She sipped her Lucky draft and drew out another cigarette to light. "Oh you're a funner," she said. "I always like a guy with a sense of humor. We only go around once in life's my philosophy, and I believe we might as well enjoy. You know what I mean?"

He nodded. "I know what you mean." In the mirror he watched the barmaid lean toward the cowboy.

The Queen lit her cigarette with the Cricket lighter and slipped it back into her purse. "Well," she took a deep draw and let it out in a single burst. "I almost hate to say this and I just hope it's between you and I. If I'd thought when Shirley asked me to come she had this in mind I would be taking a warm hot bath right now. I mean, I just thought we'd drive up to Green River and have a few Jack Daniels and maybe dance a little. Do you like to dance? Shirley just surprised the life out of me. I don't judge other people. She has a right to her own life, I'm not going to say nothing." Her face turned neon green then blue then red.

"She leave you stranded?"

"You might say so. Oh I don't mean she won't drive me back. We come in about two hours ago and there were three guys and we were the only gals, so it was natural we got together and danced a little. It was snowing to beat the band outside, what else can you do, just for a little fun? And before long Shirley is over against the wall rubbing against this guy, I've never seen him before in my life and neither has she. I mean it was embarrassing. So one of the others, one of the other guys, I mean, his name was Hock, he put his hand under the table and starts running it up and down my leg. 'Hock, I'm not that kind of person,' I said, and I'm not. I come out for a little fun and dancing, but I'm not that kind of person. So Hock stands up and does a little get-to with the guy who's got his hand by this time all over Shirley and she's got hers all over him. I was so embarrassed. And all of a sudden they're gone. Well I went out to check just as mad as could be, I was just blistering, but Shirley's blue Plymouth was still parked outside, so they've taken one of theirs, don't you see? So I cooled off a little since I figure it she'll have to come back for the car. Did you see a blue Plymouth parked right in front?"

He thought he remembered one when he came in but he couldn't be sure.

"It really surprised me about Shirley, she's always been so sweet, she's divorced too, but only once, so I never expected. But I ain't going to suicide myself over Shirley, say you never did guess my age, ha, ha."

Marvin Mifflin took a deep breath. Up on the wall Buffalo Bill was gazing off into the sunset. "Oh, I suppose you're . . . maybe, thirty or so."

"Well, aren't you the corker. You know I've got a good sense of character. I knew when you came in, I said there's a good character even if he does dress a little fancy. Just one look at them shoes and I could tell you weren't from Wyoming."

He felt the heaviness creep up the back of his neck and weigh down his head. The clock behind the bar had a lighted face over a tumbling waterfall. Several smiling salmon were jumping upstream. It was 11:37.

She punched him with her kunckle. "Forty-five," she said. "But you're not the only one, don't feel bad. Everybody thinks thirty because I still believe I'm young, you know what I mean? I believe I'm young." She looked intently at him to stress the point.

He said, "I never would have guessed forty-five."

"Did I tell you my name was Lou?"

He finished his Lucky draft and pushed the empty glass away from him. Behind Buffalo Bill two old cows were looking off in the same direction he was, their eyes sort of misty, like they were longing to be rounded up. They might have been shaggy horses. It was hard to tell in the dark.

"Everybody calls me Lou. My folks come from Louisiana only they moved to Wyoming during the depression and I was born and raised and it's home to me this very day."

He stood up from his stool and fished two dollar bills from his pocket. Lou crushed her cigarette in the ashtray and gathered up her things.

"Where to?" she asked.

The juke was singing softly. *Down in Nashville where lovers lie, my gee-tar sings that old goodby.* The cowboy in the glowing hat had his arm around the barmaid. She was running her fingers inside his sequined shirt.

"I'm pretty tired," he said. "I'm driving to Reno tomorrow."

"I thought we were having a good time, of course I don't judge people, that's one of my philosophies, I'll just walk around in the snow until Shirley comes back, she'll be back pretty soon now."

She had turned on her stool to face him. The Coors sign glowed behind her. A crown of neon shimmered around the stiff outline of her hair. Her face was in shadows.

"I just came up here because I believe in living. I believe to be young." She was talking softly. "Actually, I'm fifty-one but I don't feel old so I'm not old, and I can still dance longer and stay up longer than the younger ones. They're always saying to me, how do you do it, Lou? And I say I believe I'm young, of course none of them knows I'm fifty-one, I never tell how old I am."

Marvin pulled on his coat and jingled the car keys in the pocket. "I'm sure she'll be coming back soon."

"OK, so I do have a bridge. The rest of them's my own." She looked up at him and grinned. "You take care of your teeth and they'll take care of you."

He backed away and the Queen of Deer Creek sat like a lady on the bar stool with her hands folded properly in her lap. Shadows darkened her face and he could no longer see her eyes.

Outside, the snow had stopped falling. The sky was dark but the town seemed bright from arc lamps reflecting on the blue snow. The wide western street was deserted. He could hear a freight train slumbering through the station at the end of town. The blue Plymouth was gone. At the end of the block his own rusty Subaru sat alone with a skin of snow over it.

"Maybe you could take me somewhere." She had come out behind him and was looking at the empty parking space where the blue Plymouth had been. She pushed her hands down into the pockets of her fake Leopard skin coat. "Somewhere they got a phone."

He walked her a block to Rustler's All Night Cafe. Incandescent lights buzzed on the ceiling. Taped to the wall above the counter were small signs. Home is Where You Go After Your Mother-In-Law Leaves. No Shirt, No Shoes, No Service. God Bless Us All, We'll Need It After Eating Here. The counter man wore long sideburns. He glanced up as they came in, then turned back to a flickering image of Johnny Carson on black and white T.V.

Lou sat in the phone booth and dialed and smoked. Her legs propped open the folding door. Blue veins showed through her nylons. "I tell you about when Gen and Dory and me went to the basketball game in Pocatello? We met the coach there when they was playing Weber and he is a good looker and more fun than anything, so he invited us all up special to watch his team play. We got to sit right behind the bench and cheer for Pocatello."

She hung up and dialed another number. Her bracelets jangled as she dialed. The cafe smelled like German cabbage. Lou's cigarette smoke curled up around the light inside the phone booth. "Dory got so excited she jumped up and yelled, kill the shits, which I couldn't help but laugh, Dory's just that way, it was so cute. Then after, we all went out to celebrate with the coach and two other guys that were very nice, believe me. They really treated us right—surf and turf and the whole works. You could tell the coach liked me best, and he was always telling jokes and saying things like where'd you get them basketballs, only he meant my boobies, you see, and I laughed so I almost fell off my chair."

Marvin Mifflin leaned back against the counter and wondered how he had come to this. He had always had the suspicion he was destined for something special. Maybe not great, but something meaningful at least. He had felt it for years when he was a young man, a vague urge that kept him going. And then he got a bald spot on his forehead and his Adam's apple began to bulge.

She hung up and dialed another number. Her face looked thin and tight against the bones as she waited, this time silently while the phone rang. "What he didn't know," she said, hanging up, "was I got a partial mastectomy. They wanted to take 'em all, but I wouldn't let them and I'm glad I didn't even though it meant a couple of extra operations to build 'em back up, only they still don't look quite right. I never tell anyone about it, even Charley Severson doesn't know." Her voice faded away. Johnny Carson was telling a joke about Peoria. The audience laughed.

"Perhaps you could call one of your children," Marvin suggested. His head ached. She crushed the butt of her cigarette on the tile floor, then tapped out a fresh cigarette on her purse in her lap.

"Donald Lee lives in Indiana and Doris lives in one of those condominiums in California. They'd be the first to come and help if they knew I was stranded, they'd come right now if they knew. When Homer Richards had his heart attack we were on vacation in Zion's, you ever been there? And Doris came right now, she didn't even hesitate, came all the way from California in a day, that's the kind of person she is. She had a new Mustang with an FM radio. Of course Donald Lee couldn't get away from his job that fast, he's in Mental Growth, I like to kid him about it and say he could use a little himself, ha, ha. He's not much for funning, I never knew why. More like Baker, he never cracked a joke in seven years. Of course Baker was a Jack Mormon."

She leaned back in the phone booth, one elbow propped on the tiny shelf under the phone. She blew smoke at the ceiling and watched it rise, then pushed off her shoes and crossed her ankles. One big toe pushed up through a hole in her nylon like a mushroom. The toe looked blue in the incandescent light.

"I had to have a hysterectomy after Donald Lee. They took out the whole thing, not just the tubes. Charley Severson brought me a certificate that said I was officially spayed, he was just the cutest thing, but I got even with him when he burned his hands in the explosion. I know this friend in Logan that makes the cutest flower vases out of white urinals, so I took him one while he was in St. Bens and he just laughed when he saw it and said I got him that time. It was the cutest thing."

Marvin Mifflin looked out the dark plate glass window of the cafe. Snow had begun to fall again. He could see his own reflection with snow falling through it. It made him feel like a ghost.

"I didn't tell that to anyone, of course, you got to be a good listener as well as a good conversationist to get along. I picked up that from Donald Lee. It's all part of Mental Growth." She reached out and dropped her cigarette on the floor again. "Doris doesn't believe in Mental Growth, but I'm not so sure."

In the plate glass window Marvin thought he saw the barmaid stretch out on the bed in his motel room, the fringe falling open on her thighs. She was looking at him and maybe just shaking her hair back out of her eyes while she slowly unbuttoned the top of her blouse. If he went back to the bar there might still be time to talk to her.

Lou sat forward in the phone booth and buried her face in her hands. That was all he needed. He could see it all coming. She would get hysterical or start crying. She would scream and try to swallow pills from a bottle in her purse and the police would come.

She straightened up and held out her hand, two tiny crystals of light reflected in it. "Contacts," she said. "But you didn't know. I used to have a nice pair of glasses, you know, with rhinestone frames, but I got to thinking they made me look dated. Believe me I suffered a long time to wear these contacts, everybody thought I was crying, but I just said it was the asthma so of course nobody ever knew it was contacts."

Marvin dropped down on a vinyl covered stool at the counter. "Look," he said. "I'm really tired. I don't want to be rude and I know you're in a jam. I've got a twelve hour drive tomorrow."

"Honey, I'm not going to impose on you one minute. There's probably a Greyhound," she said. "I'll just take the old Greyhound back to Ogden and won't bother you no more, you've been so nice and helpful, I just can't imagine what got into Shirley to do this, I'll tell you she's on the blacklist from now on. That's one of those sayings I picked up from Homer Richards, he was always putting everyone on the blacklist."

She bent over and massaged her left foot. "You've been such a gentleman already and just done so much for me I don't know how I could ever repay you. Of course I won't sleep with you, I might as well just come out and say that because a lot of guys ask me and I got to admit you're a good looker but I'm just not that kind of person, so I don't want to hurt your feelings or anything. I mean I read the *Sensuous*

Woman, ha ha. I know lots of ways to please a guy beside sleeping with him and some of them's real cute once you get used to it. The only problem is sometimes my bridge comes loose."

"You folks want anything?" The counter man had come over during a commercial. He had a cold sore on his lip.

"No," Marvin started to say.

"You betchya," Lou said. "We'll have a piece of that apple pie and some black coffee. Might as well do the town right, that's my philosophy." She punched Marvin Mifflin in the arm with her knuckle and sat on the stool next to him. She slapped both high heel shoes on the counter, gold lame with dirty water marks from the snow.

The counter man went to get the pie. Marvin leaned over close to Lou and tried to talk in a low voice. "Look, lady. My head hurts. I been driving all day. I don't want to do the town, I don't want to sleep with you."

"Well, who the hell offered?"

Marvin was trying to whisper. "I just came west for . . ."

"I come out for a little fun and dancing, but I'm not that kind of person," she said loudly.

"On my way to Reno."

"Listen, Mr. Snooty. Homer Richards was a lot cuter than you and didn't wear no fancy shoes to make him look taller like some I know."

The counter man came back and held two slices of pie in his hand.

"You just think you're acey-ducey in more ways than not but I could of gone dancing or bowling or anything fun because I believe it. I believe it!" She was breathing through her nose in heavy bursts.

Marvin tried to calm her with his hands.

"Don't you touch me!" She stood up and yanked her shoes off the counter. To the counter man she said, "I told him I'm not that kind of person and I'm not. He's an old man, a lot older than I'll ever be." She walked in her nylons to the door and threw it open. A cold wind burst into the cafe. She leaned against the open door while she put on her shoes. Dry snow swirled across the tile floor. "Sons of bitches," she said as she went out. "This ain't the last cowboy town in the west."

Johnny Carson was introducing an aging Charo who was

saying gootchy-gootchy. The audience laughed. She kept saying it. Gootchy-gootchy. The audience applauded.

"You want the pie?" the counter man said.

"No."

He took the pie back to the shelf. "Who was the broad?"

"I don't know. The Queen of Deer Creek."

The counter man settled down in front of the T.V. "Ain't nothing in Deer Creek but a ghost town."

Marvin Mifflin sat for a few moments watching the snow blow through his image in the dark plate glass window. When he went out gusts of heavy snow wrapped around him. He walked with his face down until he reached the end of the block. Snow had not yet filled in the square of pavement where the Subaru had been parked. His head throbbed and he leaned back against the lighted window of a taxidermist shop, his hands stuffed deep into the empty pockets where his car keys should have been. A stuffed dog stood in the window with cobwebs between his legs. Maybe it was a coyote. He had never seen a coyote. The coyote bared its teeth and twisted its neck over its shoulder, staring at him with level dusty eyes. And for a moment Marvin Mifflin had a vision of the Queen of Deer Creek as a young girl, maybe sixteen in a long calico dress, standing side by side with that coyote out on the Wyoming prairie. Like an antique oil painting. Snow covered the ground and she had one hand on the dog's head. Both of them gazed up ardently, longingly, at a wild Western moon. For one purifying moment Marvin Mifflin wanted to call out, but the wind gusted about him, and his own dark image—wavering and transparent—reappeared in the glass. All the way back to the cafe he held his hand over his Adam's apple to ward off the chill. ■

THE OFFICIAL FRISBEE-CHASING
CHAMPION OF COLORADO
Robert Hill Long

The Navajo word for *unleaded* was not
the most absurd thing on my mind
that arid evening as we rolled
into the fever-colored hills
of Monument Valley: I had been
scaring my five months pregnant wife
with a Readers' Digest real life horror
—a Mormon sedan broke down in the desert,
summer, the whole godfearing family
having to chew melted crayons, tire rubber,
drink each other's piss and finally
slaughter their old chihuahua—
and now, with the fuel tank's *empty* signal
lighting up like a bad cowboy-movie-sunset,
I was sorry for passing Last Chance
This and Last Chance That
but sorry was not enough, I needed
a minor miracle and I got three:
all of them Navajo and not a one
over eight years old, chasing
a bald truck tire across the highway,
slapping it wobbly as if it were
a sick black goat or a priest caught
buying tequila with last Sunday's tithes.
I hit the brakes and jumped out
onto the twilight asphalt, shouting
—my wife hissed "Be nice!"—shouting
"Over here, I need to show you
something!" The car shuddered slightly,

died. The Navajo kids edged up to it
suspiciously and why not? I was
the only gringo around, tearing through
the back seat mess for a camera,
they probably thought, but what
was to prevent me from swinging around
with a knife and adding three more scalps
to the annals of genocide?
But it was a frisbee I produced,
the old worthless-trinket-trick
with a twist: a whistle behind it
was our old hound who, I lied,
was the unofficial frisbee-chasing
champion of Colorado.
And despite his broken teeth
and hips that shimmied with arthritis
he put on a world-class display,
snatching sand-skimmers, long range bombs,
kicking up his bad legs like a puppy
and fetching that orange disk back to me
like it was a sun he wouldn't let sink
until everyone agreed to make his title
official. Which we did amid much
ceremonious laughter and chatter,
trading names, quick stories,
all the invisible commerce of friendship.
They touched my wife's ripening belly,
pointed to a butte glowing in last light:
"The first people were born up there."
The desert was stealing our shadows
while we talked. I asked my tourist favor:
the oldest said if we pushed the car
a little way, there was a hill
curving down to a Texaco. For thanks
I gave them the frisbee and the young one asked

"Can we keep the dog too?" Was this how
disappointment came into the world,
an easy question chasing a hard answer
into the darkness? The dog sat grinning
with exhaustion, my wife winced
and looked away. Shadows bigger
than any of us were listening as I knelt
and looked into the boy's bean-black eyes:
"That dog's not worth ten dollars—
he'll die in a year. Let me buy
him back for five." He understood.
A minute later as the car glided downhill
I thought five dollars was cheap
ransom for such a narrow escape
from bitterness. I let out a whoop
and imagined cowboy harmonica music
swelling over the whole fading-to-black scene,
I was that glad.

PEACHES
Deborah Pope

Last night I dreamed I turned to you
from the low porch chair,
we were old,
but in your eyes I was still
the girl you followed
into another life,
hair long, feet small,
my back the exact span of your hand.
You tucked my blanket closer,
we held hands.

Tonight I will dream
I am in the yard, perhaps,
bending stiffly in the garden, apron pinned,
amid the late beans and zinnias.
I will lift my head and see you
coming over the grass, and wish again
that I might see you always so,
moving towards me.

It will be September.
We will note another summer gone.
The ash will shimmer its small change,
the ground be covered with crabapples
that six months past were blossoms
white and pink in new light.
Over us, towhees, swallows stroke and sail
the updrafts of a few, last perfect days.
The years will have peeled us
thin as ash, white as apple blossoms.

We come from tending the rows,
find ourselves walking on
windfall peaches in the north yard.
They will be all over the ground,
gold dusted, giving softly
under the balls of our feet,
size of apricots, no good for eating,
but the smell will be
delicious.

THE JUNGFRAU
Carrie J. Knowles

Mrs. Craeger tapped the band of her heavy gold ring against the edge of the table in an annoyed gesture. When that failed to get her daughter's attention, she cleared her throat and pointed to the thick grey haze covering the mountains outside the carefully cleaned dining room window.

"Rain, probably even snow on the Jungfrau again today," she said in a loud voice as though she were slightly hard of hearing, even though she wasn't.

Her daughter looked up, then went back to buttering her croissant. The waiter came with their polished silver pots of fresh hot coffee and steamed milk.

The old woman continued on as though she and her daughter were engaged in a pleasant conversation, "This will be my last chance to see the Jungfrau. We leave day after tomorrow, and tomorrow we're scheduled to go to Gruyere. I'll probably never be able to make a trip like this again." She sighed heavily, then looked at her daughter, and leaning closer to the table she went on, "I'm not well, you know, and certainly not young enough to even dream of coming here again."

Her daughter didn't move. Mrs. Craeger continued, "It's a shame the weather has been so bad. Your Uncle George was right, like I tried to tell you before you made these arrangements, you just can't count on the weather in the mountains in spring."

"This is June," Lydia said, looking up from her croissant at the cold frosted mountain top. She hadn't been listening, couldn't bear to hear the same conversation again. The weather had been cloudy. There had been some good days too, but none good enough or clear enough to go to the top of the Jungfrau.

"I know it's June. That's obvious." Her mother was annoyed, she hated for anyone to correct her. "But," she continued coolly, "it's early June and June is still spring in the mountains." Her mother wiped the edge of her mouth with the smooth linen napkin and placed it on her lap signaling that she was finished with that particular conversation.

"I don't want to go shopping." Mrs. Craeger continued, starting a new conversation. "I've really had enough of it. How about you?"

"Fine," said Lydia, looking out the window down the rain dampened street, "let's go sightseeing. Maybe go to Spiez, take a ride on the boat that goes across the Thunersee to Oberhofen, and then see the castle there. It's supposed to be rather charming."

"I don't see the point in taking the boat from Spiez to Oberhofen. If it's overcast here, then it's overcast there. We wouldn't be able to see a thing. If you want to see the castle, then let's drive there. But taking a boat ride just to be taking it when there's nothing to see doesn't suit me."

"We don't have to see anything. We could just enjoy going for the ride." Lydia picked up her knife and cut the end off a stiff dark roll, then she buttered it and covered it with orange marmalade.

"Really Lydia. You shouldn't eat so much butter. You know it's not good for you. You're not young anymore either, you know. You should pay more attention to what you eat."

"Do you want to go to Spiez and take a boat ride?" Lydia looked straight at her mother as she ate the thickly buttered end of her roll.

"I still don't know why you insisted on coming here this soon. I don't know what was so important that you had to come now and couldn't come later. It's a shame, you know, I'll never see this mountain again."

"I work. Don't you remember?" She didn't mean to say this, not really. Sarcasm rarely worked. It was not the right tactic to use when she wanted to try to get close to her mother.

Her mother began drumming her ring against the edge of the table again. "Of course I know you work. But, this was important to me. I don't understand why you couldn't have tried harder to schedule your vacation later. I would have thought that you would have been more considerate of me."

"Why not go up the Jungfrau today?" Lydia wanted badly to be able to move the conversation up the mountain, away from the table. "The weather is so unpredictable here, one minute there's rain, then the next it's as clear as a bell. It takes almost two and a half hours by train to get up the Jungfrau. Maybe by the time we get to the top, it will be clear. And, even if it's not, you can say that you went. That you saw the great mountain and that the weather was wretched."

"There's no point in going if you can't see anything. I don't want to go if I can't see anything."

"Then," countered Lydia, in a practiced move, "let's go over to Spiez and take the boat to Oberhofen and see the castle, or just explore the old city of Spiez. It's supposed to be quite beautiful, you've told me so yourself."

"I said that when your father and I were here Spiez was lovely. But, that was years ago. Since then, I've heard that it has become built up, a little commercial. Your Aunt Margie's neighbor was here two years ago and she told Margie that it wasn't as nice as it used to be."

"Maybe she was wrong."

"Why would she tell Margie something that wasn't true?" Her heavy ring rapped against the edge of the table again.

"I didn't accuse her of lying. I merely suggested that she might be wrong and that we should check out Spiez for ourselves, not depend on Aunt Margie's neighbor to do it for us."

Virginia Craeger looked hard at her daughter as though she were trying to see through her, detect if there were some lie lurking behind her eyes. She couldn't understand her daughter, didn't know why she was so independent, why she wasn't more considerate, more accepting of her. "Well," she said, her voice as flat as the dark wet street outside, "if it's that important to you, then we should go to Spiez. But I don't see the point of taking a boat ride if it's not even going to be clear enough to see across the lake."

The two women drove the short ride in silence. Lydia cruised at a pace that was just slightly faster than her mother appreciated. It was a foolish thing to do, almost childish. But, there were times that Lydia went out of her way to get a rise from her mother. Lydia never knew what would happen if she pushed her mother far enough, she thought maybe, just maybe, she might be able to create a small crack, a hole in the thick stiff veneer that surrounded their interactions.

"Look at the mountains," Lydia pointed to the crisp scenery out the front window of their car. There along the shore of the brilliant blue Thunersee were dozens of clean white-washed homes, with curved weathered red tiled roofs. And, every house had a garden bursting with blazing red gardenias.

"Mountains," her mother snorted, "those aren't mountains. Those are foothills, and low ones at that. We haven't yet seen the mountains. Hasn't cleared the whole time we've been here. Been a bad spring. Even the woman at the desk said so. I told you that spring just isn't reliable here."

"Maybe it will clear tomorrow." Lydia was sorry she was speeding. Sorry they had had to come when the weather was so bad. Sorry that they could never seem to just enjoy being together.

"Tomorrow doesn't matter," the old woman whined slightly, "we're scheduled for that tour. The one to Gruyere. Even if it does clear, we can't go up the Jungfrau."

"We'll cancel." Lydia wanted to make this work. Wanted for the moment to make the best of things, to make her mother happy.

"Then we'll lose our deposit. The brochure said that you have to give a 48 hour notice to cancel your reservations or you lose your deposit."

So what, Lydia started to scream. So what. She started to point out to her mother that the deposit was only for eight American dollars. No big deal. She started to, but she didn't. She didn't want to get into it with her anymore. She wanted peace with her. She wanted right then to be sitting in a cafe at the water's edge, drinking espresso, laughing and talking with her mother while they watched the boats pull to shore, load up, then pull away and sail across the crystal clear sea.

"We're here." She said with a forced smile in her voice, as she eased the car into the parking lot to the entrance of the boat dock and the old city of Spiez.

Her mother opened her car door, then swung her legs out in a stiff almost crippled movement. When she stood up, she stretched slightly, arching her back, and placed her cane in her left hand. Then, clicking her heavy ring against its ebony handle, she stepped away from the car.

"When your father and I were here," she said, her voice sounding light and young as she walked awkwardly to the side of the car where Lydia stood, "we spent a whole day just walking through the streets of the old city. We didn't do a thing, just walked. The flowers were beautiful that day. This is a city of exceptional gardens, of brilliant flowers and lush green trees. It was really brilliant that day, the air was clear and warm. Everything was perfect."

"Why don't we take a walk," Lydia jumped at the chance to keep her mother happy, keep the moment light, "we can see the gardens, and you can show me the places that you and daddy saw."

"No," she said, waving her hand in the air as though she were shooing flies. "I'm too old to walk that far anymore. Besides, it wouldn't be the same. Those are the kinds of things you do when you have someone special to share them with."

"You have me," Lydia said, quietly, trying to ease her way into one of the cracks.

"Yes," the old woman smiled a moment at her daughter, then, taking her cane in her right hand, she began to walk steadily away from her, "I do have you. But that's not what I'm talking about. Perhaps if you and Alan had managed to stay together and he were here with us today we'd walk through the town." She looked back at Lydia who was by then locking the car. "You should be with someone special when you have something special to share."

Lydia felt as though she had been hit and had momentarily lost her balance from the blow. She closed her eyes against the bright noon sun. If Alan were here. If things had worked out. If they had stayed together. Her mother had never asked her why they split. Never once wanted to know why it happened, or how she felt. It struck her, as she drew in a deep breath to regain her balance before she had to catch up to her mother, that her mother had never once in her life asked her how she felt about anything.

By the time Lydia caught up to her, her mother was seated on a straight backed bench, waiting for Lydia to purchase their tickets.

"First class," she shouted above the rumble of the approaching boat and the chatter of the people who were standing around waiting for the boat to dock. "You know I only like to travel first class on things like boats or trains. Don't care that much for local color."

Lydia wondered how many people standing around waiting to catch a ride across the Thunersee spoke English. How many people her mother had offended.

"Two, first class," she told the agent in her clear but limited German.

When the boat docked she showed the two tickets to the boatsman, and they were ushered unceremoniously up a set of tight steep stairs to the upper deck.

"I told you first class," her mother snapped. "If you didn't have enough money, you should have told me so, I would have gladly given it to you."

"This is first class," Lydia said, helping her mother into the small upholstered wooden deck chair near the railing along the top deck.

"You know I have trouble with stairs," she said again, this time sarcastically, "especially narrow ones on rocking boats."

"I didn't know there would be stairs." Lydia's first reaction was to blame herself for not asking about the stairs, then on second thought, she realized that there was no way in the world that she could have known or even suspected that first class would be up a flight of stairs. There was no reason to think there would be a problem, no reason to blame herself for her mother's short fuse, her foul moods. "I had no idea that first class was on the top deck," Lydia said at last, speaking slowly, counting silently to herself as each word crept out. She wanted for once to not be apologizing for something she really didn't do.

"Well, I certainly hope we don't have to ride up here on the return."

"I imagine," Lydia said, catching the rage in her voice before it could escape, "that since we have first class seats we can sit anywhere we damn well please."

"There's no need to curse, young lady. I was just saying that I hoped we didn't have to ride back on this deck in these same seats. You have a tendency to overreact to everything that I say. You should work on that a little. It would improve your social graces immensely."

The sky had cleared. All along the banks of the Thunersee Lydia could see the clean clusters of houses with their delicate terraced gardens. All over the mountainside, gardenias mingled with ageratum and the cool frosted gray of her favorite herb, Lamb's Ear, to create a mountainside carpeted in the strong petals and soft stroke of flowers.

The view was magnificent. All around them were mountains. Not great ones like the Jungfrau, but majestic ones like the graceful Saxeten, the blunt nosed Harder and the towering Morgenberghorn. Lydia felt safe, cradled almost in the arms of the ancient mountains. The air was fresh and springlike, the breeze warm yet refreshing, and for the first time in ten days, the sun was shining in a deep blue sky.

They rode to Oberhofen. It was as the brochure had said, a perfectly lovely castle, appointed with an exquisite collection of antiques, paintings and fine furniture. It was a lovely place to just wander about. There were, of course, stairs: some broad and polished made from curving oak, some roughly hewn pine that were narrow, straight and steep. Her mother walked up one flight, then, leaning heavily on her cane, she asked Lydia to help her back down. There was nothing in the castle, she declared, worth seeing.

Lydia walked with her to the garden and fully intended to leave her mother sitting comfortably on a bench watching the boats traverse the Thunersee while she toured the castle. But, her mother, upon sitting, smiled up at her and said with the slightest of sighs, "There's nothing more lonely than someone else's garden, is there?"

Lydia sat with her awhile in the garden, then they walked among the flowers and the sculptures to the castle gates and the small gift shop. Lydia bought a book with color pictures detailing the restored castle interior, including the sparse almost pristine chapel and the seductive, slightly garish, private harem room in the uppermost turret of the fortress. Her mother, refusing to go into the gift shop, didn't buy anything.

They walked down the cobblestone path from the castle to the edge of the lake shore, her mother holding on to Lydia's arm for balance, careful not to clutch her too tightly, or touch more than the sleeve of her coat.

Walking down the slick path of worn cobble stones, her mother felt frail against her side, precarious. Lydia wanted to be closer, to somehow hold her. They never really touched, only brushed cheeks occasionally in a rather ceremonial greeting that seemed to be required but only punctually observed. Lydia tried to move closer to her mother, to give her more support, but as she did, her mother transferred her cane from her left hand to her right, and as the cane dangled from her tightly closed fist it hit against the leg of Lydia's pants and created a greater distance between their walking.

"There's a cafe near the boat dock. Why don't we have lunch there?" Lydia moved closer to her mother even though she knew she might just as quickly move away.

"I hate tourist traps." Mrs. Craeger slowed her walk, then abruptly shook her arm free. She was feeling claustrophobic. She couldn't stand to have people be so close.

"It's not necessarily a tourist trap."

"If it's near anything that has anything like a view, then it's a tourist trap."

Her mother's ring tapped against her cane as it jabbed against the old cobblestones. It was a strange rhythm, her short labored steps syncopated against the sharp thump of her cane and tap of her ring, an awkward song. Lydia kept walking towards the cafe as though she had no intention of eating anywhere else. If you can't get what you need, she thought to herself as her mother's cane and ring kept tapping and thumping, get what you want.

"It looks like a lovely cafe. There's even tables and chairs outside. I'd like to just sit there for awhile and have some lunch and watch the boats sail across the lake. It's turned out to be a beautiful day." Lydia took her mother's elbow firmly in her hand and continued to guide her down the road.

"I don't see the point of paying a fortune for a second rate tourist trap meal just so you can watch the boats."

"Lunch," Lydia said with a smile, "mother dear, will be on me."

They sat in the cafe watching the boats for nearly two

hours. The pork loin was slightly overdone and the potatoes a little too buttery, but the beer Lydia drank was cold and bitter and she enjoyed it so much that she ordered another.

Once Lydia paid for their meal they left the cafe and boarded the return boat. They sat on one of the long backless wooden benches on the lower deck. It was nearly four-thirty by that time and the bottom deck was crowded with mothers and children, businessmen, shop girls and packages. The sun was still bright and warm, but was lost in the shadow of the upper deck, and the exhaust from the heavy lumbering boat engines curled up from the ruffled blue Thunersee and stayed trapped between the two floors.

She had wanted this trip to be pleasant. To give her a chance to get close to her mother. Her mother was going to die. Not soon, perhaps, but sometime in the near future.

Lydia hated her for that. Hated the box that arrived unannounced six months ago at her apartment, packed by professional movers, containing her grandmother's good gold-banded china.

The package was accompanied by one of her mother's cryptic notes: By rights these are yours. I want things settled before I'm dead.

Nothing, Lydia realized, as the boat cut its way past the sun-dappled Saxeten and the rich-wooded Morgenberghorn, would ever be settled.

The clerk at the desk had said it was going to be clear and warm tomorrow. A perfect day for the Jungfrau. They would go, however, to Gruyere, as planned.

They would return home the next day. Her mother would tell all her friends that their trip was lovely, but the weather a bit uncertain. She would, of course, always mention that they never did go up the Jungfrau.

And Lydia, fighting to bring her mother closer to her now before she was gone, would try hard to forget that there were ever any harsh words, any difficult moments. Instead, she would remember only how bright the sun was, and how sweet the breeze felt as it blew against her face on the ride from Spiez to the Oberhofen that day on the Thunersee. ■

KEY WEST, 1953
Marnie Prange

for my mother

A woman skin dives
in the blue water of the Gulf.
She is not afraid
as she waves to her husband
who is moving away from her,
just now moving
out of reach. She waves
and the curious fish
curve away from her fingers.
Now her surprised hands
choreograph an imitation
of water: the fish move
where she wants them to move.
Soon a whole sea of fish
and she forgets the sea
she came for. She thinks
of Venice and the pigeons
circling an old man's head, diving
for pellets of bread balanced
on a hat rim; or, of something
more precise. She is beyond thought.
How could it be otherwise?
All elements are fish, her body
the question they answer.
She sways and the fish sway
with her. Wrapped in a movement
of silver, she becomes the fish
the silver curtain moves

on its current. She might
be taken out to sea,
to the sargasso weeds
at its center, wear a wreath
of mourning to her evening bed,
dress herself in coral.
Or, she might stay here forever.
Become translucent as fish,
sea-softened back
into an earlier, easier shape.
The danger in this escapes her
until of the magic of fish
comes her husband. He takes her hand
and she kicks her legs, following.
Safe from the secret underwater
touching, her body turns
back into itself. Here
are her ankles, her impossible
thighs. She will not undress again
in this hall of mirrors,
before these underwater eyes.

HARD WEATHER
Roger Sauls

After first light my windows blur
with the crosshatch of an early snow.
The muffled beating of stiff laundry
drifts in from the line, a man
calling out in his sleep.
By now my mother would be up,
making coffee, sorting the wash.
In the stove, a fire just catching hold.
If she thinks of anything, it's how
little it's changed, her life
of rising early, alone, her work repeated
like the hundred sparrows
bickering above dead rye fields.
                            And she'd pull
the knit cap hard around my ears,
tell me if I loved her to go out
in the hard morning, do my part.
I was the man of the house.
But in my strangeness I grew
away, living in the pasture
where I'd feed the dray horse,
its large head floating
toward my hand inside clouds
of its own breath.
                    In cumulus
sparrows are hovering this morning
above the house. They veer in
from the east, familiar as old
worries. I feel the troubling emptiness
of this house and remember

that my mother never spoke
to me of her loneliness.
She would stand in a tile of light
next to the window, saying
nothing as I went out
fat with coats to gather the hard
frozen clothes, missing my father,
his shadow taken by the sparrows,
and I'd bury my face deep
in the shirts' whiskered frost.

NOVEMBER BIRDS
Roger Sauls

1.
Lost in some requirement of gravity
to stay close to earth, a nation
of sparrows has hovered over this cornfield

long past the last harvest. The stalks
without color, so limber
they're old men's heads bent

to reading. The field's text says
the real ease is the grace
of hills under the simple poplars.

2.
I'd wake every morning to precise
and grieving songs from doves nesting
at the edge of my sleep. Always

the day itself shuddered to stillness
the moment the world fell
to thinking about itself. A kind of death,

I couldn't help wanting to walk
to the end of it, noticing every small
feature about how dark disappears.

3.
Beyond my uncle's peeling barn
was sky tracked by traffic
of migrating birds. I prayed to be

like them: able to disappear in clouds
on the way to another home. I could hear
their parlance darkening the going.

On the ground the slightest breeze
only made the cornstalks
recite their own death rattle.

from
THE MAN WHO LOVED DIRTY BOOKS
David Guy

IV.

Finally, late in the afternoon, it had rained, long and hard, washed the low gray clouds out of the sky. The dining room, where Matt liked to sit in the evening with a beer, was a dark room anyway, and as he looked out the window to their little backyard, the foliage was heavy, dripping with water; the evening seemed dim, and green, and cool. From the kitchen—it was Laurel's night to cook—came the sound of pork chops frying; he could hear her banging around to wash the potatoes. From the living room, behind him, came the blare of the television; Jonathan was finishing up his allotted television time, watching a show about a typical American family who had somehow become stranded on another planet, where they kept running into western heroes, famous buccaneers, man-eating plants, and gory monsters. Matt sat with his beer—he had bought the kind of heavy rounded glass that was used in the best old-time bars—and puffed on his pipe, staring out at the yard.

After a while he walked out to their little kitchen, where the floor sagged with his steps, the wall above the stove was grimy from years of frying. The phone was out there, on the opposite wall.

"I think I'll try Wolf again," he said.

Peeling apples at the stove, Laurel nodded.

Matt felt an odd mix of emotions. On the one hand, there was nothing like a spine-snapping orgasm to lift his spirits; it had left him feeling cheerful all afternoon. What incredible luck! to wander into such a situation and encounter, almost literally, the woman of his dreams. On the other hand, he had lost track of Bollinger completely, came out of that little room only to find only Celeste sitting there, no help whatsoever; she didn't know whether Hugh had stayed or gone. He had looked Hugh up in the phone book, spent the afternoon trying to call him, even drove by his house to see if he was there, but had no luck. He felt sheepish calling Wolf with nothing definite to report, but thought he'd better.

"Yo." Wolf had answered the phone.

"Wolf. Where you been all afternoon? I tried to call."

"I spent the afternoon in the parking lot of the Howard Johnson's Motor Lodge. Divorce case. The most exciting thing I saw was when they came out for an ice cream cone. But I am now a witness to a suspicious circumstance. A couple spent four hours of an afternoon in a closed motel room. And when they finally came out they exchanged a lingering kiss. That's the word I'm using. Lingering."

"Good word."

"How'd it go with you?"

"I talked with Droge. I don't think he'll be much help."

"Goofy-looking guy."

"He also didn't see much. I mean he says he saw it all. But when you get right down to it he's shaky on the details."

"Wonderful."

"But I found another guy. Who I used to know a little. Hugh Bollinger."

"And he saw it."

"I think he did."

There was a prolonged silence on the other end of the line. "You forgot to ask?"

"He saw the accident. We didn't get down to details. But I'm getting back in touch with him. And he'll look a lot better on the witness stand. Downright respectable. If we can keep him sober."

"Jesus Christ."

"He's the best I can do so far. That's not the easiest place to look for a witness."

"I know, I know. Anything's better than Droge. But you got to get on it. Talk to this guy as soon as you can. If we got nobody, we got to know that."

"Okay."

"Give me a call when you have something."

Matt hung up, heaved a long sigh. It could have gone worse.

There had been the problem, earlier, of what to tell Laurel about his day. He didn't want to make it sound as if he hadn't done anything; on the other hand, he didn't think he'd better go into absolutely everything he had done, or that had been done to him. He knew she'd be fascinated by some of it. He tried to make the part with Bollinger sound a little less sleazy: they had traveled to an exclusive men's club where, for the delectation of the members, certain highly erotic acts were featured. She had been interested in all he had told her about the dancer, somewhat less interested by the details of the movie ("I don't want to hear about your obsession with the size of a man's penis." "I'm not obsessed with it. I'm telling you what happened in the movie." "All men are obsessed with it. There's nothing stupider."), and utterly disgusted by what happened at the end of the movie. "No woman should put up with that. No matter how much she's being paid." Matt had left out any account of the end of the morning. He made it sound as if Bollinger had had to leave suddenly and they'd parted ways.

She was slicing up apples to cook with the pork chops when he hung up the phone.

"Does he think this sounds promising?"

"Maybe. Anyway, he wants to hear what Bollinger has to say."

"I'm not sure he'll be so reliable a witness as you make him sound."

Ever since he had come home that day—in fact, whenever in the past month he had brought up the subject of his work— she had taken the same attitude: a certain wariness came into her voice, and her face tensed, almost winced, as she looked at him. She watched him as he talked as if he were marginally insane, kept her mouth clamped tight as if biting off the words she would like to say. He couldn't tell her the simplest details of his day without facing this attitude.

Suddenly—perhaps because he was at a point where he was least sure about his job, was going through incredible contortions to put a good face on it—he'd had enough.

"Laurel." He sat down at the little table where they kept the toaster and where, most mornings, they ate breakfast. "I don't appreciate your attitude toward my work."

"Oh." She turned an utterly blank face toward him. "What is my attitude?"

"You act like it's something an idiot would do."

Her whole body, as she stood at the stove with the paring knife, was taut. She looked as if she wanted to launch into a passionate speech, say all the things she had never said, wave the knife around, perhaps use it to carve up his face a little and then plunge it into his midsection. She seemed to be holding all those possibilities back. She spoke carefully, her face only twitching slightly.

"You're sure you're not projecting that," she said.

"I *knew* you'd say that." He slammed his fist on the kitchen table. "You always say that. You're always trying to put it back on me."

"Arguing again!" Jonathan shouted from the living room. He did not like it when his parents argued, especially when one of his favorite shows was on, and when they did he shouted at them louder than they were shouting at each other.

He had made a point, though. They were only starting once again an argument they had had many times before.

"You always put it back on me!" Matt shouted.

Laurel was facing away from Matt, seeing him just from the corner of her eye, her mouth tight and trembling, as if she were selecting the proper plan of attack.

"All right," she said. "Let's say I am the way you're saying. That is the way I feel. Should that matter to you?"

"Of course it should. My own wife."

"Would you rather I'd pretend to feel another way?"

"I'd rather my wife would support me in what I'm trying to do."

Those words, which so simply expressed a reasonable request, which in fact expressed what—in her own way—she was trying to do, touched Laurel. She put the knife down, turned her body to face him.

"Matt. I do support you." (The unfortunate double en-

tendre made Matt flinch.) "I support you in what you're try-
ing to do. To find some work that will be important for you.
I can't always agree with you about what that is."

"You haven't approved of a thing I've done since we left
school."

"That's not true."

"It is true. It is. First it was you and your counselor
friends, sitting around looking like you were going to die every
time I mentioned something I'd done. As if I spent all my
time practicing police brutality."

"Don't put it off on my friends."

"But that's where it started. Where you started off on this
stuff. As if I should spend the whole day sitting around eat-
ing yogurt and talking about my sex life, like all of you did."

"Now you're attacking my work. This isn't necessary."

"Then we moved here because you found a job, that was
just ducky for you, and when I scraped around and finally
found a way to make a few bucks you didn't like that either,
couldn't stop talking about how crummy the school was,
how stupid all the teachers were."

The things he was saying were true enough, but he made
it sound as if she were tearing him down, when really she was
just trying to keep him from sinking into something that
wasn't right for him.

"I felt terrible, Matt. I felt this horrible guilt. That I had
found just the job I wanted, and you were having to work at
that scummy place."

"Don't feel sorry for me. Don't pity me. That's the worst
thing there is. The most condescending thing."

"I know, I know. I'm sorry."

"I took the job. I did what I could with it. I didn't com-
plain. But now when I finally get away from it, I get some-
thing close to what I really want, you don't like that either."

Couldn't Matt see the long downward arc, from a police
job in a college community to a third-rate private school to a
sleazy private detective agency run by one man? Anyone could
see he was accepting scraps, reaching for less and less.

"Matt. I have no objection to police work."

"You do. You always have. You can't go back on that now."

"It isn't necessarily what I'd choose for my husband to
do. But if that's what he wants—I just don't like to see you

putting up with things. Settling for less than what you are."

"I have to live in the world. I have to settle for what there is."

Laurel's face had quietly calmed, as if she had come to a decision.

"I saw that office, Matt."

Matt reddened. "What." He spoke the word dumbly, not like a question.

"I went down to the Highland Building and saw that office. Where Wolf has his detective agency."

Matt looked away, annoyed and embarrassed. "What'd you do that for?"

"It's pitiful, Matt. It's pitiful. The building's falling down all around it. There are two years of cigarette butts in the hallway. Dust and dirt all around. They don't bother to change the bulbs in the light fixtures."

"Wolf just keeps that office as a convenience. He doesn't really use it. He's hardly ever in there. And he's that kind of man. Uses makeshift things." Matt had to smile, thinking of that incredible car.

"Now you're on this supposed case. With a man you actually know, from that other creepy place. Chasing through dirty-book stores after a worn-out alcoholic."

"Laurel. This case isn't what I'm doing. God. This case is not what I'm doing."

"A man is doing what he's doing, Matt."

"It's just a crazy thing that happened to come up. We've just got to get it out of the way. We probably have it out of the way."

"I can see it being one thing like this after another. Checking up on somebody's husband. Looking for a homeless kid. Any poor lost soul who can scrape up a few bucks can ask you to do anything he wants."

"Things won't always be like this. You've got to believe me. Wolf looks like a funny old guy, but he's one of the sharpest men in the business. In the city, anywhere."

Laurel didn't believe him. He could tell to look at her that she didn't believe him.

"I wish you were doing something else," she said.

"God!" He jumped from his chair, slammed the heel of his fist against the wall. "I wish I were doing something else. I wish I were doing it somewhere else. Anywhere but here."

"You'll crack the plaster!" Jonathan shouted from the living room.

Laurel sat limply, her hands in her lap, her eyes sad and defeated.

"I wanted to be a ballplayer!" Matt shouted. He was storming around the little kitchen, in the small space between the stove, table, refrigerator, and pantry. He was a big man, who looked as if he could wreck the place with a few quick swipes. "I was a ballplayer. A damn good one. My fastball could break a brick wall. My arm went dead."

"You could go on in baseball somehow. Coach."

"I just did coach. At that dumb fucking little school. How'd you like it when I did that?"

"I don't mean coach at the worst hole in the city."

"You have to work at the places that are there."

"There are other places."

"I didn't want to coach. I wanted to play. So I went into police work. Because my old man was a cop. I grew up with that all around me. I was proud of him. I loved him."

"It was a good thing." There were tears in Laurel's eyes, tears of frustration. They had been over it so many times, this litany of failed hopes. "It was a good thing to do."

"Then we had to move. I agreed we had to move. I wanted you to find a good job. But I couldn't be a cop here."

"You can be a cop here. The jobs have to open up eventually. If you can just wait."

"I have to live in the meantime."

"We have my salary. My parents can help us out."

"I mean I have to live." As hard as he had pounded the table, he hit his own chest, with his fist. "I have to live with me. As a man."

Laurel stared through her tears at this passionate angry man who was making almost no sense.

"I have to have something to do!" Matt shouted.

Jonathan ran into the kitchen, his face rapt with fury. "I can't hear my show."

"Take your fucking show and shove it up your ass."

It wasn't really his show he was worried about, but his parents; he burst into tears and ran out of the room.

"There are things I'd like to do," Matt shouted. "There are

things I'd like to do. I can't do them." He was staring into the dark abyss—Laurel knew it well—of nothing worthwhile in his life to do. "I have to take what I can get. I have to do what there is."

He bolted out of the house, slamming the back door behind him.

Laurel hurried to the living room to see about Jonathan.

Matt was wearing his cloth bedroom slippers, and the grass in the backyard was long, and very wet (he kept meaning to mow; somehow he got less done when he was around the house a lot than when he had worked full-time). His slippers immediately got soaked. He walked around the perimeter of the yard a couple of times as if he were taking laps. Little flecks of drizzle had started falling out of the sky, prelude to another shower. In his anger he grabbed a branch of the cherry tree and started to shake it; cherries started plopping all around him and so did a shower of rain from the leaves, wetting his hair and soaking his shirt. He noticed the elderly woman next door watching him through the venetian blind of her kitchen window. It was all he could do to keep from giving her the finger. He started his laps of the yard again, soaking wet. He felt like an utter fool and didn't care. After a while, in the evening breeze, he actually started to feel a chill. He walked around the side of the house and in the front door.

Jonathan and his mother were sitting together in one of the chairs, Jonathan still sniffing a little.

"Is it raining again?" Laurel said.

"Only on me," Matt said.

Her eyes were weary. "You look terrible," she said.

"I'm sorry, Jonathan," Matt said. "I was just mad."

"It wasn't a nice thing to say."

"I know. I'm sorry."

"It makes no sense, anyway."

"I know." Matt started upstairs to change his clothes.

Jonathan spoke to his father's back. "I missed the end of my show."

Laurel had gone to some trouble with the dinner, pork chops lightly fried and then steamed, stewed apples, mashed potatoes, and green beans, but for Matt the food had almost no taste: he chewed it listlessly, running everything together. His glass of light white wine might as well have been Kool-Aid.

Afterward he played a game of checkers with Jonathan, saw that he got a bath, read to him from a comic book.

"I'm glad you're a detective," Jonathan said while he soaped himself in the tub. "That's what I want you to be."

Matt leaned down and ruffled his hair.

Downstairs he and Laurel read for a while, Matt leafing aimlessly through one magazine after another. He couldn't find anything he liked; the rattling of the pages got to be almost continuous. Finally Laurel got up, came over and sat on the arm of his chair. "I'm sorry," she said. "The whole thing really isn't any of my business." He was too tired to answer, didn't want to get into all that again, but if he had he would have said she had been right, he had spent his adult life going from one pitiful job to another and was ashamed of all of them. (They should have changed sides and argued those positions for a while.) They walked upstairs to make love, but their hearts weren't in it; their bodies, as they lay together, felt strange in one another's arms. Matt's orgasm was mild, and came, he felt, too soon. Laurel's seemed to take forever, so that his hand almost cramped up as he touched her; when she finally finished she gave one loud shout as if in anger. Afterward they lay awake, not talking, both staring at the ceiling. Laurel was thinking, if the truth be known, of her young hungry ardent lover, who adored her spirit and fed on her body as if it nourished him. Matt, on the other hand, was thinking of that mysterious woman who gave exquisite pleasure, who asked nothing more of him than to give him pleasure and who disappeared as quickly as she had arrived. ■

POSSUMMA
Michael McFee

for William Harmon

These things are real, children:
Who needs to make things up?

INVOCATION

"O possum,"
you apostrophize to the pet-sized specimen
slumped in the headlights of your old Nova,
                    the '63 Oxymoron,
"if, as a hick once joked in a movie,
            the state animal of Mississippi
        is a dead dog in the middle of the road,
I nominate you, O most ancient of days,
            for national mascot!"

THE MANIFEST WITNESS OF HISTORY

1. American
                    At precisely
mid-millennium, Senor Pinzon, envious chief
of the Niña, presents a New World *didelphis*
                    to his dubious patrons,
Ferdinand and Isabella. The court murmurs
        as their majesties poke thier fingers
            in its pouch. *Zerigüya!* They are delighted!
In Jamestown a century later, Captain Smith,
                    new Adam in pantaloons,

interrogates the Indians
for native names to give the animals.
"And this?" "Ugh—Possum," growls the chief.
"O-possum!" proclaims
Smith to his scribe, fixing the vestigial vowel.
"Animal mirabile," his brethren
scratch in their diaries by candlelight,
"with an head like a Swine, a taile like a Rat,
& of the bignes of a Cat."

Further on, M. LaSalle,
at the heart of the midwestern wilderness
later to claim his name for a de-luxe model
with wings and whitewalls,
encounters a pair of *rats du bois* in the bushes
and dispatches them with his baton.
Soon he swaggers back to camp, possums slung
from his belt. *"Voila!"* he cries. *"Tableau!"* thinks
his artist, title ready:

"LaSalle at the Portage."
If only Franklin had known the possum's pedigree,
150 million years, more venerable than even
his beloved turkey!
Would the Congressional delegates have voted it
a place on the Great Seal, clutching
thirteen arrows in its prehensile tail
and persimmon branches in each foot, *possumus,*
e pluribus unum?

2. Literary

Consider: why did Eliot,
fastidious Anglo-Catholic, Royalist, lapsed Yankee,
call himself Old Possum? And would he have been able,

           Blessed Gabriel Rossetti,
to keep a less likely Pre-Raphaelite pet
           than the possum that slept on his table?

3. Natural
        "Nature amazes me," as someone summed up
a workshop-worn poem. That the possum is called
        "living fossil"—cousin

           to wombat and bandicoot,
contemporary with gingko tree or horseshoe crab,
the mammals' ace white-haired knuckleballer
           in the World Series
of evolution—is curious enough. But the male
        sports an anatomical feature,
        stranger than fiction, stranger than the fact
of the female's dozen-day gestation, that firmly
           clinches the prize.

           It's simply this:
the possum has a forked penis, a by-God genuine
twi-night doubleheader. This gave rise to the rumor
           of a nosy pioneer
that possums mated through the lady's snout
        and that, after incubation in the sinus,
        the missus sneezed the measly naked litter
into her pouch—yet another triumph of fecundity
           over intelligence.

BENEDICTION

        When McPhee wrote, "Be
a possum is the message, and you might outlive God,"
he had the species in mind, not pea-brained heroes

                    trying to scramble to
the other, greener side of suburban autobahns.
           The last thing your late possum heard
       was rubber thunder behind headlights' lightning,
then a bald four-part descant, some EAT MORE POSSUM
                pickup fading away.

                 Now he balloons
for the ants' Thanksgiving parade, a memento mori
grinning from the road's cold shoulder. If only he
              could shake this swoon
for a final wish, it might be what any body asks:
           to play himself again, to resurrect
       blinking from the rotten ditch, to shuffle
across the way toward some immortal shade and climb
                into the sky to sleep.

ONTOLOGIES
Buck Poole

Show me a man's ontology. Heidegger said that. He's not saying it anymore, though. He's dead. I am saying it now. Perhaps someone else is saying it right now; perhaps, too, that simultaneous saying matters. But probably not. Truthfully, I cannot even imagine that it's being said. I walk from window to window in my tiny bedroom and say it. Show me a man's ontology. Yes, goddamit, *show* me a man's ontology. I shout it. *SHOW* me a man's ontology. Show *ME* a man's ontology. I can shout now, my wife isn't here for me to disturb anymore.

She left me on the same day Jerry Lee Lewis's fifth wife died. They found her on the double bed asleep, dead. Jerry Lee's wife, not mine. My wife and I decided to separate by mutual agreement. It was a mutual decision. When it comes to men and women, I always wonder how mutual these decisions are. Isn't one the lover, and one the beloved? Isn't it always that way? What the hell difference does it make, anyway. I am concerned with ontology.

Underfoot the old wooden flooring is bare, smooth, it feels like the surface of smooth new cardboard against my bare feet. This room, tiny and shabby, an attic room. The walls, thin sheets of plaster, molded to the angles of the peaks and valleys of the roof. I can feel beams and joists pressing in on me at oblique angles. The walls have been poorly plastered and are ridged and pocked beneath the harsh overhead light.

But mostly they've been papered, and repainted, and under my fingers the paper bubbles up. The low bit of ceiling between the sloping walls is peeling and water-spotted.

All day I have been rethinking it and taking notes. A man's ontology—you catch it in a gesture, a snort, a glance. If in words, just a few. Three or four. No more than a sentence.

My east window looks out on the treetops; the spokes of the sun's rays radiate from a hub western, low. They lay on the roof, they light the leaves scarlet and gold. Like the moon, these leaves take the borrowed light as their own, and, like the moon, they illuminate a parasitic transition-time, an underside of time.

The window reaches from the floor to the ceiling. I stand before it, resting my forehead on the window frame, bumping my shins on the sill. Far below the leaves' muted beacons the cars pass one another on the little strip of blacktop. Those west-bound climb the hill, then double back around, under my western window. Beneath that window a motorcycle booms by, no mufflers, just straight pipes. The floor pulsates rhythmically beneath my feet. I run over to that window and see a Harley-Davidson pulling up the hill. Its rider is slumped along saddle and tank and rear fender, between his legs the engine's iron carnival of motion.

A few high school kids walk in the road, watch him pass out of sight. They wear black leather jackets and their hair is in their eyes. Their T shirts say "Dogman" and "Sexboy" and "Don't mess with this shit." Above them smoke curls from the tall smokestack of the town's tannery. The sun is setting on this sad little town, it pushes beneath the crest of the hill. Only a red afterglow remains.

I witness this event, this transition. Across the road is a bank of woods, and above the woods the highest point in town, a hill where the streets leading to its summit are almost vertical. Behind this hill the sun now hides, behind this swelling of horizon.

Another small ending. Let me deny this ending, this cycle of beginnings and endings, the concern with which some call ontology and some adolescence. I could run down the stairs and up the hill and see the sun again. And then, a third time, after it had once more dipped below the edge of the world, by scaling the water tower, hand over hand, rung by rung, and gathering in that last red sun, a moribund sun. The day is leaking out there. A small ending, this little death, by which we intuit a larger one. This sun sets, stars are burning out; perhaps my wife is creating some new ontology at this moment, engaging it as one cog engages another.

An ontology—is there to be something beyond this dull succession of appearances? What of the screams for the actual, the true, behind the veil of Sais? Plato emerging from the cave blinking, spectre-like, dust in his hair, as some workman from a city-street manhole? The sublime, the numinous?

But those things are not the ontology I know. The one I know is out of the corner of the eye, offhand, intuited, everyday. It's not a lightning bolt of ontology, but a bit of static electricity. A little bit of something, as when the TV camera is trained upon the evening newsman an instant too long and he is forced to shuffle his papers and clear his throat.

Or a deeper something, as when Jerry Lee Lewis, "The Killer," as he has always called himself, tells his audience during his "25th Anniversary in Entertainment" show that "the only person The Killer was trying to kill was . . . himself." Then they find his wife of four months with ten times the normal dosage of methadone coursing through the tangle of her veins. Just a little glimpse behind the scenes, no worlds-layered-on-worlds. A little glimpse, like a partial eclipse of the sun, or a small fragment of some forgotten civilization.

Now the sky is inky. Down below, the car's headlights are so small. Riding their Z of highway which loops up the big hill in switchbacks, as if this little summit were a peak in the Sierra Nevadas. I look down into the tiny valley, then up toward the summit, here on my half-way perch, my promontory. This twisted matchbox of a bedroom in this old white-slate covered frame house. There are two more rooms below, each atop the other, and so the three rooms are stacked one on the other like chunky vertebra, the enduring backbone of this old house.

I pace from one window to another. Cars sail by in the night. Through the narrow dormer window to the north, just above me, headlight beams slide and angle along the white wall of the house next door. Ontologies. Mostly you just sift the rubble of the everyday with them. Simple class concepts, metaphors. Life is a bed of roses. Life is a tangle of thorns.

Life is just a good night's sleep and a laugh with your friends. It's realizing one's potential. It's leaving the world a little bit better place. People is what it's all about.

There is a great cloud of sound between my house and the hill. The little bank of woods dances in headlight beams. It is a gang of Harleys. The staggered cadence of exhaust notes is audible in the rush and roar of engines. There is something clean, pure in the throbbing of the pipes. The V of the big cylinders, the bandanna and black leather jacket. At least a simplicity. On a little run with the brothers. Stop for some beer in a roadhouse. Maybe some booze. Zoom.

In the headlights of oncoming cars is silhouetted a woman sitting behind the rider on the lead bike; her arms are joined at jaunty angles before his chest, her head thrown back. She looks like Charlotte Rampling. Her features are sharp, pretty, disdainful, in the frozen headlight moment she is a figurehead on some ancient sailing ship. She and the bikers seem so close. The windowpane rattles before my face. I feel I could reach out and touch them as they pass. Their rush and roar recede into the distance. Bikes, brothers, broads.

Ontologies come in threes these days. A leaf, a stone, a door. Liberty, equality, fraternity. Salut, Amor, e Pesetas. The good, the bad, the ugly. Eat, drink, and be merry. Three easy bits of meaning. As easy as one—two—three; rhythm and adequacy. Two aren't enough and four are too many. What about the holy trinity? And don't forget Hegel. Ontology by threes.

Here too it must be admitted that Wittgenstein began his severe search of the *Tractatus* at just this place, quoting Kurnberger: ". . . and whatever a man knows, whatever is not mere rumbling and roaring that he has heard, can be said in three words." The directives of nakedness, necessity, revelation, but polished, palatable, homely. Show me a man's ontology.

Maybe I'll market ontology like the Encyclopedia Britannica or the Great Books. The Mortimer Adler of ontology. Maybe a supersales method will emerge. The ontological method.

Perhaps I'll hold my own ontology tent meetings. Give me a good amen, that's what they yell at the revival camp meetings. Give me a good ontology!

I see two figures across the road; what are they doing there?

Maybe they're hitch-hiking. One day my wife and I were here and two people stood across the road. They kept staring at the house. It was afternoon, a time we weren't usually home. Maybe, we thought, they were considering breaking in and looking for something to sell. They stood there for half an hour. Occasionally one of us would lift up and look. Finally I saw one of them raise a thumb as a car went by. They were simply hitch-hiking.

What a sad afternoon that was. We had driven into the town as schoolbuses and factories emptied their contents. The quiet town was filled with schoolchildren's cries and the streets were jammed with workers' cars. The dull storefronts and the drab colors of their clothing and the leaden sky were all of a piece. In the afternoon paper were DWI cases and old people and schedules of veterans' organizations meetings and beano games and obituaries. The town's ontology seeped backward and forward in time and space like a stain.

My wife and I made our way through the gray light of that afternoon to this bedroom and removed our clothes and ran our race through the columbine and larkspur. Afterward, we held one another tight to keep the leaden sky and the town's late afternoon ontologies from rendering us cold and null, foreign to one another.

Outside, the two figures are placing a slipped chain back into place on a ten-speed bicycle. The man holds the baby in one arm as he tugs at the chain with the other. The woman holds the handlebars and awkwardly mounts it as he puts the chain in place. She rides fifteen yards until a big battered sedan, riding low to the ground, muffler chuffing, slows down beside her. Someone leans out from the back seat and slaps her on the butt. The bicycle sways crazily and the car takes off in a frantic spewing of exhaust smoke and the man runs forward, yelling, you sons of bitches, at the top of his voice. Then the bicycle straightens and she slows and stops and he holds her in one arm and the baby in the other.

I wonder what The Killer is doing right now. Maybe he is swimming at the bottom of a bottle. Maybe he is with another woman in another bed. Maybe he is passed out on his piano keyboard or waving around a pistol in one of his Rolls-Royces on some southern highway. Maybe some precious white substance is dancing behind his eyes.

I saw him perform a year ago. Onstage he was pale and wan. His gleaming smile and frilly shirtfront were odd and incongruous. After the show we waited in the alley for him to come out of his Winnebago dressing room. For autographs. But when he came out there were no autographs. He appeared exhausted, ill. Phalanxed by several chunky men with defiant eyes and slicked-back hair and sport shirts, he walked carefully and slowly, eyes on the ground, to his new cream-colored Lincoln Continental. After they climbed into the Lincoln, it shot backward through the narrow alley, its headlights receding from us, at fifteen or twenty miles an hour. Jerry Lee sat between two of the men in the back seat, his head hanging down wearily.

It's half an hour after midnight. I lie on the bed staring at the wrestling poster on the wall. There's Growla the wrestling bear and Rick Flair and Blackjack Mulligan. The ontology of wrestling. The babyface, the heel, and the city of pain. They don't come to see the babyface win, a wrestler once told me, they come to see the heel get beat. Maybe The Killer would say that there is only his work, something that is bad for his work, and another which is over in half an hour.

When I awake the clock reads five a.m. and the room is flashing blue through the dormer window and the window on the road. The police cruiser is directly below the window, idling high, breathy. A busy official sound. If I took three paces out the front door I'd bump into it. A thin white shaft of light is jerking about over in the woods. I hear the crashing footsteps there, I hear a man's moans and cries. There are words—"no no, go away, ohh." His words become one long wailing word of confusion and drunkenness and pain. The beam of light catches him and he grabs at the policeman, who loses his footing and they are both sprawling in the woods.

My brother-in-law, he is yelling and crying. My brother-in-law, but the cop quiets him somehow, and soon he is sitting drunk and dishevelled and beaten in the back seat of the cruiser. The ontology of come on, we're taking you down to the station. The officer calls in; the radio crackles and resounds in the night. Then he slams the driver's door and puts it in gear and the tires squeal on take-off. Zoom, they're gone.

And now it is quiet in this awful time just before dawn. One night I stayed up until dawn finishing the *Phenomenology of Spirit.* I reached the end, the Golgotha of Absolute Spirit, and knew Hegel was absolutely and finally right, and the greatest philosopher who ever lived. But still I had to shower and go about my business that day. Somehow it didn't fit together. Later I decided that Hegel was as right as a philosopher can be, but that that right wasn't quite right enough.

I began to take an interest in the little way, ontologies of the everyday. Not ontology, but a man's ontology. Show me that ontology. Those ontologies. Since my wife's flight they're even more important. The simple, the tragic, the bizarre. Money, crime, and passion. Mercy, pity, peace.

Here's the sun again, offering itself up, having yoyoed around the world. I do a few toe touches, wash my face, pack my ontology notes and a pair of clean underwear and a Sony walkman into an attache case. Then I dress and descend from my matchbox promontory and settle beside the highway. A woman walks by, her body soft and sensual, her face hard. She carries one child in the crook of her arm and leads another by the hand. Her blue jeans are worn thin and smooth and she has a chain-drive wallet like a biker. Her fingernails are red as port wine and her eyebrows thin and arched. The wallet rides her ample hip as she walks.

I put out my thumb for a car, but it doesn't stop. The sun is rising on millions of American ontologies. The sun is rising and I am free, white, and twenty-one. Even The Killer sang "Over the Rainbow." Show me a man's ontology. ∎

THE SWAN STORY
Betty Adcock

to Don

> but the youngest was left
> with a swan's wing instead of
> an arm, for one sleeve was
> wanting to the shirt of mail.
>
> —*from* "The Wild Swans"
> by Hans Christian Andersen

1.
If you take my hand
and what you hold is instead
the prickle and broken
knuckles of feathers, dismantled
fingers of flight,
                    stay with me anyway
where we walk in the year's last snow.
If I tell you only a child's tale,
its fragment of singing, its unkempt
puzzle not worth it,
                         stay.

2.
Once, wisteria grew round
like a cave or a purple room
where I hid to read long afternoons
that tilted the house and barn toward miracle.

Something flew out of the stories,
my eleven years not yet memory

flapping voiceless and spellstruck
over the derelict kingdom, over
the listing farm, pickets and wild grass,
the exiled orchard.

Without brother or sister, I wore
all the faces, played sibling
to henyard flocks,
pouring out a teacupful of sand.
In graceless tumble and shit-bloom,
possum-robbed, sad-tailed, the hens
scratched their dotty alphabet in dust.

3.
In the orchard pond, sun looked
at itself through green.
Frogs leaped into flowers
of shattered light.
The dead mother was a black mirror
where my face wouldn't grow,
its other side only pond-silver,
only the known true world
but hidden still, and unwilling.

Night after night,
over sleep's waters burning blue
in their permanent glacial sun,
I flew the changeable journey,
a cradle of feathers under me,
a kinship, a wonder.
Down there, the day-shadows drifted
undone in the sea's glass dance.
Beautiful as fishes, the nightmares to come
were clotting into reefs.

In dream's icy candescence,
the heart knows how to fall
—*that to fall into darkness*
is to be human awhile—
its landmark the rock-shape of loss.

4.

String and tatter, a life
is what it can find
growing wild in woods and churchyard,
houseyard, abandoned orchard.
At the edges where Word *and* Doorsill *die,*
the fieldmouse will stay, and the thrush
under the hawk's eye. The ant will build
at the foot of the apple, and that tree
let down its poor bundles for birds.
There burns the green to be crushed,
to be spun in earth's turn,
the garment our bones wear
weaving itself of humus,
of light the dead are.

Becoming the stung palms of grief.

5.

Possums my father blasted from night's tree
lay flat and stiff on the spread mornings,
flies in their teeth,
and the farm's dog nursed a worm-hole deep
as an eye-socket in the breathing flank,
crossed with bloodless tendon-strings.

How did my mother go
out spark by spark? I could just
remember the box of churchlight,

the strange crowded roses.
I thought she'd left to be
that dun stone angel whose hands were broken off
before I was born into the name it wore.
The whole farm was buried
under a grainy light, the necessary
word sinking deeper, and the missing
hands of the stone.

The pantry's vegetable years
dimmed in their jars;
the milk pan glowed like a downed moon
and the wine darkened,
hissing its way up.
On the dark parlor table, a blown glass swan
lifted clear wings, a flight of rain.

6.
Mornings after storms I watched the light
tip its arrows in every brief and bush,
even the possum with his bloody smile,
even the dog eaten down to the bone
and the grave stone clear across town
shining.

Nettle, thorn and sandspur,
the world stings itself into summer.
It can open the hands like stars.

Already the future was threading
green fires. I would startle forward
like the hens shoved out of silence
by the predator's pink bright eye.

7.
From love to death to love
spirit in a splintering bone-cart
jounces, rags and tangled hair,
in silence
always toward the last fire;
and still with its green-burnt hands
weaves.

When the bird—for rescue—alights
like flurries of white air, like snow,
when the body's yet-wanting green
is flung over that whirling flight,
O makeshift forever—
dry sticks piled for a killing flame
will burst, every time, into blossom.

8.
Broken then
from the heat-blister of childhood
into fragrance of snowrose and firerose
bud and thorn-nub stirring in flesh
ready to crave and go out,
I woke to no kin but myself
of the long making.
All the winged brothers were folded
under my own skin,
this unfinished shift all I'd have on my back
for the rest of my left-handed life;
all I'd have in one hand this
web, quill and featherbone
to shadow my path with a draggled trace
like a one-sided angel in snow.

Then was the dog unstrung, gone up
like a kite, the worm
blown out of its tunnel.
The hens rose straight out of their tracks.
Tooth by tooth, the possum let go of his grin.
And the stone took up her hands of earth.

9.
Long ago the sky came down,
pond water full of refracted birds,
and the grounded kingdom lifted its heavy wings.
In the dark mirror whose face I know,
my mother's hands become a stand of simple weeds.

10.
If this is a story, it ends here,
halfway to knowing how.

Only the earliest dream is hollow
and sings. Only that reed
is not filled. Wise bone, flute,
it breathes old stories
into the savage wind that never closes.

Love, tonight we walk in snow
where the creek is nettled with ice.
It grumbles and clinks
beneath a slick suburban moon.
Under flurries that break like pigeons from the pines,
we are freezing and following
rabbit tracks in the blue shadows.
We will laugh our way home, our bodies ready
to clothe each other with hands.

11.
What are you and I
but the one dreamed story
that out of time breaks into many?

We walk toward our winter fire
under the sky's downfall.
Bird-Loose-Feather whitening our hair.
Dear one, hold on. We are
only halfway there.

WAITING AT DACHAU
Reynolds Price

The camp itself—its active life—only lasted twelve years
('33-45). Twelve years after that, we parked by its gates.
Now, twelve years after that, I still don't know; the question
has gathered force with every year's distance—why did you
balk and refuse to enter Dachau, letting me, forcing me to go
in alone? I need to know several things—my version, your ver-
sion, then the truth.

Is the answer simple?—you were sick or tired or fed-up
with sights after six-weeks' traveling? Or were you miffed
about the night before, or—being a little younger—you may
not have seen my urgent need, as a radio-and-newsreel child of
the Forties, to test my memories against the source? (Dachau
and I are almost exact contemporaries; I'm one month older
than it and still running.) For months in advance, I'd braced
for the prospect. Me at the Alps—*us*, don't you see?—the heart
of darkness head-on, between the eyes. (What did I expect?—
to stagger? vomit? No, I knew all wounds would be internal,
all effects delayed.) Or maybe you understood quite well—you
and your Imagination of Disaster—and were only invoking
your famous policy of kindness-to-self. Surely, though, your
chances of bearing-up were as good as mine—we'd been told
the camp was hip-deep in flowers! Couldn't you have entered
as a simple gift to me?

Well, you didn't. You waited. The last time you waited—

for me, at least—and I still wonder why.

My version is this: we'd planned it from the first. Christmas vac. of my first Oxford winter you'd flown from Paris and we'd stretched on the frigid floor of my digs, maps and budgets around us, and plotted the summer (should it ever come: your nosedrops had frozen on my bureau Christmas Eve!)—a slowly warming arc. You would join me again in mid-July. We would ship my new Volkswagen—Newcastle to Bergen. Then we'd push slowly on—a week each for Oslo, Stockholm, Copenhagen; then a non-stop plunge through Germany to Munich. Dachau.

Why Dachau at all? We passed within twenty miles of Belsen, Nordhausen, Dora, Buchenwald, Ohrdruf, Flossenburg. Dachau was never a major death camp. Only a third of its inmates died. Yet I never considered another camp. Three reasons, I think: I knew it was there (most others were razed); the name itself was the perfect emblem, as it was for the Germans themselves, it seems—anyone who disappeared was assumed "to be in *Dachau*." (Something inheres in the name, the sound—pronounced correctly it contains an unstopped *howl*. So does *Auschwitz* but Auschwitz could be—for Americans born after 1950—a brand of beer; *Buchenwald* could be a national park; *Belsen* a chocolate factory. *Dachau* seemed to me then—and seems now—only a terminus; last-stop, as Auden knew in '38—

> . . . *the map can point to places*
> *Which are really evil now—*
> *Nanking. Dachau.)*

And then nearby was Salzburg, as antidote—*Figaro* with Schwarzkopf, Fischer-Dieskau, Seefried, Karl Böhm. Then we could slowly climb the Rhine to Cologne (still without a whole building), the Hague and Vermeer, Amsterdam and Rembrandt; then (healed by now, stronger for the burns), we would ship back to Oxford, take a look at our gains, our chances, maybe marry. You'd pack up your chaste tight paintings in Paris (adjectives yours—triangles, oblate spheroids, cubes, all aching with loneliness in empty space) and join me for a last Oxford year on my thesis; then we'd sail home to all the books I'd write (my dreams of extracting love from my past, the boneyard of my childhood)—having already, well before we were thirty, faced the worst that life had ever offered any human pair, the final solution.

We made it to Munich precisely on schedule, only slightly in the red and apparently in love after four weeks of cold-water hosteling, cold roadside meals—canned potato salad, canned corned beef; we had bought a case of each and would only need bread every day at noon. I keep a photograph of one of those lunches—even without it, I'd have it in my head. We have stopped for lunch by a lake somewhere between Geilo and Oslo. Clear sky, the light a lemon yellow. You sit on a large stone, ten yards from the water, surrounded by smaller stones round and large as baseballs. The sounds are: our feet in those stones, water stroking, your opening of cans. I squat watching you warmed to fragrance in the light, adding to my luck only one more sound—in my head, the voice of Flagstad. She is still alive, a hundred-odd miles from here in retirement, playing solitaire and knitting—and that voice like a new lion in a zoo, *intact*! If she'd sing now we'd hear it cross valleys, through pines! (she will of course return to make those last recordings which calmly eliminate all future need for Wagnerian sopranos). You speak—"Sir, your lunch." You are holding out your hand with a plate of food but you have not risen. I must come to you. Halfway is halfway. I rise and go. *The happiest day in all my life*—I say that silently, moving toward you. Now, twelve years later, it is still unassailed. There hasn't been a happier. Yet, how do I have this photograph of it, in which your hand and the plate of food are blurred, moving toward me? Did I force you to offer it again for the camera or had I waited, shutter cocked, for the moment? Why did you let me complicate your simple service?—you smile in the picture but you have at least the grace to refuse to meet my eyes. Your refusal has begun; your heels are digging in. I am drowned, though, in what tastes to me like good fortune; so I fail to notice for weeks, days or nights.

In the days I could see you—walking gravely past acres of Norwegian painting (every painting since the war in shades of pink and yellow) to smile and say at last "A nation of fairies!" Or sitting in a Stockholm park, eavesdropping on a Swedish girl and her compact rapidly heating French boyfriend (the girl so liberated that I all but expected a taut diaphragm to pop out and roll to rest at our feet when she uncrossed her legs), you said, "Knock her up and she'll wail like Queen Victoria!" Or stopping in the midst of tons of bland Thorwaldsen marbles in Copenhagen (all like variations on the head of Mendelssohn)—"Well, I like the *Danes*. They're crooks." Setting those down makes you sound studied, tough; a big reader of Salinger and Mary McCarthy. But I *saw* you. You were then, every minute of those long summer days, the perfect customized answer to all my optical needs. You seemed—you threatened!—to lack outer boundaries, integument; to vibrate within only vaguely held limits which, each night, permitted—welcomed!—me in to form a perfect compound.

Was I wrong, self-deceived, about that as well? I could even see you then—by the Midnight Sun; the birds never slept. Were you merely drumming time through all my happy hours of artful plunging? (the years spent studying van de Velde, Eustace Chesser)? It's accurate, I know, to say you never turned to *me*. I was the one to initiate action. But once I had laid a hand on your hip, you would rock over toward me and open like—gates! Very earnest, weighty gates that not every man could move. And you'd smile and *thank me*! Always at the end—and you almost always made it or threw Oscar-winning acts—you would say (not whisper; have you still never whispered a word in your life?) *"Thank you"* as though I had zipped the back of your dress or made you a small expensive gift (when there stood my donor capped with high-smelling rubber, Reservoir Tipped to *block* small expensive gifts). And that in the Fifties before the Revolution, when ninety-eight percent of the girls I'd had still shuddered at the end and asked forgiveness—asked me, Count Vronsky! I would lie some nights for hours, too grateful to sleep. You'd be gone in ten seconds.

Was I really wrong? Wasn't the only bad night the one in Munich? Where did we sleep there?—some station hotel or with one of our specialty, war widows with lace-curtained bedrooms to rent and permanent frozen killing smiles propped round government-issue teeth? I can't see the room but I heard the silence—that I took you, really *had* you, against your will for the first time ever. You were tireder than I; but even then you laughed and when I'd hacked to my reward, all huffs and puffs, and questioned your stillness. You said—*said!* surely our *Witwe* heard you—"Riding shotgun in a Volkswagen daily leaves a body badly tuckered." Well, pardon me, Sara—twelve years too late, if you even remember. Hadn't all the other sex till then though been mutual? Wasn't it *love?* We had known each other for ten years exactly, grown up together. We knew all the ways—more than half of them hidden—to protect each other; and any damage was a slip, inadvertent. We could have lived together as easily as dogs; and I'd thought—till that day at Dachau—we meant to. If we didn't love each other, who ever has?

—The de Wieks anyhow, if nobody else. You won't have heard of them. I hadn't till two years after we parted—in Ernst Schnabel's book on Anne Frank. A Dutch Jewish husband and wife flushed from hiding in 1943 and shipped to Auschwitz, where the husband died and the wife survived to remember Anne Frank's death. But this is the thing I want you to know—Mrs. de Wiek's memory fifteen years later of a moment on the packed train threading toward Auschwitz:

> *I sat beside my husband on a small box. The box swayed every time the wheels jolted against the tracks. When the third day came and we had not arrived, my husband took my hand and suddenly said: "I want to thank you for the wonderful life we have had together."*
>
> *I snatched my hand away from him, crying:: "What are you thinking of? It's not over!"*
>
> *But he calmly reached for my hand again, and took it, and repeated several times: "I thank you. Thank you for the life we have had."*
>
> *Then I left my hand in his and did not try to draw it away . . .*

There is no photograph in the book of him or her; but they've walked, since I read that, as clearly in my head, as in *Daniel* three just Jews walk safe through the flames of Nebuchadnezzar's furnace. Shadrach, Meshach, Abednego—and a fourth, their angel. The de Wieks walk alone, two stripped Dutch Jews, dark-eyed, grinning, safe in my head; to Hell with *my* head, safe through all time should *no one* know of them, sealed in the only knowledge that turns fire—to have loved one another through to the last available instant, to have *known* and then had the grace to say thanks.

Were you just not that good—that strong and pure—or did you choose not to be that good *for me*?

I see them in their flames (or you by your lake) much more clearly than I see Dachau. My world-famous total recall deserts me. Or does it? Can it have been the way I remember? (I've never gone again.) The latest *Britannica* gives this much—that Dachau is a town eleven miles northwest of Munich, population ('61) 29,086, first mentioned as a market village 805 AD and continued as a village till 1917 when an ammunition factory was built there—the site in March 1933 of the first Nazi concentration camp; that the town stands on a hill at the summit of which is the castle of the Wittelsbacher and that the other sight is a parish church (1625).

What *I* remember is driving through sunny fields of potatoes and grain, you watching for road signs and calling the turns (German roads then were still under heavy reconstruction; and one of your frequent bursts of song was *"Umleitung* —there's a muddy road ahead!"). Wasn't my right hand holding your thigh, except when a farmer waved from a yard? Wasn't the town still a village after all, merely houses (no business street that I remember)?—low white houses with small sandy yards, green gardens in front? Don't I remember screened porches, green rockers, dusty ferns in cans, geraniums in boxes? A gray frame railway depot and platform? Didn't I ask to stop and walk awhile or to drive slow and aimless (we had hours till the camp closed) through the loose grid of streets that seemed home at last (were they really unpaved, ankle-deep in white dust?)? But you led us on—"Turn right; here, here." Your unfailing sense of where we were, where we must go. I was ready to wait, stop short of the camp. The village itself, your warm proximity, had eased my urgency for confrontation. What we had—there and then—seemed tested enough by time and chance, to require no further *pro forma* buffeting. It was you—I'm sure of this—who forced us on. An Ariadne who—calm in her beauty—perfectly aware of the course she's set—calmly leads dumb Theseus back into the lethal heart of the maze, its small tidy utterly efficient death chamber, the patient minotaur who has only played possum and waits now, famished.

From the parking lot (!) on—in my memory—it does seem a room, not ample but sufficient and sturdily enclosed. The new small gates (where are the old ones?—*Arbeit Macht Frei*), the cyclone fence thickly threaded with vines, the no-nonsense sign (*Maintained by the Corps of Engineers, U.S. Army*), the clear sky, the light—seemed interior, roofed, sheltered, shrunk or a model scaled precisely to a larger form. Is that why I didn't lock the car?—after weeks of paranoia, left out luggage available to any passer? Or had I started guessing you would stay behind?—guessing and hoping?

You had got yourself out ("Chivalry ends here," you had told me in Stockholm) and stood in sun that suddenly had the weight of sun at home, that seemed each second to be loading you with burdens. Also the color—you were bleaching as I watched. Yet you took off your sunglasses and stood by your shut door, hands at your sides, squinting straight at me.

I came round to you and extended my hand. You accepted. I took a step onward and engaged your weight, gently.

You said "No." You were planted. Your hand stayed in mine but your face refused.

I said "No, *what?*" and laughed.

"Not going," you said.

I didn't ask why but said what my father always said when I balked—"Are you sick?"

"No," you said.

"Then you promised," I said.

You had not; you should have laughed. But you shook your head.

"If I ordered you?" I said.

"You wouldn't."

"If I did?"

"I wouldn't go."

I said "*Wouldn't* or *couldn't?*"

"Wouldn't," you said.

We had not smiled once!

You took back your hand.

I said "Will you wait?"

You nodded yes.

"Where?"

"I'll *wait*," you said. You half-waved behind you, a cluster of trees, shady grass beneath.

So I moved again to go—to leave in fact—not looking back, and entered the camp. Dachau. Left you waiting, as you chose. Are you waiting still?

You have never seen it and, as I've said, my otherwise sharp pictorial memory is dim on Dachau; so to write this, I've spent three days trailing information through volumes of war-crimes trials, memoirs, histories of the S.S., photographs (forty Jewish women—nude, mostly pot-bellied, three of them holding children—queue up for a massacre in some Polish ditch: two of them are smiling toward the camera). Guess what a good three days I've had—to learn very little more than this (the memoirs on Dachau specifically are in Polish and German, shut to me): Dachau was opened in March 1933, a pet project of Goering and Himmler. The site, a mile square, was equipped for 8,000 inmates. At its liberation in April '45, it contained 33,000—90% civilians, 10% war prisoners. The civilians, from the first, fell into four groups—political opponents, "inferior races" (Jews and Gypsies), criminals, "asocial elements" (vagrants, pimps, alcoholics etc). Further divisions were recognized by the colored patches on prison clothing (selected with a grinning irony)—black for "shiftless elements," yellow for Jews, pink for homosexuals, purple for Jehovah's Witnesses. Though the oldest camp and the popular symbol for all, it was classified in the S.S. scale as a class-I camp—the mildest rating (Auschwitz was III). Only 70,000-odd inmates are estimated to have died there (4,000,000 at Auschwitz). The existing gas chamber was used only experimentally. Indeed, experiment was among the camp's functions—the famous experiments of Dr. Signund Rascher in chilling prisoners to 19°C., then attempting to thaw them with live whores stretched on their bodies (Himmler regretted that the chosen whores were Aryan). Or locking prisoners in mock altitude chambers to observe when they'd die of oxygen starvation. Or the study of asepsis by inducing infections which were left to gangrene.

—You know most of that. Everybody over thirty does (though to anyone not there, as prisoner or liberator, it has never seemed credible). What I'd like to tell you is what I saw, twelve years after its liberation. I have the four photographs I took that day. I can build it round them.

The gates were unguarded. I walked through them onto a central road wide enough for trucks but closed now to all but lookers like me—there were maybe a dozen in the hour I was there. To my left, one compound (the only one or the only one saved?)—a four-acre piece of flat tan dirt enclosed by stretches of concrete wall (seven-feet high, electrified on top), relays of barbed wire and, in each corner, an all-weather guardhouse (twenty feet high, all empty now). No trace of barracks, no sign of shelter. Where were the famous "dog cells" in which prisoners could only lie on their sides and were forced to bark to earn their food? Razed apparently (on a partial diagram I count thirty barracks). A few weeds grow and, in my picture of a stretch of wall and guardhouse, a leafy branch decks the upper right sky. (Good composition. But how old is the tree?) No entrance there, no gate in the wire. To the right, though, free access—trees, grass, flowers, buildings.

All the people were there. I remember them as old and all of them women; but my photographs show one man (late forties, his suit and tie American—was he a prisoner here?) and two children under ten (a boy in *lederhosen*, a girl hid behind him)—otherwise, old women in long cheap summer dresses, stout shoes. All in clusters of two or three, simply standing akimbo or reading, their lips moving drily at the effort. There are no talking guides, no sign of a staff to question, only scattered plaques and inscriptions in German—the single attempt at a monument, modest, signified, undistinguished, a ¾ths-lifesize gaunt bronze prisoner gazing across the road to the compound, head shaved, hands in his scarecrow overcoat, feet in wooden shoes, on his marble base DEN TOTEN ZUR EHR, DEN LEBENDEN ZUR MAHNUNG ("To Honor the Dead, To Warn the Living") and an urn of red geraniums. Granite markers maybe twelve inches square set in beds of geraniums—GRAB HUNDERTEN NAMENLOSEN (that's from memory—"Grave of Hundreds, Nameless"; was it *hundreds* or *thousands?*). Then twenty feet onwards—it is all so small—six or eight women wait beside a building. It is one-story, cheap brick, green tile roof, straight as a box car and only twice as long. At the pitch of the roof there are turret windows; in the end near me, one large brick chimney eighteen feet tall. Along the side, frequent windows and doors. The only sign was a single black arrow aimed toward the far end (the end farthest from the compound and hidden). I followed, past a post-war willow tree, and found at the end a door —normal size, no wider than the door to my own bedroom.

From here I am on my own—no pictures. I think I remember the logic of progression, each small room labeled in German and English, giving into the next like a railroad apartment —*Disrobing Room, Disinfecting Room* (roughly ten feet by twelve, nine foot ceilings, unpainted plaster walls scratched now with the names and hometowns of GI's). Then another normal-sized wooden door opening into a larger room—maybe fifteen by twenty, shower spigots, soap dishes, floor drains, a ceiling window.

—I've built that effect outrageously—I'm sorry—to the oldest surprise of the twentieth century. The shower was gas, Zyklon B; the window was a deathwatch; the drains were for hosing down the products of surprise and suffocation. The next room was small again—*Storage Room.* The walls were printed from floor to ceiling with dirty bare feet, all turned neatly up. Corpses stacked like cord wood for the ovens. Next room, the ovens. The largest room and last, *Crematorium.* Four or five brick ovens spaced six feet apart, their iron doors open on seven-foot grill racks. The walls bore sets of black iron tools—tongs, prods, pokers, shovels. Behind the ovens, in the wall, were little doors—ash chutes to outside, for the *Namenlosen.*

End of tour. No more sights—oh an old woman kneeling by the farthest oven, clicking off her rosary. Otherwise nothing else to linger for but sunlight, geraniums. Or to make you wait awhile. I thought you were still waiting; and I thought, retracing my way toward you, that I was returning.

You could easily have stood it—have I made you see that? It lacked—now I understand the vagueness of my memories— the mystery of place. There are places, objects, quite literally impasted with the force of past event; places in which one is pulled up short by the pressure of actual atoms of the past. Almost never in America—our shrines being ruthlessly scalded and scoured if not bulldozed—and almost always in sites of suffering or wickedness. The Borgia apartments in the Vatican still are oiled with the presence of Rodrigo Borgia's rotting body; electrons that witnessed, sustained, his life still spin in the plaster, the stones underfoot, can be gouged (brown and rank) with a quick fingernail; unaltered atoms of hydrogen and oxygen that occupied his holy dissolving lungs in 1495 rush over one's lips and teeth with each breath. Or the Domus Aurea of Nero, subterranean now and leaking, where I rounded a dark corner on an elderly English gentleman masturbating (English by his clothes). Or the dungeon beneath the Capitol in which Caesar strangled Vercingetorix —45 BC. Or—another thing entirely—the crystal reliquary in Santa Maria Maggiore which one Christmas Eve mass was borne toward me, immobile in the crowd, its scraps of wormy wood, whether hoax or not (the remains of the Manger), as immanent with promise and threat to my life as a gram of radium bombarding my eyes. Dachau is one month younger than I. It saw—caused—the agonizing unwilling death of tens of thousands while I was still paying half-fare at the movies; yet its huddled remains bore me less of a threat, less pressure of the past than Williamsburg, than any plastic Hilton lobby.

—Why? That's *my* question. Why was I unshaken, unmoved? Anger with you? Tourist fatigue? (I who could weep years later in Chillon at the pillar to which Byron's Prisoner was chained?—and that after ten days of hiking in the Alps.) What had I expected?—a Piranesi prison with eighty-foot ceilings, thick brown air, torture wheels staffed by malignant dwarfs? No doubt that would have helped. The physical remains of Dachau are so mindlessly disproportioned to the volume of suffering they were asked to contain, the literal volume of agonized breath expelled in that square mile in those twelve years. The slaves who died building pyramids are at least survived by pyramids, not tarpaper shacks and geraniums.

But no—don't you see?—I'd expected *home*. It's taken me twelve years to understand that even—my curious memory (dead-wrong surely) of the town itself as a scene from my childhood (porches, ferns, dust!—eastern North Carolina) and my readiness to dawdle there with you, my near-panic at the camp gates when you refused. I had secretly thought through all those months of planning that this would be our home, that if we could enter Dachau together, face and comprehend its threat and still walk out together, then we'd be confirmed —a love not soluble in time or death. *Home* in the sense of birthplace; we'd have been born there, our actual marriage, a perfect weld-job in the ultimate crucible.

Nonsense, you're thinking. Were you thinking it then? Is it why you refused?—you would not be a party to soft-brained theatrics?

But surely you're wrong. Sappy as my whole secret plan may have been—so sappy it was even secret to me; a Fiery Consummation!—it was not a fool's plan, not built on lover's lies. I wrote of "comprehending the threat of Dachau"— hadn't I done that already, in advance, by insisting on this visit? Its final horror—and that of all the camps, class I-III— was not the naked fulfillment by a few thousand gangsters of their fear and hatred on impotent objects (that, after all, is everyone's dream) but precisely the threat to human attachment, loyalty. The ghastliest experiment of all was not one of Dr. Rascher's mad-scientist pranks but the high voice that pulsed out its desperate need like a hypertensive vein—and at first uncertain of its power to enforce!—"Let me set you apart. Mothers here, children there. Husbands left, wives right." And millions obeyed, even the de Wieks—the most successful human experiment in history.

No, the horror is not that the camps did not revolt, that Treblinka stood alone—the horror was accomplished, ineradicable, the moment any one man entered Dachau—but that no husbands, wives, parents, children *stood*—by their radios or sofas or milking stools—and said, "No, kill us here in our tracks together." Oh maybe some did—then why are they unknown? Why aren't their statues in every city center, our new saints of love?—so far surpassing Tristan or Abelard or Antony as to burn like constellations over fuming brush fires. We are only left with endless processions of pairs who *agreed*—to abandonment, to separation by other human beings (not death or time). You know that there were mothers who hid from their children on arriving at Auschwitz—buried their own heads in coats or crawled through knees—to escape immediate death? Can they be forgiven that?

Every American over thirty has his favorite obsessive Holocaust story which he's read or, rarely, heard and retails ever after as his version of Hell. An entire sub-study might be done of these stories and their relevance to the teller. I *heard* mine, and after we parted. A colleague of mine—age 38—is a west-Polish Jew. His mother died of TB early in the war. There were no other children and he lived with his father, a practicing dentist. When the roundup came in '42, my friend was eleven. In warm July weather he rode with his father in the packed train to Sobibor—two days, I think, stopping and starting—and once they were there and unloaded on the siding and a doctor came round to eliminate the sick, my friend's father said that his son was consumptive. It was news to my friend; but being a child, he only thought, "Of course he's right; they kept it from me." But his father never touched him and my friend was led off, presumably for gassing or a lethal injection. Some ball-up ensued, his death was delayed; he never coughed once, chest sound as a stone. But he never saw his father. He was strong enough to work, my friend— farm the camp potatoes—so he managed to live through two more years and a transfer to Auschwitz. Then one day—age thirteen—he was standing in a compound when a line of new men passed. One man fell out for a moment and came toward him. My friend said, "He thought he was running; he was creeping" (too weak to run). Of course, it was his father. They both knew that. But they didn't speak and, again, didn't touch; and a guard beat his father into line—fifteen seconds. Never met again.

Well, in the immortal words of King Lear—"*Howl.*" My friend thinks the question in his story is *why?*—why his father did that. I'd never tell him but the question is *how?* There are degrees of offense at which motive is irrelevant. Can he ever be forgiven?—that father (out of Dante) stumbling on his appallingly vital son whom he'd lied to kill? Can any of the millions ever be forgiven?

Can you, Sara, ever? And not just by me. It was you who refused. Only you were not killed. You could have walked into that tamed camp with me; you could have had the guts to settle it *inside*—to have seen it all with me, to have armed it with the threat which without you it lacked and then (if you needed so desperately) have said to me, "No, I will not live for you." Instead, for your own no doubt clear reasons, you lurked outside on the shady rim, half-sadist, half-coward —unwilling to choose, thinking you could wait and that I, having waited for half an hour beyond a wire fence among debris as meaningless as M.G.M. sets, would presently return.

□

I did and didn't. When I came back through the gates, I didn't look for you but went to the car and sat in its oven-heat. I already knew that I was not waiting and had not returned, not to you at least; but—stopped short of panic or the courage to act my feeling—I was not prepared to abandon you physically, to leave your bags on the empty parking space and drive off for Salzburg with your twenty-dollar *Figaro* ticket in my wallet. So I thought in the heat, "I may go under but I won't go looking."

In three or four minutes you walked up slowly, got in and sat, facing forward. How did I feel to you? What vibrations, what aura? Or were you receiving? Had you ever been?

What I felt was hatred. What's *hatred*, you ask?—the wish that you were absent from my sight, my life, absent from my memory. I had put my hands on the wheel for steadiness, and I thought my hatred was shaking the car. Then I saw, in my head, a Volkswagen jittering-away in the sunkist parking lot at Dachau; so I cranked up and moved.

You said "Where are you going?"

I did not want to stop now and look at you—I must keep my hands busy. I said "*I*? To Salzburg."

"Am I coming?" you said.

"Unless you jump," I said.

I think you took that to mean you were forgiven. You behaved as though you were. Slowly through our drive to Salzburg you loosened, slowly became the girl I'd thought I needed—smiled at my profile and, then when we'd got in sight of hills, you sang the whole final scene of *Figaro* (from "*Gente, gente, all'armi, all'armi*"), taking all the parts, chorus included.

Your text was letter-perfect, your Italian B+; only your baritone plunges failed. Yet I knew your motive far better than you. It had nothing to do with the coming evening. It all bloomed out of your need and wish to sing five lines—

THE COUNT:
    Contessa, perdono.   [*Countess, your pardon.*

THE COUNTESS:
    Più docile io sono   —*I'm gentler now*
    e dico di sì.   *and I'll say yes.*

ALL:
    Ah! Tutti contenti   —*Ah! Everybody's*
    saremo così.   *happy with that.*]

That, I think, was the climax though the day (and this piece) had a good while to run. I took that to mean you were pardoning *me*—for not having cheerfully granted your independence back at Dachau, for not having bought the metaphor your refusal offered (we'd be hitched to one load but in separate yokes). So I thought I would launch a spot of unforgivability. When you'd sung through the orchestral *tutti* to the curtain, you faced forward resolutely—no bow in my direction. That meant I should applaud—right? Well, I drove a good mile before making a sound; and then I said "One question."

"What?"

"Why in all your extensive *reconciliation* repertoire"—can you still do Cordelia, Marina, Fidelio?—"is it always the *lady* dispensing largess?"

You'd have bit off your tongue before admitting you hadn't noticed. You said, in an instant, "It's the way the world's built."

"Many thanks," I said and by then we were threading the fringes of Salzburg, its castle as stunned by the day as I.

I said that this would be my version, what I remember and understand. The rest of the day—what I thought was the day—is necessary; then tell me yours; I genuinely need it. Yet, again, my memory of *places* is vague, my grip on surfaces.

You've greased my hands, greased every wall; or is it only some new lubricant from myself, manufactured now in me—suddenly—in response to your refusal, to ease me away? Anyhow, it's still produced. Some days it pours.

Mozart's *Geburtshaus*—we saw that together but what do I recall? Two or three pokey rooms, white walls, dark brown woodwork, an early piano on which (the guide told us) Harry Truman had just played. Was there even a *birth*-room? Were they sure of which room? I couldn't say. It seemed more like the birthplace of some dry chip—say, Metternich—than the Sublime Foul Mouth. And didn't you recognize that? When we'd made our separate rounds and I passed the guest-book on my way downstairs, I saw you'd signed with your comic alter-ego—*Veronica F. Pertle and traveling companion.* We were already lethal, in under three hours—we'd agreed to be a team of cut-rate Midases, transmuting all we touched to chalk.

I slept through a good deal of *Figaro*—all that endless nocturnal business at the start of Act III, the confused identities. I've slept through greater performances than that—Melchior's Lohengrin, Welitsch's Salome—though always before from travel fatigue, biting off more grandeur than I could chew, but here I wasn't tired. I'd slept eight hours the night before, driven ten miles to walk maybe five hundred paces round a concentration camp, then eighty miles farther on a good wide road. No, I was retreating. The great death wish, Sleep Mother of Peace—if I couldn't lose you, I could lose myself. You woke me toward the end with a firm elbow—"Don't miss the forgiveness." So I can still hear that (Schwarzkopf's perfect frailty, a bulldozer disguised as a powderpuff); thanks for the elbow—the trip was not in vain.

What I think I remember—as clear as the Norwegian day, your offered food—is the rest of the night. Correct me on this—

We had late coffee in some hotel lobby which seems, in memory, entirely upholstered in 1938 Pontiac fabric, and were spared conversation by a pair of purple-haired American ladies drinking *Liebfraumlich* six feet away. They had also heard the opera and debated the performance. One defended it stoutly but the doubter trumped her in the end—remember?— "Lena, all I know is, when I hear great singing something in me swells up. Tonight it didn't swell."

—"Mine neither," you said and stood and we left, heading

toward Munich still hungry (no supper). Yet you didn't mention food, barely spoke at all; and what did I feel? —that really I was racing, to end this night, the trip, what we'd had and you'd failed, that I could go without food and sleep for days, an emergency encystment for however long it took to deliver you to whatever door you chose.

Then on the edge of Munich you said, "I'll never sleep without some food."

It was pushing two a.m. So I had to hunt awhile; but we found a place open somewhere in Schwabing, down a flight of stairs thickly cushioned with dirt.

"More dikes than Holland," you said going in; but in what light there was, they seem more like gypsies to me on hindsight.

You wanted fondue but we settled for something merciful and a good deal of wine; and with all the eating, surely we hadn't said fifty words when the two men entered with the lion before them. If they weren't gypsies I'll surrender my license—they laid down about them that heavy metal air of offense and threat I've known all my life (they still roamed the South when I was a boy, telling fortunes and offering odd skilled services no one would accept, though by then in trailers not painted wagons; and their squat swart women with the Carmen earrings and their men whose hard faces all wore livid scars are high in my childhood pantheon of menace).

They picked you at once. Do you still think I signaled them? I *saw* them see you the moment they entered, even the lion.

He was straining toward you on his red dog-leash—maybe six months old?—and no one held him back though I swear the rear man—the one with hands free—passed the huge lady-owner a small piece of money in their rush to you. Were they illegal, bribing their way? The lion was smelling your foot before you saw; and of course you didn't flinch—a male lion cub in a Bavarian dive at the end of a day comprising Dachau and Mozart: oh.

They were photographers—take your picture with a lion; best American Polaroid, instant result. I told them No—didn't I? I'm almost sure I did—but the contact man (the one with the leash) held the lion up and said "See, he *begs*." With his free hand he clasped the cub's front paws together in a mockery of prayer (its high tight testicles were pink as salmon, utterly vulnerable). The man's English seemed more Italian than German but maybe just basic PX English—"He begs you to warm him; four dollars for picture, give to your husband. He lose his mother, he lonely here." The cub's eyes were shut, so lonely he was dozing.

You continued eating but you asked him "Did you kill her?"

That seemed the terror-button. Surely these two oily small-time spivs had not been poaching in Kenya; yet at your question, they both threw grimaces at one another, and the talker said, "Look. No charge for you." He extended the lion, eyes still shut—"He need your help."

"He's asleep," you said.

The man jogged him hard; he looked out, groggily.

"No," you said.

But I said "Do it" and produced my wallet. I wanted you to do it and I wanted to pay.

Looking at the lion not me, you said "Why?"

"I want the picture."

I extended twenty marks to the man and you stood.

"You sit," the man said, "then we take you both."

"I'll stand," you said. "It's me he wants." You stood and reached out. You were in the black dress with narrow shoulder straps—much white skin showed.

He moved close against you and hung the lion on your shoulder like a child. The photographer—the silent man—backed off and raised his camera; the talker said "Big smile."

You smiled sideways, no teeth. The other diners paused, awaiting the flash. It came. In its light, blood streamed down your arm.

The lady-owner bellowed, came waddling forward. The two men leapt toward you. The lion was clamped into the meat of your shoulder.

I was still in my chair.

"Stay back," you said.

They understood and stopped a foot from the table.

"What's his name?" you said.

The talker said "Bob."

The lady-owner babbled coldly in German. They must get him out, get out themselves, *die Polizei!*

You were stroking the back of Bob's locked-on neck, simply saying his name again and again—the two of us the only calm people in the room, only still ones at least. Us and the lion—he was motionless, teeth deep in you. What nourishment was he taking?—what pleasure, fulfillment? What did he think you were?

—A lion-tamer, anyhow. You stroked him free; he looked round at his owners. You had never smiled, talked baby-talk to him, given the odor of fear or asked for help; you had saved your day. You handed Bob over to the trembling talker.

He slapped him once across the nose, laid my money by my plate; and they left at a trot—the owner behind them, maledicting.

(*I don't have the picture.* Have you thought of that? Did we ever mention that? Of course, I didn't pay but a picture was taken, at the instant of the bite. Does it still exist in some gypsy's pocket?—an image of a bad night, another close call, image of his *life*, assault and impotence, the helpless witness of another's competence to solve hurtful puzzles? I would give a lot for it. What is on your face?—still, after twelve years? What did I miss in the moment of flash, your moment of sudden unexpected pain? Whom were you blaming? I need that picture badly.)

Before I could stand up to check the damage, you had asked a bystander, "*Wo ist die Damen?*" and loped off to that.

So I sat again and was wondering what next when the owner pounded back with a rusty first-aid kit and stopped at me, aghast.

"*Wo ist ihre Gattin?*"

I said that the *Fraulein* was in the cabinet, washing.

She considered attempting to wither me for negligence but no doubt remembered that in her situation *die Polizei* was a two-edged blade; so she said, "*Nicht toll, nicht toll. Er ist nicht tollwütig*" (*not rabid*) and headed for the *Damen* to disinfect you.

I ate on and in five minutes she returned to say you were all right, would be back soon and would we, in recompense, have a free dessert? I thought that seemed uniquely German— for a lion-bite, dessert—but I accepted and she quickly produced two enormous wedges of obscenely moist chocolate whipped-cream cake. I thanked her, she assured me again

"*Nicht toll*" and that you were fine. Then she left.

I waited awhile—thinking what? Most likely, nothing. (I can sit for whole half-hours, thinking nothing, my consciousness a bowl of thick soup, cooling. You'd never accept that; so often, on the road, when we'd ridden in silence, you'd say "What are you thinking?" and when I'd say "Nothing," you'd clearly disbelieve me. *Why?* What mutterings filled *your* silence? It is how I understand the life of objects. Keats said that he could inhabit a sparrow and peck in the gravel. I can inhabit, say, a walnut log or the white blind heart of a loaf of bread.) Maybe though I thought a few calm sad thoughts on our imminent split—*past* split, in fact; it was hours old. But I know I wasn't yet asking *why?* I was now an engine geared for one purpose—the expulsion of waste parts, self-starting restored. And when, in five minutes, you hadn't come, I began my cake and called for coffee. In ten more, I'd finished; you were still absent; and the owner walked past me—no word or look—to check you again.

She returned and I managed to understand through her fury that now you had the outer door locked and had spoken to her but would not open.

I couldn't think of how to say "Give her time"; so I must have stared blankly till the owner said in English in a python-hiss (discovering *Ssss* in two *s*-free words)—"Go. *You* go!" She'd have punched me in the breast bone with her short fat finger, but I leaned back and stood and went to the *Damen*.

I knocked and called your name.

You must have been against the door—no sound of steps—but you took a few beats before turning the lock.

When I opened, you were standing three feet away, by a grimy wash basin, your back to me, your head down but silent.

I said "Are you hurt?"

You turned to show me. Your face was splotched from crying; but you weren't using that—no mercy pleas. You pointed to your shoulder. One single strip of bandage, one inch by two.

I looked from where I was—I'd entered entirely but the door was cracked open (for needy *Damen*). It didn't occur to me to take another step, touch you gently, peel the bandage back and check—was that all my fault? Weren't you throwing off a field of volts that I'd never have pierced, however determined?

"One tooth," you said, "one canine puncture."

"Good," I said. (I knew you'd had tetanus shots and, now from the owner, that Bob was not rabid.)

You said it to my eyes (I grant you that), "*Good?* Well, I guess"—another three beats, no shifting of gaze—"Yes, *marvelous.* Something *in* me finally. And a permanent mark." You pressed the bandage. "I'll carry a little white scar to my grave, the size of a navy bean—a real lion, my summer in Europe. I can show my children." You reached for your purse and, as you came toward me, said "Chocolate on your teeth" (was I grinning by then?). Then you said, "I need air. Please wash your mouth and I'll meet you at the car." You went out past me, half-closing the door again.

So since the room was empty I went to the basin. In the mirror I seemed unaltered though my teeth were socketed in chocolate. I was flushing my mouth when (I never told you) I saw your little message—to the side of the mirror and in small printed letters but quite clearly your hand (the only graffito, your color of ink, of course in English). Before I could read it, I knew it was not for me. You'd had no way to know I'd enter the *Damen*—or had you? did you wait to force me to come and see the two lines? Is it why you wouldn't let the owner in? How could she have minded? She'd have never understood. Who on God's earth would?—

Jesus, will you help me now?
I will. I have.

I thought at once of Salinger's *Franny*—mystical union in the Ladies Room—but I knew that, even if you'd read the story you'd have thought it unforgivably corny to mimic its action, like quoting Edgar Guest at a family funeral. In any case, Franny only squeezed her little book, *The Way of the Pilgrim*; you addressed Jesus straight and claimed a straight answer. You were surely not drunk, surely not joking. I dreaded facing you. What help had you got? What new fierce power; How much farther could you thrust me?

But I went, paid the bill, thanked the owner for her help and the chocolate cake—she smiled but despised me—and climbed to the street.

The car was parked five steps away—no sign of you. I looked toward both dark ends of the street—nothing, empty. I stood yearning to run—to enter the car silently, crank and drive away. You had your passport and traveler's checks. And I'd taken a step—would I have done it?—when you rounded the corner, stopped in the cone of light. I waited for you to come on to me.

But you pointed behind you down the hidden street and held your place.

So I went to you, more curious now than dreading. You were back in darkness before I reached you—I was both spared and deprived full sight of your face. "You're all right?" I said.

You didn't answer that. You pointed again toward the end of the street—what seemed a small park, a knot of trees.

I said, "Do you want to walk?"

You said, "No, I've got something to show you."

I walked beside you but you were leading.

The park was two concentric rings of sycamores that all but filled the dark space above with limbs, leaves. Only a pierce of sky twenty feet square, say, was visible; but despite the glow of Munich and the few park lights, there were stars—oh a dozen. You took us to the center.

I looked round—alone; all benches empty.

Then you said "Straight up!"

I looked, half-thinking you had lost a screw? even one-tenth wondering if you'd stab my unprotected gut (you who trapped spiders in my Oxford rooms and conveyed them, live, outside to grass).

Again you were pointing. "See those two stars there?"

"Yes."

"Now shift to the right and down an inch or so."

I did.

"See that blur?"

I waited, straining not to blink; then I saw it—a faint smear, an old chalk fingerprint. "Yes."

You moved closer on me and, there as I was, hands loose at my sides, head back, throat stretched taut, I considered again that you might have plans and means to kill me—a sacrifice to what? Your Jesus-of-the-*Damen*? Some Eastern star god?—Ishtar, Ahura Mazda? For that moment, it seemed an acceptable fate—or not to over-dignify it, *acceptable next act*,

Tosca and Scarpia, *finalmente mia*! (Is it from this whole full day that my total fearlessness emerges? Death would startle me, granted, but roughly as much as an air-filled bag popped behind my ear. I face all prospects quite nicely, thank you; let Nothing mishear me though and apply misfortunes.)

But you only spoke. "Do you know what it is?"

I said "Do you?"

"NGC 224."

"Is that a space ship?" I said (no satellites yet, though the Russians were cranking up, a little to our right).

"No, the great spiral galaxy in Andromeda."

I had vague recollections of boyhood astronomy, photographs in *My Weekly Reader* from Mount Palomar; but I certainly made no leap of awe.

You said, "Do you know how far away it is?"

"No."

"One million, five hundred thousand light years. And what its apparent diameter is?"

"No," I said.

"Sixty thousand light years." Your hand was still up, no longer quite pointing but in a sort of arrested Boy Scout salute; and your lips were parted—you were just beginning.

Yet my dread, such as it was, was ebbing. The worst possibility now seemed clearly nothing more than a Thornton Wilder sermon on Just-us and the Stars—you *were* drunk, I thought; this was way below standard.

You dropped your hand but continued silently looking up.

So I felt I had to speak. "What am I supposed to do?"

"Forgive me," you said.

That was meant to be worse than a sacrificial knife. It was. I must have wobbled. At some point I said "For what?" I was facing you now—or your dim profile; you would not look downwards.

"You know," you said.

"For waiting back today at Dachau?"

"More than that," you said.

"Say what then, please."

"For not thinking you were safe to follow."

"Into poor Dachau? It's a national park. There are not even bears."

"Don't joke. *You* know."

I didn't know but I didn't ask—because, just then, I didn't want to know and, after the whole day, couldn't care much. Simple as fatigue.

You apparently knew—had thought through your balking and, in asking for pardon, were asking your way back into my life. I was safe, after all, to follow?—was that it? Or safe as you guessed you could hope to find? Or maybe you'd realized after all that you'd led, not followed, all those years in any case?

I wasn't standing there, in silence, asking questions—again I was locked in simple fatigue.

Then you looked at me and said "You haven't answered."

"What?" I said.

You said again "Forgive me?"

I should have said Yes. It was surely the instinct, the reflex of my feeling; but with Yes in my mouth, I balked and thought, "I must wait till tomorrow. It would be my tiredness talking, and the wine." It would—I know now—have been my heart but wait I did. I said "Give me time."

You nodded, gave it and went to the car only slightly before me.

But in two further weeks on the road, I never answered. (Not that I forgot; it was all I thought of—a glaze of scum which I laid across all those Rembrandts and Vermeers that might have saved us if they'd cared enough to fight. They survived it though, my self-surrendered vandalism. You and I didn't, no masterworks.) And you never asked again. You should have. Why not? You had led so much of the way. Your silence and patience only fueled my flight, stoked a natural warmth of sadism in me which let me ride beside—*lie* beside you—for weeks more and still wish that you would vanish, speaking civilly but coolly, touching you only by accident. (If you were awake—and I did wait until you were breathing like sleep—I beg your pardon now that twice in those last weeks I lay beside you, not ten inches away, and took what pleasure my head demanded from my own dry self with my own dry hand: dry to keep the slapping down. Fun, fun.)

Why? You never asked that even. Why, after years of

assuming I required you—daily sight of you, daily touch—
after gladly embracing the prospect of *life* with you, your
one false move in the parking lot at Dachau thrust me from
you in a helpless irresistible rush? Worse than helpless, *grin-
ning*. I was glad, I thought, to go. Blessed clear space at hand
—empty, free—toward which I flew at stunning speeds like
your galaxy.

Well—Jesus—we've uncovered the secret of Dachau, of all
the camps, every act of submission, why no one refused, even
the de Wieks—they were glad to go! In secret glee, which they
could not have borne to face or seek themselves, millions like
us were permitted to abandon all human contracts, bonds—
duties!—to shed all *others* like last year's skin and to stand, if
only for a few hours, free; breathing free air (unshared by
wives or children) till the air became gas. There were two
women smiling in that photograph, remember? holding their
children for the last heavy moment before pitching forward,
dead in a ditch, but alive maybe one moment longer than the
child. After such knowledge, what forgiveness? We should
never have acquired it, by chance or intent. Yet you forced it
on us—by your simple refusal twelve years ago at Dachau.

I'm back where I started, Sara—why did you refuse?

Never mind. I won't care now. But one more thing—your
astronomy lecture, so unheralded that night in the Munich
park, when I thought you'd gone nuts if not homicidal (mes-
sages from Jesus and NGC 224)? I've been working on that
lately—what you might have intended, short of an open-air
homily on the need for love in the drowned depths of space.
I've read up on your pet galaxy Andromeda—Fred Hoyle, the
Larousse Astronomie, even old Sir James Jeans' *Mysterious
Universe* with its chilling, exhilarating, unanswerable conclu-
sion—

> *We discover that the universe shows evidence of a de-
> signing or controlling power that has something in
> common with our own individual minds—not, so far
> as we have discovered, emotion, morality, or aesthetic
> appreciation, but the tendency to think in the way
> which, for want of a better word, we describe as*

*mathematical. And while much in it may be hostile to
the material appendages of life, much also is akin to
the fundamental activities of life; we are not so much
strangers or intruders in the universe as we at first
thought. Those inert atoms in the primaeval slime
which first began to foreshadow the attributes of life
were putting themselves more, and not less, in accord
with the fundamental nature of the universe.*

Were you making one last try, that night, to accord us with
the universe?

I've bought its picture—your galaxy's. After years of won-
dering and stumbling across it, badly printed and dingy, in
various books, I ordered its photograph from Mount Palomar.
For two weeks now it's hung above my desk—only just below
Jesus, your other messenger (Rembrandt's Hundred Guilder
print, in a first-class fake). So it watches me this minute (as it
watches perpetually, day-sky or night). The picture (through
the 48″ Schmidt telescope) is in color—the great spiral itself
in white, rose and lilac on a matte brown sky pierced by single
stars. If I didn't know, it could be several things—a Miami
lady-decorator's dream of the ultimate ballroom chandelier.
Or—for me most pleasing—the loveliest toy ever made. It could
be that (sixty thousand light-years across)—a cooling circular
platter of light that whirls round its billowing center in utter
silence, having no final rim but diminishing slowly into thin-
ner clouds of stars and finally night; my dream of a mobile to
hang in my bedroom to wake to at night; or the sort of gift
that God the Father might have willed for the Infant Christ
(trumping the Magi) in a Milton ode (what if Milton could
have seen it?)—

> *And for a sign of My delight in Thee,*
> *I hang this tilted wheel above Thy bed,*
> *Attended at the rim by Hosts who smile*
> *And, smiling, face the axle drowned in light*
> *Whence My eternal love for Thee streams fire.*

Did we really see it that August night? Was that smudge
above Munich really it? Or were you lying? Or did you not
know? I haven't yet found in any of my reading whether or

not the Andromeda galaxy is visible ever to the naked eye—and if so, was it visible in Munich that particular night (or early morning)?

Look. I'm going to assume that you really thought you saw it and that—calling me and pointing up and reeling off those almanac-facts as prelude to asking forgiveness—what you meant to say was something like this, another effort at the poem you were always aching to write (your poem, not mine; mine would be better but that's my job, right?)—

There it hangs, a million and a half light years away, sixty thousand visible light years across, composed of billions of separate stars all drowned in isolation yet all wheeling round a common center at something like a half million miles per hour, a stroke of radiance on your retina dimmer than the luminous dial of your watch. Or there it hung *a million years ago, for the instant it took to launch this present light in its unimaginable outward flight toward the curved walls of space.* Flight *from what though?—the Big Bang? Maybe. But maybe flight from us, simply you and me, the two repellent objects at the core of space from which all other matter hurtles at speeds increasing till they pass the speed of light (and hurtled for millions of years before us in anticipation of this one day). Or a little less narcissistically—in flight from the blue planet, home of men. For elsewhere, all creatures desire perfect union—desire not require—and each one's desire is silently achieved. Parallels meet. It is how the world is made. Andromeda—the millions of other universes, the billions of planets—is swarmed with pairs who serve each other. Or, barring that, is empty; has the grace to be empty. We will not be forgiven for forcing their flight.* Turn. Return.

I'd add only this—it is all no doubt grander, funnier than that. God only watches comedies, can only smile. Waterloo, Dachau. The end is planned. There are no options.

Sara, come back. ∎

HOURGLASS
Fred Chappell

O is Time still that kingdom
of pathless winds, of maze
in maze reflected, blaze
of oblivion? The bloom
of fury's rose, doom
inevitable as days
stumbling always
downward home?
Is it a fire
of sunsnow
and star
throe,
pure
No
?

```
O  is  Time          kingdom
  of  pathle          of maze
   in  maze  r        ed,  blaze
    of  oblivi       The bloom
    of  fury's       ose, doom
      inevitab       as  days
       stumbli       always
        downwa       home?
         Is  it       fire
          of  s      snow
          and        tar
           th        e,
            p        e
```

```
            nd
           oms
          stella
         the  quest
         Time  can
```

```
O  i              gdom
  of             maze
  in             laze
  of             loom
  of             doom
 ine             days
  stu            ways
 down            me?
   Is            ire
    o            w
```

```
     shall
     ds:   th
     far be
      capac
     row  as
   on  and  as b
  he atoms that
    interstellar   spa
 Time the question p
 only Time can ever
```

O,
Time
can no
man limn
in shallow
words: theme
too far beyond
those capacities
as narrow as bliss
of iron and as blind
as the atoms that wend
the   interstellar   spaces;
as Time the question poses
that only Time can ever end.

O is Time still that kingdom
of pathless winds, of maze
in maze reflected, blaze
of oblivion? The bloom
of fury's rose, doom
inevitable as days
stumbling always
downward home?
Is it a fire
of sunsnow
and star
throe,
pure
No
?
O,
Time
can no
man limn
in shallow
words: theme
too far beyond
those   capacities
as   narrow as bliss
of iron and as blind
as the atoms that wend
the   interstellar   spaces;
as Time the question poses
that only Time can ever end.

AFTERWORD

This book isn't meant to be a 'Best of North Carolina' anthology. It's a miscellany, and as such displays the diversity of styles and concerns of contemporary North Carolina writers. By North Carolina writers, I mean present or past residents.

I've decided not to include biographies of the contributors, because I prefer to let the work stand on its own. I hope this will encourage readers to browse through this anthology and find pieces which appeal to them personally, rather than turning first to those stories and poems written by writers with the more extensive publication records.

The submission process for *Cardinal* was open. No one was guaranteed acceptance. Some 500 writers were notified personally; calls for material were listed in nationally-distributed writers' publications; the larger North Carolina publishers were solicited; and letters were sent to everyone on the North Carolina Arts Council's list of minority writers. There may have been a few writers I missed, but it wasn't by design. I apologize to those writers whose work was good enough to appear in *Cardinal* but, because of space limitations, didn't make it. I make no apologies for the absence of work by writers who did not submit material.

I hope this book brings you many hours of reading pleasure.

Richard Krawiec
Editor